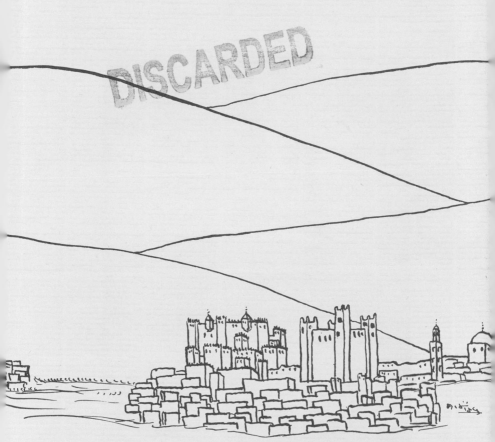

Lords of the Atlas

GAVIN MAXWELL

Lords of the Atlas

The Rise and Fall of the House of Glaoua
1893–1956

E. P. DUTTON & CO., INC.: NEW YORK
1966

For queries on an empty page;
For rams and expiated sin;
For desert dust and falcon's cry.
For tempest in a ruined inn.
For sunrise, and the mountain's age
A vulture on the sky.

Contents

Illustrations

Following page 158

T'hami El Glaoui, Pasha of Marrakesh, in the early years after Madani's death

Hadj Idder, T'hami El Glaoui's Chamberlain and confidant
Reproduced by courtesy of René Bertrand

The ramparts of Marrakesh, with the High Atlas in the background
Reproduced by courtesy of René Bertrand

Marrakesh: the Koutoubia Mosque and the High Atlas beyond
Reproduced by courtesy of René Bertrand

Marrakesh: the Place Dj'mma El F'naa – 'a sort of perpetual fun fair'

Tribal reception for El Glaoui: the *achwash* dance
Reproduced by courtesy of René Bertrand

Mounted warriors at a tribal reception

The *kasbah* of *Caid* Omar El Glaoui at Taliouine

Telouet: the *kasbah* of *Caid* Brahmin El Glaoui, the 'palace of 1,001 nights'

Telouet: the *kasbah* of *Caid* Brahim during the golden years
Reproduced by courtesy of René Bertrand

Telouet: the *kasbah* of *Caid* Hammou, the village, and the *kasbah* of *Caid* Brahim

Men of the Glaoua tribe

Telouet interiors

T'hami El Glaoui with his son *Caid* Brahim at Telouet
Reproduced by courtesy of Office Marocain du Tourisme

Telouet: the *kasbah* of *Caid* Hammou in 1961

Telouet: the *kasbah* of *Caid* Hammou from the *kasbah* of *Caid* Brahim, 1961
Reproduced by courtesy of René Bertrand

T'hami El Glaoui during the height of his powers
Reproduced by courtesy of René Bertrand

Following page 222

A Glaoua *kasbah* in the Dadès valley

T'hami El Glaoui and Marshal Juin
Agence France-Presse

The brittle alliance: *Caid* El Ayadi of the Rehamna and T'hami El Glaoui
Reproduced by courtesy of René Bertrand

The heart of the conspiracy: the Glaoui's palace at Marrakesh during the plot to dethrone the Sultan Mohammed V, 1953
Reproduced by courtesy of René Bertrand

T'hami El Glaoui and Abd El Hay Kittani plot to dethrone the Sultan Mohammed V, 1953
Agence France-Presse

Rebels' banquet: kous-kous covers for a reception of notables at the Glaoui's palace in Marrakesh, 1953
Reproduced by courtesy of René Bertrand

Minstrels in the Glaoui's palace in Marrakesh, to entertain the rebels' banquet, 1953
Reproduced by courtesy of René Bertrand

The puppet Sultan Ben Arafa about to sacrifice a sheep for the *Aid El Kebir* at Marrakesh, 21 August 1953. Extreme left, Abd El Hay Kittani; third from left, T'hami El Glaoui; left, behind the Sultan, *Caid* Brahim El Glaoui. Sacrificial stone in the foreground
Reproduced by courtesy of René Bertrand

The Sultan Ben Arafa leaves with T'hami El Glaoui to entrain for Rabat. In the back of El Glaoui's Delahaye are General d'Hauteville, the Sultan Ben Arafa, and T'hami El Glaoui. In the front passenger seat, Hadj Idder
Reproduced by courtesy of René Bertrand

Children of Telouet

T'hami's Sultan, Ben Arafa, arrives at Rabat by train from Marrakesh. *Left to right:* General d'Hauteville, T'hami El Glaoui, the Sultan, Commandant Franqui, *Commissaire de la ville*
Reproduced by courtesy of René Bertrand

The first attempt on the Sultan Ben Arafa's life, Rabat, 11 September 1953; an open car charges the Sultan's horse as he rides to the mosque. The imperial parasol has fallen at right of picture
United Press International (UK) Ltd

The grenade thrower, Ahmed Ben Ali, immediately before he was shot by T'hami El Glaoui
United Press International (UK) Ltd.

The second attempt on the Sultan Ben Arafa's life, Marrakesh, 8 March 1954;
the Sultan bleeding from a grenade thrown at him in the Berrima mosque.
Hadj Idder at centre
United Press International (UK) Ltd

T'hami El Glaoui, spattered with the Sultan's blood, advances to shoot
Ahmed Ben Ali
United Press International (UK) Ltd

Rabat, 26 October 1956. T'hami El Glaoui enters the throne room to submit
to the Council of the Throne
Agence France-Presse

Paris, 9 November 1956. At the château of St Germain-en-Laye T'hami El
Glaoui kisses the feet of the Sultan Mohammed V whom he had deposed
Keystone Press Agency Ltd

T'hami El Glaoui shortly before his death in 1956
Studio Lorelle

*All unacknowledged photographs, except that of T'hami El Glaoui opposite p. 158
are by the author*

Maps, etc.

Author's Foreword

THE preparation of this book has involved a great deal of research over a period of several years. What written information is available is scattered throughout a very large number of French books and documents, most of them not easy of access; the references are fragmentary, too, so that the production of a narrative has been like collecting and assembling widely dispersed pieces of a jigsaw puzzle. The literature in English is meagre and for the most part trivial, (with the exception of Rom Landau's *Moroccan Drama*), but early on in my reading I chanced upon the late Mr Walter Harris's *Morocco That Was*, published by Blackwood's in 1912. Mr Harris was *Times* correspondent in Morocco from before the turn of the century until after the establishment of the French Protectorate; he could, and often did, pass as an Arab, and enjoyed the personal friendship of several Sultans. While his book covers a period of less than twenty years, and is mainly anecdotal and episodic, I realized at once that to use his information while changing his words would be unthinkable; for his style, both moving and hilariously satirical, must have been unique in his epoch. I therefore approached his nephew and literary executor, Mr Peter Harris, who has been generous enough to allow me to reproduce long extracts verbatim. This I have done, not always in sequence, cementing them, as it were, by factual material from other sources. Thus all passages in Book One that are placed between inverted commas are his unless otherwise acknowledged. It has, in fact – since the book was short – proved possible to use the greater part of his text, and I am sure that many will share my pleasure in the republication after so many years of a neglected virtuoso.

A select list of published sources is given at the end of this book. Beyond this I have relied upon a great bulk of verbal communication and unpublished notes that have been made available to me; these, at the request of the donors, I have not acknowledged to individuals, but I express my great appreciation of the time and trouble they have given to my project.

Any biography of a ruler necessarily involves consideration of much of his country's contemporary history, and it is difficult for the biographer to determine at what point to arrest examination of an outside sequence of events that may have affected his subject. Thus, for example, the Istiqlal or Moroccan Independence Movement merits a separate volume at least as long as the present one, and discussion of the Arab Berber problem in Morocco has had to be kept to the minimum for understanding of the narrative. The select bibliography is crammed with tangential fact, which may be described as 'further reading'.

I am indebted to Lord Brockway for allowing me to reproduce his letter published in the *Manchester Guardian* on 10 June 1953; and to the Trustees of the late Agnes, Lady Grove for permission to quote extracts from her *Seventy-one days' Camping in Morocco*.

The decorations in the text were drawn for this book by Ahmed Ben Lahcen Tija, a Berber from Marrakesh, originally of the Haha tribe.

Tighremt'n Oughzen, Dadès valley

Table of Principal Events

Book One

1912–
1914 French use El Glaoui, El M'touggi and El Goundafi to conquer the Southern tribes.
1914 Outbreak of World War I. Madani El Glaoui swears allegiance of his family and that of El M'touggi and El Goundafi to France.
1914–
1918 Subjugation of the South continues under these three.
1918 Madani's favourite son, Abd El Malek, killed in battle against Southern tribes.
1918 Madani dies; his place as chief ally of the French is taken by his brother T'hami, Pasha of Marrakesh.

Book Two

1918 T'hami El Glaoui, Pasha of Marrakesh, nominated by the French as head of the Glaoui family. But his nephew-in-law Hammou remains *Caid* of Telouet and in control of great lands beyond the Atlas, and shows himself strongly anti-French.
1922 End of T'hami's strictly military career.
1924 End of El Goundafi's fief.
1927 Death of the Sultan Moulay Youssef, and accession of his younger son Moulay Mohammed V.
1928 End of El M'touggi's fief.
1930 Early stirrings of the Independence Movement; French reply with the Berber *dahir*, aimed at dividing the Arab and Berber populations.
1932 Publication of *Son Excellence*, a violent attack upon the power and personal character of T'hami El Glaoui.
1934 Hammou El Glaoui dies, and T'hami consolidates the Glaoui Empire.
1935 Pacification of the South officially completed.
1937 French exile leaders of the Independence Movement.
1939 Outbreak of World War II. The Sultan Mohammed V swears allegiance to France until she is victorious, though by now he aspires to an independent Morocco.
1943 Casablanca Conference (Roosevelt, Churchill, de Gaulle, etc.). Roosevelt has private meeting with the Sultan, and expresses himself in sympathy with the Independence Movement.
1944 Gabriel Puaux becomes Resident-General in Morocco. Further arrests of Independence Movement leaders. Riots and repressive measures.
1946 Erick Labonne succeeds Gabriel Puaux. Independence Movement leaders freed.

1947 Riot and massacre in Casablanca. The Sultan's speech at Tangier. General Juin replaces Erick Labonne. French pursue repressive policy.

1950 The Sultan and El Glaoui visit Paris. The Sultan receives no satisfaction to his aspirations for a future independent Morocco; El Glaoui remains in Paris after he has left.

In December, the Sultan quarrels with El Glaoui, and orders him never to set foot in the Imperial Palace again.

1951 Juin demands that the Sultan denounce the Independence Movement. The Sultan refuses. El Glaoui's Southern tribesmen march on the capital in a 'spontaneous uprising' against the Sultan. The Sultan signs compromise documents.

Juin replaced in August by General Guillaume.

In October the Arab Group demand that the Moroccan question be put before the United Nations.

El Glaoui urges the deposition of the Sultan.

1952 Massacres in Casablanca. Mass arrests of all connected with Independence Movement.

1953 Conspiracy between El Glaoui and Abd El Hay Kittani, brother of Mohammed El Kittani, who had been flogged to death by Moulay Hafid. They plan with the French to depose the Sultan.

El Glaoui attends coronation of Queen Elizabeth II as a personal guest of Winston Churchill, but his gifts are refused.

El Glaoui's warriors march on the North for the second time. Representing this as a second spontaneous uprising, the French depose the Sultan and send him to exile in Corsica. His elderly uncle Moulay Mohammed Ben Arafa is declared Sultan.

Riots and massacres throughout the country.

First attempt on Arafa's life.

1954 Continued riots and repressive measures. Second attempt on Arafa's life.

Guillaume replaced by Francis Lacoste, nationalists liberated.

1955 Lacoste replaced by Gilbert Grandval. El Glaoui uses every measure to prevent return from exile of the ex-Sultan Mohammed V. On the anniversary of his deposition French are massacred all over Morocco. France recognizes that there is no solution but to recall Mohammed V, and bring him to France. El Glaoui, defeated, accedes, and makes his act of allegiance.

1956 Death of El Glaoui. Morocco independent.

1957 Members of the Glaoui régime dispossessed or exiled.

Olive jar

Genealogical Table

of the

House of Glaoua

ABDESSADEK
Chief of Mezouara Tribe, mid 19ᵀᴴ century

HAMMOU BEN ABDESSADEK
(But Glaoua ruled by a woman). Succeeded by

HADJ MOHAMMED 'TIBIBT' BEN HAMMOU
Caid of Telouet 1859. died 1888. Four wives, of whom two known, Lalla Yjja and Lalla Zora, otherwise Om El Heir, mother of Madani and Thami El Glaoui.

MADANI 'El F'ki'
b. 1866. d 1918. Grand Vizier to Sultan Moulay Hafid, 1909. Minister of War.

THAMI
b. 1879 d. 1956. m. Chems (Turkish), Kamar (Turkish), Zineb El Mokria, daughter of Grand Vizier El Mokri and ex-wife of Madani El Glaoui, Halima (Turkish), Zoubida (Tamdacht). Zim Fatma (Telouet) and a daughter of El Hadj El Mehdi El Menhebbi, who was Knighted at the Coronation of Edward VII.

HAMMOU
(Mohammed) Eldest son. d. young.

MOHAMMED EL ARBI
Eldest son. Minister of War to Sultan Moulay Hafid at age 18. Banished to Ouarzazat at the fall of Madani's first régime.

3 Daughters.
m. Caid Abdallah El Ouriki, Ben Driss and Derdouri.

LALLA RABIAA
m. 1910, Sultan Moulay Hafid.

LALLA HALIMA
Married Hammou, Caid of Telouet, who died 1934 (also Caid of Zagora, Tinerhir', Ouarzazat, and Commander of the South). She later married Thami El Glaoui.

LALLA R'KKIA
Sainte-femme or Marabout. Intermediary between Thami El Glaoui and Byaz. m. Boubker Ben Bachir El Ghandjaoui, rich Marrakesh merchant.

LALLA AICHA

LALLA MALIKA
m. Caid Brahim El Glaoui.

4 Children of marriage to Lalla Kamar.

2 Children of marriage to Lalla Zineb who was previously married to Madani El Glaoui.

BRAHIM
Caid of Telouet, Ait Ben Haddou, Ouarzazat & Skoura. Eldest son, by Lalla Kamar. Intermediary between Byaz and El Glaoui. The only son, who followed his father's politics. m. Lalla Malika, daughter of Caid Hammou of Telouet, 2 daughters living (in Marrakesh). Also m. 1950 actress Cécile Aubri, by whom 1 son Mehdi. Divorced 1958. Sentenced to 15 years exile in 1957. Lives in Paris.

ABDALLAH
d. 1952.

AHMED
Caid of Haouz (Guich). m. Daughter of French Industrialist. 1 daughter. No Politics. d. 1959.

HASSAN
m. daughter of Edward G. Robinson. Painter. Lives in Paris. No Politics.

MADANI
Unmarried, lives in Marrakesh. Member of Istiqlal, and imprisoned by El Glaoui, alternately at Telouet & Ait Ourir.

ABDESSADEK
Held title of President of the Chereefian Tribunal of Marrakesh. Khalifa. Interpreter to El Glaoui after 1955. Member of Istiqlal.

HAMMADI (Mohammed)
Khalifa at Ouazarzat. Inhabited
Taourirt at centre of oasis.

HAMMOU BEN MOHAMMED
Caid of Telouet etc. m. Lalla Halima, daughter of Madani.

ABDALLAH BEN HAMMOU Adopted by T'hami.

ALLAL
Caid of Demnat.

HASSI
Pasha of the Kasbah
of Marrakesh.

AHMED ZEMMOURI
Khalifa at Marrakesh after
Byaz, and Vizir de la Justice.
Epileptic.

ABD EL MALEK
b. 1899. d. 1918.
Favourite son.
Caid of Demnat at
17. Killed in action
against troops of
Sidi M'ha, at Bou Yahia.

ABD EL HAMID
died 1928.

OMAR
Caid of Demnat
& Taliouine
(Sektana tribe).

MOHAMMED EL KEBIR
m. 1918 Jehane Sabey
(nurse in French Hospital).
Lt. French Army
1ˢᵗ World War; wounded.
He divorced her 1925. was Khalifa at Marrakesh.

TAYEB
Khalifa at Anzal.

ABD WAHAB

MADANI

SMAÏN Died 1927.

Children of marriage to Lalla Zineb.

MOHAMMED EL FAKI

HOUIRYA
A daughter.

MINA
A daughter.

2 Children of marriage to Lalla Halima,
ex-wife of Caid Hammou of Telouet.

2 Children of marriage
to Lalla Zim Fatma.

1 Child of marriage
to Lalla Zoubida.

MOHAMMED
Ex-Caid of Ait
Ourir (Mesfiouia).
No Politics.

LALLA FATOOMA
d. 1949. Ex-wife of
Mohammed El Hajoui
functionary at the
French Residency-General.

MEHDI
Killed at Monte Cassino
2ⁿᵈ World War.

LALLA KHEDDOUJ
m. Abdesselam
El Mokri, son
of Grand Vizier.

LALLA SAÄDIA
b. 1944, the only
child of El Glaoui
born after 1940.

BOOK ONE
Madani El Glaoui

I

The Castle

THE castle stands at an altitude of more than 8,000 feet in the High Atlas mountains of Morocco. It and its scattered rookery of crumbling predecessors occupy the corner of a desert plateau, circled by the giant peaks of the Central Massif, all of them rising to more than 10,000 feet, and some, such as the great Jebel Ghat to the eastward, reaching 12,500. When in the spring the snows begin to thaw and the river below the castle, the Oued Mellah, becomes a torrent of ice-grey and white, the mountains reveal their fantastic colours, each distinct and contrasting with its neighbour. The hues are for the most part the range of colours to be found upon fan shells – reds, vivid pinks, violets, yellows, but among these are peaks of cold mineral green or of dull blue. Nearer at hand, where the Oued Mellah turns to flow through the valley of salt, a cluster of ghostly spires, hundreds of feet high and needle-pointed at their summits, cluster before the face of a precipice; vultures wheel and turn upon the air currents between them.

Apart from a sprinkling of evergreen shrubs upon the lower slopes, the mountains are bare of vegetation, for only close round the castle walls are there real trees; the tenderness of new leaf and the glory of blossoming almond intensified by the mighty desolation of the back-cloth.

Even in this setting the castle does not seem insignificant. It is neither beautiful nor gracious, but its sheer size, as if in competition with the scale of the mountains, compels attention as much as the fact that its pretension somehow falls short of the ridiculous. The castle, or *kasbah*, of Telouet is a tower of tragedy that leaves no room for laughter.

The double doors to the forecourt are twenty feet high. A giant Negro slave opens the lock with a key a foot long and sets his shoulder to the iron-bossed wood; the door gives way reluctantly, inch by inch, creaking and rasping upon rusty hinges. A kestrel hawk, disturbed from its nest in the wall above, flies out scolding with sharp staccato cries. The surface of the courtyard is an uneven rubble, sloping sharply to the left, down to the curtain wall, where row upon row of dark doorways lead to the stable quarters. Above them are castellated look-out posts facing the Jebel Ghat. There is sheep-dung scattered among the rubble, and the reddish curling horn of a Moroccan ram. To the right rises the whole mass of the *kasbah*, tower and rooftop: ill-ordered, ill-planned, but majestic in its proliferation and complete absence of symmetry. There are three colours only – whitewash, red stone or clay, and brilliant green roof tiles. Above these the ever-present birds of prey, the vultures, ravens and kites, weave slow and intricate patterns upon the hard blue sky. There is no sound but their calling, and the clacking bills of the storks which nest on every tower.

The slave unlocks an intricately carved door in the white wall to the right of the forecourt. The number and weight of keys that he carries is so great that in order to support them he wears a heavy silk rope about his shoulders, concealed by his *djellabah*, an ankle-length white woollen garment with a hood, and further hidden by his *selham*, a black woollen cloak, also with a hood, which envelops all.

He carries sixty-seven keys. He has been in sole charge of Telouet for three years, but even now he does not know his way through the labyrinth that was constructed intentionally as such. He can find his way to the kitchens (I counted two hundred and thirty-eight paces and twenty-two doors unlocked), but he cannot find his way from these to the harem without going back to the main reception quarters and looking out of the windows to reorientate himself.

It was to these reception rooms that he wanted always to return; they were the outward and visible sign of ultimate physical ambition. They were all on one floor, but three hundred men had worked on them for three years, plasterworkers, carvers, and one painter, who covered inches rather than feet daily. This man had been paid, by Moroccan standards, an enormous wage – about £22 a week. The owner of the castle had intended that it should become the most fabulous palace in the world, a Château de Coucy, an Xanadu. It had already been called 'The Palace of a Thousand and One Nights'.

The décor was in the main based upon the stalagmite theme of the Saadien tombs (the Saadiens were an earlier dynasty of Moroccan Sultans who reigned from 1554 to 1659), but it embraced, also, every style that was luxurious, however debased, and made use of every traditional motif. A (comparatively) small salon in which the occupant entertained intimate guests incorporated continuous three-foot-high panels of silks and brocades from Lyons, rugs from Rabat, Persia, Turkestan and the High Atlas, comparatively crude work and bastard design alternating with high craftsmanship of all nations.

The harem is paved and walled with painted tiles that seem, for the most part, to be of modern Italian origin, though some have the detailed beauty of the ancient Hispano-Mauresque. The carved and painted yew wood ceilings of the reception rooms are Moorish in concept, as is the Saadien plasterwork of the noble alcoves. But deep invading cracks cut crudely through the intricate elaboration of years of work, for Telouet is empty now; only the Negro slaves, almost destitute, linger on to tend the relics of a dead dynasty.

I have various images of Telouet. The last and most enduring is after a great snowfall when more than four thousand sheep and goats in the surrounding mountains were buried and killed by suffocation. When the snows thawed and the carcases were exposed every vulture, kite and raven congregated on Telouet. As the sun went down the air was dark with them as with a swarm of locusts; they homed for Telouet in their thousands, like starlings to Trafalgar Square, till the branches of the trees broke under them, till the battlements of the castle were foul with their excreta, and still, as the last of the light went, the black wings were thronging in to alight and jostle their neighbours. It was on that night that, listening to the jackals howling, I became lost in the castle, and found my torch shining upon white but manacled bones in a dungeon. With the turbulent history of Telouet they could have been either a hundred or less than five years old.

'In every governor's *Kasbah*, deep in damp dungeons – as often as not holes scooped in the earth for storing grain – there lay and pined those who had committed, or not committed, as the case might be, some crime; and still more often, those who were rich enough to be squeezed. In such suffering, and in darkness, receiving just sufficient nourishment to support life, men were known to have existed for years, to emerge again long after their relations had given up all hope of seeing them. But there was always a chance – a chance that the Governor might die or fall into disgrace; and then the dungeons in his castle would be opened and the wrecks of his prisoners be released. And what prisons! what horrors of prisons they were, even those above ground and reserved for the ordinary class of criminal. Chained neck to neck, with heavy shackles on their legs, they sat or lay in filth, and often the cruel iron collars were only undone to take away a corpse.'

'The whole life in those great Atlas fortified *Kasbahs* was one of warfare and of gloom. Every tribe had its enemies, every family had its blood-feuds, and every man his would-be murderer.'

Work on Telouet was still in progress when the régime fell ten years ago, the only event that could logically bring it to a halt. The plasterers and tilers and mosaic-workers had a programme lasting for years ahead. There are windows still unglazed, others awaiting the addition of the elaborate wrought iron work with which they were all to be embellished. Many walls carry the bold charcoal outlines for an ambitious mosaic that was never begun, for the whole vast palace and all its uncountable rooms were to have been decorated with the same disregard for time or money. Builders were at work on further extensions to the castle itself, here a new wing, here a lofty gallery from which guests might watch feats of horsemanship on the green sward below.

Telouet presented, in fact, a picture that was almost unique, for it was not a mediaeval survival, as are the few European castles still occupied by the descendants of feudal barons, but a deliberate re-creation of the Middle Ages, with all their blatant extremes of beauty and ugliness, good and evil, elegance and violence, power and fear – by those who had full access to the inventions of contemporary science. No part of the *kasbah* is more than a hundred years old; no part of its ruined predecessors goes back further than another fifty. Part of the castle is built of stone, distinguishing it sharply from the other *kasbahs* that are made of *pisé*, or sun-dried mud, for no matter to what heights of beauty or fantasy these may aspire they are all, in the final analysis, soluble in water.

From this desolate group of ruins in the High Atlas, so far from the seat of government at Fez, there arose by a strange chain of coincidence a generation of kingmakers. They were two brothers, chiefs of an insignificant mountain tribe, and they rose in that one generation to depose two Sultans, to become the true rulers of Morocco, to shake the whole French political structure; and, with their downfall, to add a new and uncomfortable word to the French language. The name of the tribe was Glaoua, and *glaouisé* now means, in French political jargon, betrayed. Neither France nor Morocco is over-anxious to recall the tale behind the word; and for this reason, if for no other, a true reconstruction presents the historian with formidable difficulties.

A hundred years ago very few contemporary Europeans had ever visited Morocco. There were no more than a handful resident in the country, and fewer still had ever penetrated into the savage territories of the High Atlas, where wild tribes skirmished amid the barren peaks, or into the palm oases of the Pre-Sahara beyond them. The country, despite its geographical position as a neighbour to Europe, remained as unknown as Tibet, xenophobe and mysterious, guarding splendours and horrors that the wildest travellers' tales could not exaggerate. The Corsair pirates still patrolled the coasts; in the greater towns the Jews salted for public display the heads of the innumerable executed; every sizeable city held its slave market three times a week, on Wednesdays, Thursdays and Fridays; there was neither a railway nor a true road in all the land. Yet the splendour of its palaces, the majesty of its mosques, rivalled anything in all Islam.

In fact, Morocco at the end of the last century was little different in any external respect from what it had been at the end of the century before – or, indeed, the end of any other century for a thousand years or more. Since the seventh century, when the Arabs conquered and Islamized the country from the indigenous white Berbers, it had remained an independent state for thirteen hundred years, ruled over from the sixteenth century onward by Sultans who combined both temporal and spiritual power – each was both king and *imam*. The Sultans were *Chereefs*; that is to say that they were or claimed to be direct descendants of the Prophet Mohammed.

The historical development of the whole country parallels and underlines the paradox of Telouet; Fez had achieved a mediaeval richness of culture and scholarship long before northern Europe reached the same point, but there she had remained. The reasons were numerous and complex, but the most easily understood was the influence of successive assaults of Portuguese, Spaniards and Turks in the fifteenth and sixteenth centuries, disrupting through dislocation of trade routes a merchant economy which had promised stability. In any country a characteristic of absolute monarchy was an almost unbelievable disparity between the cultural standards of the court and of the general life of the people, and in Morocco this was to the last degree accentuated by the character of the terrain.

There have been many attempts to divide Morocco into convenient sections for discussion, but most of them appear unnecessarily complex; it is easier to consider an inner Morocco and an outer Morocco, the two being divided by the whole mass of the Atlas mountains running from the south-west to the north-east of the country, and the Rif mountains which turn at right angles to these and form the Mediterranean wall. From the point of view of a central government, or *mahkzen*, at Fez the governable territory of inner Morocco reached barely to the foothills of the mountain ranges; beyond this line wild tribes acknowledged no allegiance to the throne. The same rough geographical division into an inner and outer Morocco covered the terms *bled el mahkzen* – country under government control – and *bled es siba* – literally the 'lawless country', where force was the only criterion – of the infinitely greater territories of unsubdued tribes. It was from the *bled es siba*, and more especially the land of desert and palm oasis lying to the east of the Atlas, that almost every new dynasty of Sultans rose to conquer and replace the last.

The pomp and pageantry of the Sultans was unequalled anywhere in the world, but their hour was often proportionately brief; at one point there had been six Sultans in ten years. At best, the geographical extent of their rule embraced little more than half the land nominally enclosed by the frontiers of Morocco. Much of the unconquered territory was unworthy of a Sultan's attention except as a possible cradle for a new pretender to the throne, but the vast white ramparts of the High Atlas contained a greater challenge, for they guarded the rich and fertile oases that lay between them and the Sahara Desert. Sultan after Sultan led punitive forces against the unconquered tribes of the south; but, no matter what the fortunes of war, there could be no final decisive battle, for once the imperial army had withdrawn the tribes settled back into their old insolent disregard of central authority.

The present ruling dynasty, the Alaouites, have occupied the throne of Morocco for an uninterrupted three hundred years. They celebrated their tricentenary in 1964; and King Hassan II, who succeeded his father Mohammed V in 1960, is the twenty-second rightful Alaouite Sultan.

The second Sultan of the dynasty, who reigned for no less than fifty-five years (1672–1727) remained until recently the only one whose name – Moulay Ismael – was familiar to many Europeans, and familiar in a most unsavoury context, a name to be bracketed with those of Gilles de Rais or de Sade. Moulay Ismael was, in what may be described as his personal life, an ogre for whom there can be few parallels in the history of any country. Like a fox in a hen-run, he killed for sport, not occasionally, but as a matter of personal and daily satisfaction like the pleasures of the table or of the harem. There was no pretence at pretext; with his own sword he would strike off the head of the slave who held his stirrup as he mounted his horse, or several heads of his own Black Guards as he rode down their ranks; he disembowelled the living and organized displays of torture for the titillation of his senses; there was, in fact, no imaginable atrocity of cruelty and bloodlust in which he did not habitually indulge. Yet as a ruler he was one of the great figures of Moroccan history. By the maintenance of a permanent army of black slaves he did much to unify and extend the *bled el mahkzen* (though he was at civil war throughout almost his whole reign, and latterly with his own sons). He eliminated many of the foreign enclaves in his country, ejecting the British from Tangier in 1684 and the Spanish from Larache; he forced the attention of France by demanding in marriage a natural daughter of Louis XIV, the young widowed

Princesse de Conti; he built with the labour of thousands of Christian captives, whose bodies were simply built into the walls as they died, his new capital of Meknès. He left, however, the greatest of Morocco's internal problems untouched, for he made no attempt to integrate temporarily defeated Berber tribes into an Arabized Morocco.

After the death of Moulay Ismael in 1727 the whole of Morocco fell into total anarchy, while for a full thirty years his sons struggled for the throne. It was like a game of musical chairs, but a singularly bloody and noisy one. One of the sons reigned twice, another achieved four times; in between, five other Sultans scrambled briefly on to the throne before being pushed off again. Deserters from the armies of all factions formed roving brigand bands, and no life nor property was safe anywhere in the country; the *bled es siba* crept back from the mountains on to the plains.

The period ended with the exhaustion that characterizes the close of an hysterical attack. Both the country and the imperial palace were utterly impoverished. Every subsequent Sultan was faced with the necessity of leading tax-collecting punitive armies against the numerous rebellious tribes of a now established *bled es siba*, tribes who preferred the chances of war to the certainty of destitution. It was to one of these repressive sorties, more than a century and a quarter later, that the House of Glaoua owed its sudden but vertiginous rise.

The Eagle's Nest, Telouet

2

The Cannon

In 1893 the reigning Alaouite Sultan, Moulay Hassan, decided upon a tax-collecting expedition to the desert oases beyond the High Atlas, with its ultimate aim as the restoration of law and order at Tafilelt, the great palm oasis that had been the cradle of his dynasty, and which was now, as so often before, in a state of anarchy. It was creeping with his own blood relations, for it had always been the custom of the Alaouites to send home to Tafilelt unwanted members of their families. As these families numbered literally hundreds of children, and as the majority were unwanted, the descendants of the Prophet in Tafilelt were legion. It was an unusual state of affairs if there were not a few stirring up trouble.

The expedition would have meant, had all gone well, a return journey for his army of something over a thousand miles, but he was well used to this peripatetic existence. Moulay Hassan was, by the standards of his day in Morocco – and it is necessary to emphasize the qualification – an intelligent ruler. He saw the necessity of reducing the *bled es siba*, the lands of rebellious tribes, to unity with the government at Fez, but he was essentially an exponent of the tradition summed up by the dicta of his predecessors, and more especially by the cynical aphorism 'an empty sack cannot stand upright'. This implied the emptying of the sacks (destitution by tax and pillage of the potentially dissident tribes) and he never looked beyond this to a more permanent solution.

'He was no fanatic, and had he been able to break down some of the great reserve which encircled him, he probably would have been content to do so. In appearance he was extremely handsome, dark, but showing no trace of black blood, with straight regular features, and a

Sultan Moulay Hassan, 1873–94

most dignified bearing. His most remarkable feature was, however, the sadness of his expression.

'Moulay Hassan's energy was never-failing, and he maintained order amongst his lawless tribes and stamped out the constantly occurring revolts by an almost unceasing "progress" through the country, accompanied by his rabble of an army. He seldom spent six months together in any of his several capitals, and the Moors had a saying "The Imperial tents are never stored".

'The great labour, the enormous transport that these journeyings necessitated, is difficult to appreciate. Not only was the Sultan accompanied by his numerous ladies and all his viziers and their families and suites, but he had with him as well some ten thousand soldiers and a rabble of camp-followers. A large number of native merchants also joined the throng, for trade flowed to the region in which the Court was residing.

'Some idea of the results upon the country passed through can be imagined from the fact that the very name of these expeditions in Arabic is "*harka*", "the burning". No matter whether the tribes were in incipient rebellion, in open revolt, or in peace, they had to provide the food and fodder of this great horde, whose ravages more nearly resembled those of a flight of locusts than the passing by of human beings. Not only such "legal" taxation as could be extorted was collected, but the viziers and the Sultan's entourage had to be bribed and paid as well, while every soldier and every camp-follower pillaged on his own account. On receiving the news of the coming of one of these Imperial expeditions, as many of the population as could, or as dared, fled to other regions; and the Sultan often passed through a deserted country, except that the Governor and tribal representatives had to be there to pour the little wealth of the countryside into the royal coffers.'

The following description of the routine of such an expedition refers to a later march and another Sultan, but of it Walter Harris writes, 'Sultan after Sultan, ever since the empire of Morocco first came under the dominion of the Arabs, had travelled in exactly the same manner . . . in no detail had it changed. The very shape and decoration of the tents had never varied.

'Long before daylight the great camp was astir, and when, soon after 3 a.m., the morning gun was fired, a number of tents had already been struck, horses saddled, and mules and camels packed for the march. In the moonlight and early dawn the scene was one of great beauty – an indistinct medley of white tents, here silvery in the moonlight, there ruddy with the glow of camp-fires, whose tall red columns of smoke rose pillar-like into the still air. In and about the tents passed the shadowy forms of men and animals. As if by magic the scene was ever changing, as tent after tent silently fell to the ground, until with the first glow of dawn there remained of the great encampment only the canvas-walled enclosure containing the Sultan's tents, and a plain covered with horsemen and thousands upon thousands of baggage mules and camels. Already the cavalry were massed near the Sultan's enclosure, the horsemen forming an open square, in the centre of which, surrounded by the Ministers of State, lay a crimson-curtained palanquin with its couch of turquoise blue. From the entrance of the Sultan's tents to the square of cavalry a double line was formed by white-robed, red-capped officials, awaiting His Majesty.

'A bugle sounds clear in the still atmosphere, and a moment later a great cry rends the air. There is a beating of drums and a sound of trumpets, as a solitary white figure, erect and dignified, walks slowly through the bowing lines of officials, enters the square of horsemen, and seats himself upon the blue divan. Again arises the cry of welcome, as, bending forward, the tribes greet their Sultan with the salutation, "May God prolong the life of our Lord".

'The sun has risen now, his first rays falling upon the gold-orbed banners, heavy with brocades and silks that wave high above the heads of the cavalry; then upon the wild horsemen themselves, their saddles of brilliant reds and greens, half-hidden in the heavy folds of their long white garments, and the scene becomes one of indescribable beauty. One by one the Sultan's tents are struck, and the great canvas-walled enclosure vanishes under the hands of hundreds of skilled tent-pitchers. Sometimes His Majesty gives an audience to an official, a local governor of a tribe, who, barefoot, approaches the Sultan, falls upon his knees, and three times touches the ground with his forehead, remaining crouched before his lord and master during the few seconds that such audiences last. Again a bugle; and through the line of horsemen run dusky soldiers leading saddled horses, trotting them past the Sultan that he may choose upon the back of which he will perform the day's march. With a slight motion of his hand the choice is made, and the honoured steed is led up to the palanquin. Sometimes it is a white, saddled and trapped in turquoise blue; sometimes a grey, decked in rose-coloured silks; sometimes a black, his head half hidden in prim-rose-yellow tassels.

'As the Sultan mounts, the scene becomes for a few minutes one of wild confusion. The banner-bearers, the spear-bearers, the cavalry, the scarlet-and-blue mounted infantry, the high officials on their saddle-mules, the artillery, even the Sultan himself, seems hopelessly mixed in a struggling crowd. It is only for a very little while, and then from the medley emerges the royal procession, forming into order as it proceeds. The vanguard is formed of an escort of cavalry, headed by the standard-bearers, carrying flags of every hue and colour, the poles topped with glittering balls. Next come the artillery, the guns carried upon the backs of mules, and after them a troop of mounted infantry. Two mounted men, carrying long slender spears, precede the led horses, five or six of which, trapped in rich silks, always form a feature of the procession. Riding alone is the Grand Master of the Ceremonies, a dark man of fine presence, wand of office in hand. Then, after a space of some forty yards, the Sultan, a solitary white figure on horseback. At his side run Negroes, waving long white scarves to keep the dust and the flies off his holy person. Immediately behind His Majesty rides a soldier, bearing aloft, so as to shade the Sultan from the rays of the sun, the Imperial parasol of crimson and gold. The red palanquin, borne by sturdy mules, follows, and behind it a long wide line of standard-bearers, the banners rich in gold thread and brocaded silks, and the

Berber warrior

poles of one and all crowned with gilded orbs. Immediately behind the flags ride the viziers and great officers of State, followed by a rabble of smaller officials and soldiery, of black slaves and tribesmen from all over Morocco.

'There are no roads, and the procession of men and animals spreads widely out over the plains and undulating hills. Often as far as the eye can reach one can trace the great migration stretching from horizon to horizon, a rainbow of colour upon the green plains. Sometimes to cross a valley the procession narrows in, to spread out again in the open country beyond, till the whole land is dotted with horsemen and mules, and slow-gaited lumbering camels.

'Now and again a tribal governor, with his escort of horsemen, comes to salute his sovereign. Drawn up in a long line they await the Sultan's approach. At his approach the governor dismounts from his horse and prostrates himself before his lord, to rise again at a signal from His Majesty. Bending low, he approaches and kisses the Sultan's stirrup, then mounts again, and with a hoarse cry of welcome the tribesmen dig their spurs into the flanks of their barbs and gallop pell-mell hither and thither, now singly, now in line, firing their guns the while, until the horses are brought to a sudden standstill in a cloud of smoke and dust. These tribesmen are not the only people who come from afar to greet the Sultan on his march. There are beggars and representatives of all the dervish sects, from cymbal-beating Negroes from the Sudan to the Hamacha of Meknès, who cut open their heads with hatchets. There are snake-charmers and acrobats, and men with performing apes; little deputations of country Jews and Jewesses; groups of white-robed scholars from local mosques, bearing white flags; veiled Arab women, uttering shrill trembling cries of welcome, and offering bowls of milk; lepers with their faces swathed and wearing great straw hats, bearing bowls of wood to collect alms in, for none may touch them – a thousand scenes of human life, with all its pleasures and all its tragedies.'

'Usually a ride of about four hours brings the Sultan to his next camping-ground. A quarter of an hour before reaching the selected spot the bands commence to play, and the tribesmen, the cavalry, and mounted infantry gallop ahead, forming into two lines, between which His Majesty rides into a square of horsemen drawn up in the same formation as that of the early morning. The crimson palanquin is quickly unharnessed, the blue divan arranged, and the Sultan seats himself in solitary state to await the pitching of his encampment.

'No tent might be raised in the camp until the gilded globe which surmounts the Sultan's principal tent is in position; but it required only a very short time for the skilled tent-pitchers to pitch the great mass of canvas crowned with its glittering orb. It is a signal to the rest of the camp, and almost as if growing from the ground arose the white canvas town. There was no confusion, no noise. Everyone knew the right position to pitch in, and the whole system worked without a hitch. Probably the Moors are alone in the pitching of these great camps; it seems a hereditary trait in their characters.

'The Sultan's principal tent once up, the tent-pitchers turned their attention to the remainder of his camp, consisting of some half-dozen large marquees, the whole – an acre perhaps of ground – being enclosed with a nine-feet wall of white canvas, decorated in patterns of dark blue. This private encampment of His Majesty formed the centre of the camp, which stretched away on all sides, often for nearly half a mile in every direction. At the outer extremity were pitched the tents of the infantry, so close to one another that entrance and exit to the camp was only possible at certain intervals, where spaces were left for the purpose.

'The greatest interest naturally attached to the immediate surroundings of the Sultan's tents. No one but his ladies and their female slaves might enter the walled enclosure, with the exception of one small portion of it divided off from the rest, retained for unofficial audiences. His Majesty transacted all his affairs of State outside the enclosure, in a tent of scarlet and green cloth, pitched at the end of a large open square and visible from a considerable distance. Here before the eyes of the public His Majesty received his Ministers, attended to his correspondence, and sealed official documents. Near this tent, known as the "*Siwan*", were two large marquees, one used as a mosque, the other the office of the viziers. In this quarter, too, were the offices of the other Ministers of State and high officials. Behind these were the private encampments of the more important personages, often consisting of several very large tents leading to one another by covered passages of canvas. Directly opposite, on the farther side of the Sultan's enclosure, were the royal stables, where a quantity of fine barbs were tethered, their number constantly being added to by the presents brought to His Majesty by the tribal governors.

'As soon as his tents were ready, the Sultan remounted his horse, and amidst the playing of bands and the shouts of the tribesmen, rode into the seclusion of his private camp. It was generally not long after His Majesty's disappearance from view that a long line of white-robed and veiled women, mounted upon mules, passed silently amongst the tents and entered the royal precincts. As they filed through the camp every man turned his head away from the mysterious white procession. Usually the whole camp was pitched by midday, and not long after that hour the neighbourhood of the Government quarters became astir with life. The white-robed viziers sought their offices, while soldiers kept order amongst the throng of people that were always crowding near the tent doors awaiting audiences with the Ministers of State. Only the "*Siwan*" was deserted, but not for long. A bugle sounds. There is a hurrying to and fro of officials and soldiers, and again the cry, "God prolong the life of our Lord," is heard, and the solitary white figure, round whom all this great camp revolves, is seen slowly entering under the shadow of the tent of scarlet and green.

'At sunset gunfire, His Majesty prayed, and retired to his tents for the night, though almost every evening he gave unofficial audiences to his friends in the divided-off portion of his private encampment reserved for this purpose. As night fell the camp became dotted with the little lights of lanterns, often gaily decorated with coloured glass, while here and there a camp-fire showed up ruddily amongst the tents. Now and again could be heard the tinkling of stringed instruments and the soft murmur of a singer, who seemed afraid to raise his voice in the stillness that pervades everything, – a stillness only broken now and again by an order to the guards and sentries – of whom four hundred, shoulder to shoulder, encircled the Sultan's enclosure – or by the long-drawn accents of the mueddin as he called the Faithful to prayer.

'The "last post" – and as the note of the bugle dies away, a wonderful silence fell upon the moonlit camp.'

'In 1893 Moulay Hassan determined to visit the desert regions of Morocco, including far-off Tafilelt, the great oasis from which his dynasty had originally sprung, and where, before becoming the ruling branch of the royal family, they had resided ever since their founder, the great-grandson of the Prophet, had settled there, an exile from the East.'

With the Sultan at Tafilelt, though not in his official role of Commander-in-Chief of the Chereefian army, was one of the most curious figures of the day, a tubby little man commonly called *Caid* Maclean. His real name was Sir Harry Maclean, and he had been a British officer of the Gibraltar garrison. From there he had been seconded to the Sultan's Court as an artillery instructor, and had captured the Sultan's fancy so greatly that a few years later he was offered – and, after official permission, accepted – the supreme command. He habitually wore a white turban, highly polished English hunting boots, and a Berber cloak or *selham* of his clan tartan. To his men he was known as 'El Kronel', the nearest their speech could approach to 'colonel'.

'Leaving Fez in the summer, the Sultan proceeded south, crossing the Atlas above Kasbah-el-Maghkzen, and descended to the upper waters of the Oued Ziz. An expedition such as this would have required a system of organization far in excess of the capabilities of the Moors, great though their resources were. Food was lacking; the desert regions could provide little. The water was bad, the heat very great. Every kind of delay, including rebellion and the consequent punishment of the tribes, hampered the Sultan's movements; and it was only toward winter that he arrived in Tafilelt with a fever-stricken army and greatly diminished transport.

'Moulay Hassan returned from Tafilelt a dying man.'

The Sultan's return from Tafilelt was like the retreat of Napoleon's armies from Moscow. He did not try to return to Fez, but made for the southern capital of Marrakesh, separated from Tafilelt by the mighty wall of the High Atlas. By the time his army had reached the foothills the winter snows had begun; as they climbed higher into the main massif more and more of the camels, mules and horses, weak with starvation, stumbled into deep snowdrifts and died. Little but their carcases stood between the remnants of the *harka* and starvation, and the surviving beasts staggered on and upwards laden with what little meat could be salvaged from the corpses of their companions. The army was attended by clouds of ravens, kites and vultures. Hundreds of men died daily, they were left unburied in the snow, stripped of whatever rags they had still possessed.

'Often the soldiers, if they took the trouble, buried the wounded alive, to prevent their heads being carried off as trophies by the enemy. I remember being told, while spending an evening with some of the riff-raff of the army – who, in spite of their characters, were often the most jovial and cheery of companions – the story of a recalcitrant wounded comrade who didn't want to be buried alive. The incident had happened the same day. The man was badly wounded, the camp was a long way off, and his "pals" didn't mean to have the trouble of carrying him there. So they dug his grave, and began to push him in. He naturally protested. "I am not dead," he cried; "don't you see I am living?" "Be quiet," said a companion; "you were killed at least an hour ago. Don't you realize that you are dead?" The poor man still cried out till the earth covered him and put an end to his protestation and his life. The soldier who narrated the incident added, "The Moorish soldier is an ungrateful and unbelieving individual. This man, for instance, had no confidence in us, his comrades, when we assured him he was dead. I hate ingratitude," – and he filled up his little "kif" pipe and handed it to us for a whiff.'

Men too weak to carry their weapons any further dropped them and struggled on unarmed. The main arsenal, however, which included a

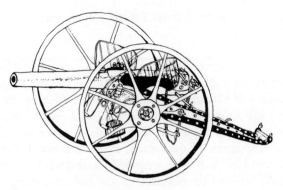

The Krupp cannon

ponderous Krupp assault cannon and a quantity of its weighty ammunition, was never abandoned. The continued existence of this cannon changed the whole history of Morocco.

This particular cannon happened to be functional, a fact noteworthy enough by itself to distinguish it from a number of collaterals whose role was purely ritual. Sultans were always buying cannon, often accompanied by a temporary instructor, but when the instructor had gone and the few instructed had been killed, the artillery inflicted more casualties upon its masters than upon its enemies. But to the people the cannons had become symbols of the Sultan's army; more, they had become symbols of the Sultan in his capacity of *imam* or spiritual leader, for it was one of the decrepit but still vocal guns called El Nouba, that announced the hour of prayer at dawn and dusk. A whole rigmarole of ritual and belief grew around the cannons. They became, in effect, ambulant representatives of His Chereefian Majesty's person, possessing his power of *baraka* or blessing, his power to cure diseases, to receive petitions and offerings, and to grant asylum. Any malefactor who sat himself upon the shaft between the cannon's wheels acquired automatically the right of direct appeal to the Sultan, an appeal which no Sultan would refuse. 'I swear by the cannon of the Sultan' was a frequent and binding oath, and the cannons also received direct prayer, addressed customarily to their muzzles. They also received offerings, in the form of the heads of the enemy, and after a victory the cannons were completely hidden by the bloody heads piled on and around them. More bizarre still, during a temporary truce or parlay in rebel territory, women of the Berber tribes could be seen kissing the big

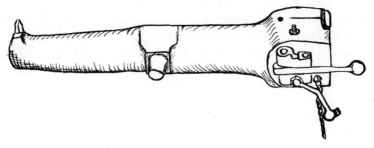

Early wall cannon

bronze gun barrels and praying to them for the defeat of the Sultan. The paradox was not apparent to them, for they venerated the Sultan as the *khalifa*, or representative, of God, and abhorred him as an oppressive tyrant of their people.

So, in various stages of sacred decrepitude, corrupt and corroded, the cannons continued to accompany the Sultan's *harkas* and *mehallas* (armies), dragged or carried by camels, mules or harnessed slaves.

The Sultan was still many days' march from Marrakesh, and he was far from certain of his reception by the mountain tribes through whose territory he must pass. An Imperial *harka* in its pomp, with banners and standards flying, was a thing to be hated, certainly, but one to be feared too; this feeble rabble, less than a third of the ten thousand with whom he had set forth, might all too easily disappear into the maw of the mountains.

Then, as now, there were but three practicable passes over the High Atlas. Each of these was controlled by a warrior tribe, organized much as were the clans of the Scottish Highlands in their heyday. All three were Berber tribes, with a greater or lesser admixture of Arab blood and that of the black slaves with whom, since the Arab conquest, every notable had surrounded himself.

Some explanation of the slave system in Morocco at that time may be helpful to the general reader. The black slaves were originally imported mainly from the Sudan and from Timbuktu. Even a petty village chief owned a few, while any notable would count several hundreds, and in a few cases over a thousand. Slaves were encouraged – forced, in fact – to breed fast and early. The children were inspected regularly for signs of puberty, and were mated as soon as they were considered fruitful. Thus their numbers increased in direct ratio to the length of time that a notable remained a notable, for at his fall all his property, including his slaves, was seized by the *mahkzen* or central government. In theory, a family that succeeded in remaining in power for a hundred years would have owned many thousands of slaves, but few families ever lasted half that time without destitution and a slow climb back to prosperity. Slaves were the absolute property of their master, who held over them the power of life and death; he might use them how he pleased, sell them, or give them away. They formed, however, part of his household in *kasbah* or palace, and were as integral to its structure as his own children – which in fact they very frequently were, for any sizeable harem contained women of all colours. There was no concept of legitimacy in the modern European sense, and from the vast numbers of daughters that any notable necessarily sired he would give away one here, one there, as a casual present to a friend or neighbour. With her went a retinue of slaves to look after her – a small or large number according to her importance and the esteem in which her mother was held by the donor. Abuses of the owner's absolute rights were rare, and slaves enjoyed a degree of protection and security considerably greater than the average free man. Favourite slaves and freed slaves often rose to positions of great power, and the inter-breeding was so constant and continuous that there were few families in all Morocco who could be certain of the purity of their blood. A rich man of thirty would have, say, a hundred children by his concubines, and of these a full half would probably be black.

While the community structure of the High Atlas was far more complex than any to be found in Europe, the superficial resemblance to Scottish clans was remarkable; thus the principal family of each tribe attached the prefix 'the' (*el*) to the tribal name, in the same way as did such Highland chieftains as The Mackintosh, The MacLachlan or The Macleod. Like these, too, they inhabited castles, or *kasbahs*, of barbaric splendour, exacted heavy tribute from their tribesmen, and made sporadic war upon one another according to the shifting alliances of the moment. They belonged, as did all Morocco in name, to the religion of Islam, though among the remoter tribespeople there had always been those who clung secretly to an older, polytheistic worship, and blood sacrifices to sacred trees, streams and stones.

Reading from left to right (or south-west to north-east) as the Sultan's army now looked up at the mountains, these tribes were the M'tougga, commanding the southernmost pass of Tiz-n-Test; the Goundafa, controlling the central Oued Nfis, and the Glaoua, dominating the pass then called Tiz-n-Telouet (now the nearby Tiz-n-Tishka). The chief of each of these tribes was officially a *Caid*, or representative of

Sultan, in his own area, responsible for collecting taxes and enforcing recognition of the central government, but such titles were often bestowed by the Sultan and his viziers as much in the hope of making a convert as in any certainty of loyalty. There was enough precedent for rebellious or treacherous *Caids* to justify uneasiness.

These were the three principal *Caids* of the High Atlas; they were constantly at war with one another and constantly changing alliance – facts that afforded the Sultan the profoundest satisfaction. All three were highwaymen in the respectable Moroccan tradition. They exacted, that is to say, heavy tribute from the caravans of dates, olives, *argan* oil and walnuts, whose trade routes led from the south through the passes they commanded, and those who refused to pay they simply pillaged and put to death. Each had his own pretentious town house in Marrakesh, much as European aristocracy used to maintain an establishment in the capital city; each longed to extend his territory into the fertile plains – or, to use the phrase of the day, 'the lands of summer water'. Without that expansion into the plains no one of them could have achieved real power, and their lives were devoted to the conquest, by force or by intrigue, of territory either to the south or to the north of their mountain massif. Each deserves a separate volume; but as the M'touggi and the Goundafi are no more than tangential to the long drama of the Glaoui, they cannot in this narrative claim more than introductory paragraphs.

Caid Abd El Malek M'touggi, controlling Tiz-n-Test, was not by nature a warrior but an intriguer, with a finger in every pie. He was a hoarder, and was reputed to have great treasures hidden away. His slaves were distinguished by a silver ring through one ear, and when they formed his escort they rode superb grey horses. The mountain lands that he owned, his *kasbah* of Bou Abbout and his five hundred slaves he had inherited from his uncle. For a long time the M'touggi's ambition to expand on to the plain lands of Marrakesh had been thwarted by the powerful and hostile Haha tribe who occupied them. At last, in 1868, the M'touggi threw suspicion of treachery upon the *Caid* who had commanded the Haha for the past twenty years. The Sultan summoned this man to Marrakesh and there offered him the choice between a glass of poisoned tea and starvation in an iron cage. The *Caid* accepted the tea, saying, 'It is written.' The ensuing chaos in the lands over which he had ruled gave the M'touggi his chance; but in a few years he too had grown too powerful for a Sultan's liking, and Moulay Hassan dispossessed him of all but his original mountain property. His nephew *Caid* Abd El Malek M'touggi had little cause to love the Government at Fez. In the year of which I am writing he was fifty-two years old and he commanded six thousand rifles.

Caid Tayeb El Goundafi, controlling Tiz-n-Babaoun, was actually with the Sultan's *harka*, and there existed between him and the Sultan what amounted almost to a personal friendship. This had begun when he was no more than thirteen years old. His intransigent father, perpetually at war with the Government, decided at last to submit, and required an emissary to send to the Sultan. He proposed his brother, who refused point blank, and the child Tayeb volunteered. The Sultan's representative in Marrakesh sent him and his slaves to Fez in chains, and they spent the first night in prison. In the morning he was summoned before the Sultan, who called for a blacksmith to cut his chains. The Sultan accepted submission provided that the Goundafi came in person to the palace at Marrakesh, where the Court was soon moving. On Tayeb's assurance that if his father would not come he would return himself, the Sultan let him go with his blessings. It took Tayeb four days to persuade his father to go to Marrakesh; when at last he did so he was rewarded with the title of *Caid*, which passed to Tayeb at his father's death in 1883. His father's resources were reputed to be limitless, and there is historical record that when the Sultan visited Marrakesh El Goundafi sent him a gift of one hundred male and one hundred female slaves, one hundred horses, one hundred cows with calves, one hundred camels with young, not to mention the customary contributions of gold and silver. (A sidelight on this gift of slaves is cast by Monsieur Chatinières, in his book *Dans Les Grands Atlas Marocains* published in 1919. 'It is said that Tayeb El Goundafi breeds slaves for profit. His Negroes are mated with Berber women requisitioned from his mountain villages. Their amber-coloured progeny, both male and female, seem to be much appreciated, and he gives or sells them to his friends.') *Caid* Tayeb El Goundafi was thirty-two in 1893 and could raise some five thousand armed men.

Caid Madani El Glaoui, controlling Tiz-n-Telouet, was of different calibre from either of the other rival war lords. He was a young man of great intelligence and limitless ambition, an outstandingly brave warrior who possessed at the same time something more than a flair for intrigue. He was known as El F'ki, a title meaning no more than 'the literate', but he had in fact also received his Koranic instruction. He had succeeded his father a bare five years earlier. During his grandfather's time the Glaoua tribe, an unimportant sibling of a larger tribe to the south, had been ruled by a woman, – a situation unthinkable to an Arab, but within the framework of Berber matriarchy. *Caid* Madani's father succeeded her. His full name was Si Mohammed Ben Hammou (Hammou is a Berber substitute for either Mohammed or Ahmed; the refusal to use the full Arab forms was a measure of Berber resentment against the conquerors) but he was commonly known as El Tibibt, which means 'the sparrow'. This nickname had a double significance; it implied that he was a holy man, because the little blue-headed sparrow is sacred in Morocco, and it implied the cockiness common to all races of sparrows. In the middle of the nineteenth century he tried to unite the scattered Glaoua and other sibling tribes – administered by a far-off *Caid* of another tribe – under his personal leadership, but failed so conspicuously that he had to seek the sanctuary of a holy place to escape assassination. From this refuge, force having failed, he began a lengthy intrigue which ended in his official appointment as *Caid* of the region in 1859. A year later he began the construction of the new *kasbah*, immediately adjoining the old, which was still growing nearly a hundred years later, and by the time of his death in 1888 he had so far exploited his official position as to bequeath to his son Madani a well-established authority and a considerable fortune. He had also made the pilgrimage to Mecca, and was thus entitled to the prefix Hadj, or holy pilgrim, before his name. His eldest son died young, and he was succeeded by Madani, son of an Ethiopian concubine whose name had been Zora, but was renamed Oum El Heir, which means 'Mother of Plenty'. Zora bore him two sons; Madani, born in 1866 and T'hami, born in 1879.

The Glaoua were almost unique among the Atlas *Caids* in that they did not owe their comparative affluence entirely to piracy and violence, for they owned an extremely profitable salt mine. The pass they controlled, known then as Tiz-n-Telouet or Tiz-n-Glaoua, lay a little to the north of that now known as Tiz-n-Tishka, whose road was finally

THE CANNON   47

completed by the French Foreign Legion in 1936. The old pass snaked upwards through the desolate, lunar valley of the Oued Mellah – the river of salt. At either hand rise mountains so bizarre both in form and in colour as to suggest an extravaganza of stage design: tapering spires of red, blue-green and yellow, sharp at their summits and void of all vegetation, take their colour from curiously localized minerals; others appear to have become limp and settled down upon themselves, leaving horizontal swags like those of a stage curtain. Underfoot, even when the season of snow is passed, the floor of the valley remains patchily white, encrusted with salt crystals against the terra-cotta red of the bare earth. A narrow defile at right angles to the main ravine leads to the salt mines, and perched high above the entrance to this corridor are the decorated, Disney-like ruins of a mud castle, a Glaoua sentinel tower dating, probably, from about the time of the Napoleonic wars. The corridor reaches a dead end at the salt mines – caves tunnelled into the red hill face, shored and propped with timber as are coal mines in other countries. Inside these subterranean tunnels one seems to be standing in chambers whose walls are of solid rock crystal or quartz, but this is solid salt, for the whole mountain is composed of it.

Salt has always been a very valuable commodity; 'if the salt has lost its savour, wherewith shall it be salted?'. To these salt mines of Telouet came camel caravans from the Sahara, from the Sudan, from Mauretania, from inner Morocco and from the great oases of the desert. At the time of which I am writing, towards the close of the nineteenth century, two hundred men working in the mine were unable to meet the demands that came mainly from distant regions. The Glaoui raised the price of salt, and demanded, too, a tax from every caravan that came to transport it. The family was by now on its way to comparative wealth but not to power, for it could command, at the most, between two thousand and three thousand mounted warriors. Any attempt at expansion to the west was effectively checked by the neighbouring and more powerful Goundafa, to the north by the Zemran, and to the south by the M'touggi. The Glaoui family understood that the only possible conquest lay to the south, and had begun to spread their tentacles into the Pre-Sahara and towards Tafilelt.

In that autumn of 1893, when what little remained of the Sultan's army was struggling upward through the snows under a canopy of ravens and vultures and with a rearguard of jackals and hyenas, the *Caid* Madani El Glaoui was twenty-seven years old, and his brother T'hami, son of the same mother, was fifteen. Madani was ugly by any standards, but with a certain refinement of ugliness that excluded coarseness. With it he possessed a graciousness, an air of feline fastidiousness, that made his thin consumptive face with its enormous black velvet eyes and irregular yellow teeth one, according to early French writers, of 'destiny and tragedy'. Both he and his brother T'hami were very dark-skinned, but T'hami was less positively ugly than his elder brother, less disdainful and enigmatic.

The Glaoua pass at Telouet lay on the Sultan's direct route to Marrakesh. Probably he did not actually choose the tribe through which he would pass; the terrible condition of his followers and his own failing health made any question of detour impossible. The Sultan had visited Telouet before, in the time of Madani's father, and left laden with the customary gifts; earlier still an army of the previous Sultan, Moulay Mohammed, had in 1864 passed the same way and been made welcome. The Imperial *harka* staggered on towards Telouet, still in possession of the cannon. Part of the army had become cannibal upon their own dead; such of these as were apprehended were themselves put to death, and swelled the long trail of corpses upon the snow.

Madani and T'hami El Glaoui heard of the approach of the defeated Sultan's army while it was as yet many miles away. Every war lord was an opportunist, and had there been at that moment a pretender to the throne it is likely that they would have chosen to take the Sultan captive and hold him to ransom, for in those days hostages were the general currency of Morocco. But there was no pretender, and the brothers knew of the reigning Sultan's plight. They did not know that the Sultan was a dying man, but they did know of the Krupp cannon. The sum of their knowledge, in fact, added up to the desirability of giving the Sultan the greatest welcome that he had ever received from a mountain *Caid*. Having taken this decision Madani put the greatest possible pressure upon all the tribespeople owing allegiance to him, and in forty-eight hours they had collected a vast number of mules and horses, an uncountable number of sheep and goats for slaughter, and special dues poured in from every corner of their kingdom in cash and in kind until, when the Sultan's *harka* was still twenty miles distant, winding its terrible way upwards from Anemetir, Madani El Glaoui was prepared to entertain the Sultan and his followers for as long as they cared to stay.

Madani, having called upon his tribespeople for their ultimate resources, wanted no misunderstanding. The Sultan must be welcomed, and welcomed as he would wish. With his younger brother T'hami, he rode out to meet the *harka*, accompanied by a bodyguard of five hundred mounted warriors, and behind him trailed the infinite army of mules and horses that he had requisitioned.

Madani observed every detail of protocol, prostrating himself before the Sultan in the snow, touching his forehead to the ground while it remained held there by the Sultan's ministers, repeating, 'Lord of all, be pleased to rest with us a while; Lord of all, accept our humble homage; Lord of all, be pleased to accept what little your slave can offer; Lord of all, be gracious, and with your illustrious presence lighten the darkness of my *kasbah*; Lord of all, bestow the favour that I may feed your *harka*; Lord of all, bestow your blessing upon my will to be your slave; Lord of all, tell me how I may serve you.'

It is difficult to appreciate the extravagance of these offers without having some mental picture of the High Atlas in winter. There is nothing; no blade of vegetation is visible above the snow, no mule-track shows above its whiteness. In that year there were snow blizzards of unprecedented severity. Food for three thousand men was a wild fantastic dream, like the image of cold, clear water in mid Sahara. Perhaps Moulay Hassan doubted the reality of these two half-Negro brothers who greeted him and promised what was seemingly impossible.

He had in any case no choice. He knew that without food and prolonged rest he and his *harka* would never reach Marrakesh. Graciously, as always, he accepted, and inside five hours he and his army were installed at Telouet; in that time the Sultan had passed from a kind of enduring polar hell to the luxuries of a palace.

The *diffa*, an endless banquet at which course succeeds course – spiced chickens and pigeons, kous-kous, and whole roast sheep and kebab and almond pastries and sweet mint tea – long after the guest can eat no more, lasted all through the night. Swaying lines of women danced to

the music of their own wild chant; the traditional boy dancers, with
painted faces and white robes drawn tight at the waist by gold-
embroidered belts, danced to the tambourines and the clicking of the
copper castanets on their fingers; in the courtyard a huge fire of
juniper logs lit the battlements of the castle; outside the *kasbah* walls,
where the *harka* had pitched its tents, the night was loud with feasting.
It was a scene more appropriate to the welcome home of a victorious
army, laden with the heads of decapitated prisoners to decorate the
walls of Marrakesh, than to the rescue of a starving and straggling
column from the snows.

By some unguessable means Madani found the resources to prolong
this situation for several days, while the Sultan recovered his strength
and his army munched its way through a few more thousand sheep. On
the day before the Imperial *harka* struck camp and set out for Marrakesh, the Sultan showed his gratitude. He made Madani his personal
khalifa, or representative in the region, giving him nominal command
of all the tribes between the High Atlas and the Sahara, and the *caidat* of
Tafilelt itself. Of infinitely greater significance, he made him a present
of a considerable quantity of modern arms and ammunition. The
exact amount of this armoury it is now difficult to establish, but it
included the 77 mm bronze Krupp cannon, the only single heavy
weapon in all Morocco outside the Imperial Chereefian Army. The
gift of something so cumbersome was possibly made, one may com-
prehend, as much from expediency as from gratitude, but its effect was
the same. From then on the surrounding tribes regarded Telouet as a
veritable arsenal of modern warfare.

Kasbah *of* Caid *Brahim El Glaoui, Telouet*

3

Whose King is a Child

WHEN the Sultan Moulay Hassan reached Marrakesh he was already a dying man, and he never returned to Fez. From what disease he suffered it is impossible to determine now, but it had already progressed far by the time of his retreat from Tafilelt. He passed the spring at his palace in Marrakesh, refusing the régime that his doctors dictated, and in May 1894 he rode at the head of a fresh *harka* to quell a new and powerful insurrection that had exploded in the region of Tadla, some hundred and twenty miles north-east of Marrakesh.

'While camping in the enemy country he died.' (It was afterwards popularly rumoured that he was poisoned by his freed slave and Chamberlain, Bou Ahmed.) 'Now, the death of the Sultan under such circumstances was fraught with danger to the State. He was an absolute monarch, and with his disappearance all authority and government lapsed until his successor should have taken up the reins. Again, the expedition was in hostile country, and any inkling of the Sultan's death would have brought the tribes down to pillage and loot the Imperial camp. As long as the Sultan lived, and was present with his expedition, his prestige was sufficient to prevent an attack of the tribes – though even this was not unknown on one or two occasions – and to hold his forces together as a sort of concrete body. But his death, if known, would have meant speedy disorganization, nor could the troops themselves be trusted not to seize this opportunity to murder and loot.

'It was therefore necessary that the Sultan's demise should be kept an absolute secret. He had died in the recesses of his tents, themselves enclosed in a great canvas wall, inside which, except on very special occasions, no one was permitted to penetrate. The knowledge of his death was therefore limited to the personal slaves and to his Chamberlain, Bou Ahmed.

'Orders were given that the Sultan would start on his journey at dawn, and before daylight the State palanquin was carried into the Imperial enclosure, the corpse laid within it, and its doors closed and the curtains drawn. At the first pale break of dawn the palanquin was brought out, supported by sturdy mules. Bugles were blown, the band played, and the bowing courtiers and officials poured forth their stentorian cry, "May God protect the life of our Lord." The procession formed up, and, led by flying banners, the dead Sultan set out on his march.

'A great distance was covered that day. Only once did the procession stop, when the palanquin was carried into a tent by the roadside, that the Sultan might breakfast. Food was borne in and out; tea, with all the paraphernalia of its brewing, was served: but none but the slaves who knew the secret were permitted to enter. The Chamberlain remained with the corpse, and when a certain time had passed, he emerged to state that His Majesty was rested and had breakfasted, and would proceed on his journey – and once more the procession moved on. Another long march was made to where the great camp was pitched for the night.

'The Sultan was tired, the Chamberlain said. He would not come out of his enclosure to transact business as usual in the *Siwan* tent, where he granted audiences. Documents were taken in to the royal quarters by the Chamberlain himself, and, when necessary, they emerged bearing the seal of State, and verbal replies were given to a host of questions.

'Then another day of forced marches, for the expedition was still in dangerous country; but Moulay Hassan's death could no longer be concealed. It was summer, and the state of the Sultan's body told its own secret.

'Bou Ahmed announced that His Majesty had died two days before, and that by this time his young son, Moulay Abd El Aziz, chosen and nominated by his father, had been proclaimed at Rabat, whither the fleetest of runners had been sent with the news immediately after the death had occurred.' (Abd El Aziz, as the Sultan's heir, had accompanied the Tafilelt expedition, as had also his mother Lalla R'kkia, a

Turkish lady who was Moulay Hassan's favourite wife. Aziz, being still a child, went ahead of the dead Sultan's cortège, with his mother and the rest of the harem.)

'It was a *fait accompli*. The army was now free of the danger of being attacked by the tribes; and the knowledge that the new Sultan was already reigning, and that tranquillity existed elsewhere, deterred the troops from any excesses. Many took the occasion of a certain disorganization to desert, but so customary was this practice that it attracted little or no attention.

'Two days later the body of the dead Sultan, now in a terrible state of decomposition, arrived at Rabat. It must have been a gruesome procession from the description his son Moulay Abd El Aziz gave me: the hurried arrival of the swaying palanquin bearing its terrible burden, five days dead in the great heat of summer; the escort, who had bound scarves over their faces – but even this precaution could not keep them from constant sickness – and even the mules that bore the palanquin seemed affected by the horrible atmosphere, and tried from time to time to break loose.

'No corpse is, by tradition, allowed to enter through the gates into a Moorish city, and even in the case of the Sovereign no exception was made. A hole was excavated in the town wall, through which the procession passed direct into the precincts of the palace, where the burial took place. Immediately after, the wall was restored.'

With the general knowledge of Moulay Hassan's death rebellion spread throughout all the old *bled es siba*. Those tribes whom his assiduous persecution had kept under at least a nominal control declared themselves openly against the throne, and more stable regions that had accepted the authority of Moulay Hassan joined the rebels at his death. This was a vaster, more menacing *bled es siba*, one that went then under the name of *es siba Moulay Hassan* – the anarchy that succeeded Moulay Hassan. Every *Caid*, even every petty chieftain in all Morocco, dreamed of riches and power. Of the total number of those holding official *mahkzen* positions in 1894 a rough calculation leads one to believe that more than seventy per cent were either dead, destitute, or chained in dungeons for life – or rather for death – by the turn of the century. The

new Sultan, Moulay Abd El Aziz, was under thirteen years old, and he
had been chosen, as was customary, by the ruling royal family, with
the approval of the *oulemas* or religious councils responsible for election.
Under Muslim law there was no compulsion upon a Sultan to nominate
his eldest son, and in the majority of cases he chose his favourite – a
choice that might be modified by the council of the reigning dynasty
or challenged in open rebellion by any of its male members. In the
absence of absolute prerogative there were, therefore, several pretenders
at the death of any Sultan. These ranged between genuine relations of
the dead king, through upstarts claiming descent from the Prophet
Mohammed, or impersonating some previous claimant who had
probably been long dead in a dungeon, but of whom, for political
reasons, there remained no trace but anonymous bones.

'The mother of Moulay Abd El Aziz was a Turkish lady, brought
from Constantinople to Morocco. Report states that she was a woman
of great intelligence and considerable force of character. She was
certainly a most devoted mother. It is even said that she played a part
in the politics of the country, and that she was consulted on affairs of
State by her husband. That she must have possessed a remarkable
personality is clear from the fact that she maintained her influence over
the Sultan till the day of his death – no easy task amidst a host of rivals –
and so assured the succession of her son. Her great friend and companion in the harem was another Turkish lady, the mother of the
reigning Sultan Moulay Youssef [1912–27]. It is curious that these two
"strangers in a foreign land" should both have been destined to become
the mothers of Sultans.

'It was only natural that the succession of a minor gave rise to every
form of intrigue at Court. There were two great factions in the palace –
the party of Bou Ahmed, the powerful Chamberlain, on the one hand,
and that of the Grand Vizier and Minister of War on the other. These
two high officials belonged to the aristocratic and powerful family of
the Ulad Jamai, and were respectively Hadj Amaati and Si Mohammed
Soreir. Now Bou Ahmed was the son of a Negro slave, and therefore
could count on no tribal or family influence. His rivals, on the contrary,
were Fez aristocrats, highly born, and supported by the influential
population of the towns. They came of what is known as a *mahkzen*
family – that is to say, a family who in the past had held Government

posts, and had a sort of traditional claim to high employment. It was evident that jealousy must exist between these two factions.

'Bou Ahmed's position of Chamberlain gave him constant access to his sovereign, whose extreme youth brought him little into contact with his viziers. No doubt, too, Bou Ahmed could count upon the influence of the Sultan's mother. He had been the constant and trustworthy confidant of her husband, and instrumental in putting her son on the throne. His own fate, too, depended upon his keeping him there, and there can be little doubt that Moulay Abd El Aziz's mother and Bou Ahmed worked in connivance.

'As soon as the new Government was organized sufficiently for Moulay Abd El Aziz to travel, the Court left Rabat for Fez – the real capital of the country. No Sultan can count upon his throne as being safe until he has been accepted by the religious and aristocratic Fezzis, and taken up his residence in the city; for Fez is the centre of religion and learning – and also of intrigue – and the influence of its population upon the tribes is very great. It was therefore very important that the young Sultan should reach Fez at as early a date as possible. His journey through the tribes to Meknès was very successful. He was well received on every side, and on his arrival at the old capital which Moulay Ismael, a contemporary of Louis Quatorze, had built, the population of the city accorded him a popular welcome.

'Meknès is some thirty-three miles from Fez, and there remained only this last stage of the journey to be accomplished.

'Bou Ahmed fully appreciated his position. He knew that once in Fez his influence must decrease. His rivals could count upon the support not only of the townspeople, but also of the Sultan's relations in the capital. To the Fezzis he was an upstart, and there would be no peace from their intrigues to bring about his fall, and no pity when he fell. It was a case of now or never for Bou Ahmed.

'There were no signs of the coming storm. The Ulad Jamai brothers were no doubt waiting till their arrival amongst their own people in Fez to begin a more active intrigue, and Bou Ahmed himself was courteous and a little obsequious to the influential viziers. A few mornings after the Sultan's arrival at Meknès, the usual morning Court was being held. Hadj Amaati, the Grand Vizier, surrounded by his white-robed followers, rode into the palace square, amidst the bowing officials and the salutes of troops. He was immediately summoned into the Sultan's presence.

'Moulay Abd El Aziz was alone with Bou Ahmed when Hadj Amaati entered. He prostrated himself, and waited for the Sultan to speak. In a rather frightened voice Moulay Abd El Aziz asked him a question. Hadj Amaati's answer was not found satisfactory, and Bou Ahmed burst forth in a string of reproaches against the Vizier, and accused him of disloyalty, avarice, extortion, and political crimes. Suddenly appealing to the Sultan, he asked for permission to arrest him. Moulay Abd El Aziz inclined his head.

'A few minutes later a dishevelled, cringing, crying creature, amid jeers and laughter, was dragged through the palace square amongst the crowd that only so short a time before had been bowing to the ground. His clothes were torn, for the soldiers were rough, and his turban was all askew. As he passed through the gate, dragged by the soldiery, the sentry at the door seized the Vizier's clean white turban and set it on his own head, replacing it by his own dirty fez cap. A shout of laughter greeted this act.

'The Vizier's brother, Si Mohammed Soreir, the Minister of War, had not yet left his house for the palace. He was arrested at his own doorway, and did not attempt to resist, but allowed himself to be led to prison.

'The subsequent history of these two men forms perhaps the blackest page of Moulay Abd El Aziz's reign. They were sent in fetters to Tetuan, and confined, chained and fettered, in a dungeon. In the course of time – and how long those ten years must have been – Hadj Amaati died. The Governor of Tetuan was afraid to bury the body, lest he should be accused of having allowed his prisoner to escape. He wrote to Court for instructions. It was summer, and even the dungeon was hot. The answer did not come for eleven days, and all that time Si Mohammed Soreir remained chained to his brother's corpse! The brother survived. In 1908 he was released after fourteen years' incarceration, a hopeless, broken, ruined man. Everything he had possessed had been confiscated; his wives and children had died, the result of want and persecution. He emerged from his dark dungeon nearly blind, and lame from the cruel fetters he had worn.'

I record Walter Harris's description of these and other hideous

happenings, because the frequency and universality of such incidents in
Moroccan history show the career of the Glaoui brothers in truer
perspective. Both at their best and at their worst they acted in the
tradition of their country. Cruelty, torture and oppression had always
been regarded as signs of strength; mercy was evidence of weakness.
No man could rule and show pity.

Black guard of the Imperial Palace

Under the regency of Bou Ahmed the child king Moulay Abd El
Aziz was virtually confined to his palace. He was Sultan in name only;
it was Bou Ahmed the freed slave who ruled Morocco, and Bou
Ahmed's faction that occupied every public position. One of his own
brothers he installed as Chamberlain, to another he gave the post of
Minister of War. When, early in his regency, he moved the Court to
Marrakesh, so that the Sultan might be recognized and established in
the southern capital, he began immediately to build for himself – at
public expense – a gigantic palace, in the construction of which every

skilled craftsman in the city was engaged for six years. (This palace, named the Bahya, or effulgence, later became the French Residency.)

He was no more free from the necessity of quelling perpetual revolution than had been any Sultan before him; these he dealt with in the 'traditional' manner. A major insurrection started in the great Rehamna tribe, who occupied a wide area of the fertile plain to the north of Marrakesh. Their leader, Taher Ben Suleiman, proclaimed Sultan Moulay Mohammed, an elder brother of the reigning Abd El Aziz. (Moulay Mohammed was characterized by a drooping eyelid which had given him the nickname of Le Borgne, and a taste for sexual orgies of a somewhat specialized nature.) His rebellion was initially so successful that rebel troops occupied the northern fringes of the town. When Bou Ahmed's troops, aided by Madani and T'hami El Glaoui, succeeded in driving them out, and at last gained a decisive victory in the rebels' own territory, his reprisals were very traditional indeed. Moulay Mohammed was taken prisoner and confined in the Bahya, from which he was later transferred to Meknès, a departure from the violent tradition that can only suggest Bou Ahmed's desire to have an alternative Sultan up his sleeve. Every single man of the Rehamna, however, who could be captured was beheaded, and for weeks the Jews were kept busy salting literally thousands of heads for public display on the city walls. (A Moroccan ghetto is even now called a *mellah*; the word simply means salt and refers directly to this practice.) 'The heads of enemies were, until the end of Moulay Hafid's reign, commonly exposed upon the gates of the towns of the interior of Morocco. In 1909, during the official Mission of the late Sir Reginald Lister to Fez, the Bab Mharouk was hung with the heads of rebels. One of these grisly monuments fell, with a resounding thud, as the British Minister and some of his party were passing underneath. The manner of affixing them was by passing a wire through the ear, which was fastened to a nail in the wall. Over and over again during my long residence in Morocco I have seen the gates and other buildings at the Moorish capitals decorated with these horrid trophies.' The women and children were given to Bou Ahmed's troops to do as they pleased with; when they had done it, what remained was sold in the slave market. The Rehamna territory was devastated, the crops and houses burned, the flocks driven away; in a few years the once fertile lands of the tribe had reverted to total wilderness. The leader of the revolt, Taher Ben Suleiman, was confined in a tiny cage made from the rifle barrels of his own dead tribesmen, brought to Marrakesh on the back of a camel for public exhibition, and then starved to death in a dungeon.

Meanwhile the Lords of the Atlas found the whole political climate exceedingly to their liking. In the words of the Goundafi, '*Allons chez les rebelles couper les têtes et travailler pour nos maisons!*' They worked so well for their houses that during the six closing years of the century, the years of Bou Ahmed's regency, each had more than trebled his territory and his riches. Everywhere there were rebel tribes waiting to be conquered in the name of the Government and pillaged in the name of the family. Submission was ritual, symbolized by the sacrifice of a sheep before the *kasbah* walls of the victor. The Goundafi, strongly bound in name anyway to the *mahkzen*, by reason of his friendship with the dead Sultan Moulay Hassan, led *harka* after *harka* even further afield and ever further on to the plains on both sides of the Atlas, and the heads of his captives poured into Marrakesh. The Glaoui, far from idle himself at this period, said to the M'touggi, 'For every one of those heads the Goundafi adds ten hectares of fertile land to his name.' The M'touggi replied, 'He is a hill man who has discovered the plains; it will not be easy to get him out of them.' These two formed a brittle alliance against the Goundafi by which they would stop any further expansion on his part and share the lands of the plain between themselves. Despite the elaborate exchange of courtesies and vows of undying mutual loyalty, this, like other Moroccan alliances, was one of expediency. The M'touggi had a wary eye upon the Glaoui's swelling territory and prestige, and the Glaoui in his turn had watched the M'touggi's increasing independence with mistrust. For the M'touggi had gone so far as to threaten Bou Ahmed with rebellion, and the Regent, preferring this able schemer to be at least nominally on the side of the *mahkzen*, had bought his temporary loyalty by adding two more tribal territories to his already immense fief.

Madani El Glaoui, for his part, had extended his lands far to the south, and the greater part of the north-eastern Pre-Sahara was now under his control. As in the case of the Goundafi and the M'touggi, this 'reduction of the southern tribes' was a purely personal venture, each conquest by slaughter or by intrigue a stage in the foundation of a private kingdom. He or his younger brother T'hami led their own *harkas*, and wherever the bronze cannon trundled into action there were ruined castles and severed heads. In some cases the mere threat of the cannon, or of other suspected secret weapons in the arsenal at Telouet, was enough to elicit submission from a powerful enemy. The greatest addition to their territory was the fertile lands of the Mesfiouia tribe, who had been in open rebellion against Bou Ahmed's decree to divide the territory into seven *caidats*. Bou Ahmed sent out a *harka* to put down the insurrection. This *harka* was not only defeated but driven back to Marrakesh with the Mesfiouia on its heels, and the rebels set siege to the town itself. The Glaoui brothers, having been promised the Mesfiouia lands in return for the defeat of the tribe, took the besiegers in the rear. This was the beginning of a systematic destitution of the Mesfiouia, whose lands remained in dispute many years later.

The *kasbah* of Telouet, as befitted Madani's personal stronghold, grew year by year; originally begun in 1860 by his father and steadily enlarged ever since, it had little of the elaborate grace of the earlier Glaoua *kasbahs* at Telouet, in which the architectural influence of the Dra and Dadès valleys – probably relics of the Phoenician colonists, whose remains can be seen at Lixus, near Larache – predominated in tapering towers and intricate decoration; the new *kasbah* took shape as a massive structure in the government tradition, and within its curtain walls was a labyrinth at whose heart one might expect the Minotaur.

Dra kasbah *and* marabout

'In 1900 Bou Ahmed died. No one cared, unless it was a few of his personal followers and attendants, who would naturally suffer by his demise. As for the rest, there was a general indifference. He had never been popular, and the immense fortune he had amassed and great palace he had constructed awoke the jealousy of others who had the same desires but not the same opportunities. He was feared certainly, for his will was indomitable, and he was cruel. A sort of superstitious reverence had encircled his life, but it disappeared when sickness laid him low; and when he breathed his last, the pent-up feelings of the people burst forth, and they rose up and cursed him.

'The death of a great personage in Morocco is terrible, and for several days as the Vizier lay expiring, guards were stationed outside his palace waiting in silence for the end. And then one morning the wail of the women within the house told that death had come. Every gateway of the great building was seized, and no one was allowed to enter or come out, while within there was pandemonium. His slaves pillaged wherever they could lay their hands. His women fought and stole to get possession of the jewels. Safes were broken open, documents and title-deeds were extracted, precious stones were torn from their settings the more easily to be concealed, and even murder took place.

'While all this was proceeding within the strictly guarded walls, Bou Ahmed's body was borne out and buried. The Sultan, weeping, followed the bier of the man who had put him on his throne and kept him there through those difficult years of his youth. He must, indeed, have felt himself alone as he stood beside the grave of his Vizier, who, whatever may have been his faults, however great may have been his extortions, had been loyal throughout. When Moulay Abd El Aziz, still weeping, had returned to his palace, his first act was to sign the decree for the confiscation of all Bou Ahmed's property. It was now organized loot, for officials and slaves were turned loose to carry out the royal commands. For days laden baggage animals, half-concealed under great masses of furniture, heaped with carpets and bedding, or staggering under safes, bore Bou Ahmed's property into the Sultan's palace. His women and his slaves were made to give up their loot, and the house was left empty and its owners penniless. A few days later nothing remained but the great building – all the rest had disappeared into space.'

Walter Harris does not mention that Bou Ahmed's two brothers Dris and Said, Chamberlain and Minister of War, both died within a few days of Bou Ahmed, or that most contemporary historians claimed that all three were poisoned by the Sultan's mother, Lalla R'kkia, who had come to fear the absolute power the Negro family wielded.

At Bou Ahmed's death the Sultan's forceful mother appointed his First Secretary as Grand Vizier, but Moulay Abd El Aziz, weary of controls, contrived to remove him after a year and substituted Mokhtar, a cousin of Bou Ahmed's, giving the post of Chamberlain to the dead Regent's own brother Hassan Ben Moussa. The Ministry of War he gave to Mehdi El Menhebbi, who had been Counsellor to Bou Ahmed. In consolidating the power of the Moussa faction, he underwrote the downfall of Morocco. For thereafter his Ministers shared only one common concern, to distract the young Sultan from all interest in affairs of State. All that Morocco could provide the Sultan already possessed; the riches, the luxury, the panoply of State, the enormous harem, had been his for years, though he was barely nineteen.

The policy of his viziers amounted to menticide. The whole emerging world of western mechanical invention was dangled before his eyes, and his palaces became vast playrooms, guarding secrets no graver than those of gramophones, toy railways, typewriters, musical stuffed birds and a great host of clockwork toys. A gold camera was imported from England. Outside, there were bicycle races with ladies of the harem in fancy dress, roller-skating, miniature rifle ranges, balloons and fireworks; even though there was no road in all Morocco, a hansom cab and a scarlet state coach reached Fez from London. The transport of a billiard table, lurching on camel-back from Larache to the royal palace at Fez was but one of a thousand bizarre extravaganzas devised by the Government in its efforts to divert the Sultan's attention from the terrible state into which his country had fallen. A crook American sold him for 40,000 dollars a British bulldog with false teeth. A German firm sold him a motor-boat; this occupied a room to itself in the palace and was tended by a German engineer, though there was never any suggestion of the vessel putting to sea. The engineer, like so

(*Courtesy* Illustrated London News)

The *kasbah* of Telouet towards the close of the 19th century

(Reprinted from Kitab Aâyane al-Marhrib 'l-Akça *by Marthe and Edmond Gouvion)*

T'hami El Glaoui as a young man

Abd El Malek El Mtouggi (left) and Tayeb El Goundafi in old age

(Both photographs reprinted from Kitab Aâyane al-Marhrib 'l-Akça by Marthe and Edmond Gouvion)

The ancient Goundafi fortified mosque of Tinmal on the river Nfis, dating from 1200 A.D.

A Glaoua village on the Telouet plateau

A sheep market in the Atlas foothills

A camel market

Black slave in the ruined courtyard of Telouet

The *kasbah* of Tineghir at Ouazarzat

Aït Ben Haddou on the route from Ouazarzat to Telouet

The *kasbah* of Tamdacht, on the caravan route from Ouazarzat to Telouet—surrendered to T'hami El Glaoui in 1901 (see p. 74)

Berber children from the High Atlas

Women of Telouet

Berber man of the mountains

Boy of the Aït Wouzgit

Entrance to the Todghra gorges

Kasbah of Aït Ani, above the Todghra gorges

Aït Youli, a typical Glaoua *kasbah* in conquered territory

many other Europeans who found themselves at the Court for com-
mercial reasons, became a friend and confidant of the young Sultan.

Poor Abd El Aziz. Weak he certainly was, but he was not by nature
either frivolous-minded or self-indulgent. He was, indeed, genuinely
interested in reform, which was the very last thing his Ministers wanted
to see; he was intellectual, and an excellent conversationalist, but his
conversation must at all costs be steered clear of politics. He was shy,
gentle, possessed of great charm and a keen, western sense of humour;
he was also a puppet Sultan enmeshed in a gigantic web of intrigue,
woven and rewoven by hundreds of spiders in collaboration.

Sultan Moulay Abd El Aziz

'These were the first days of the toys and fireworks at the Moorish
Court. For a time the latter were paramount, and almost nightly the
southern capital was illumined by the reflection of Catherine-wheels
and startled by the flashing of the many colours of marvellous rockets.
A man was brought especially from England to show and prepare the
fireworks, and he became a permanent member of His Majesty's suite.
The natives were partly amused, partly shocked. Thrifty as the Moor is
by nature, he could not overlook the wild extravagance of this manner
of spending money, and the fireworks by the time they had arrived in

Marrakesh had cost a pretty price. Freight, insurance, and the long caravan transport from the coast had to be added to the original cost, and there was an item known as commission. They were certainly very beautiful fireworks and very expensive. I was present at a display given to amuse a British Minister, who highly disapproved of this extravagance, but could not refuse the invitation. There was a set piece of an enormous elephant, and the show concluded with a waterfall of fire in a new shade of pink, just discovered, and accordingly of elevated price. It was certainly very beautiful, but it was very useless and very dear.

'One afternoon the Sultan informed me that there would be a display that night in the palace grounds, but that it was for the "palace" – that was to say, the ladies – and no men would be invited; but if I went up on to the roof of the house in which I was living, I should no doubt be able to witness something of it. I watched the beautiful rockets of every colour rise in their streaks of fire into the wonderful sapphire blue of the sky of the southern night, to burst with their thousand stars, filling the whole scene of the flat house-tops of the old city with the pale glow of greens and pinks and yellows. In the "Dj'mma El F'naa" – the open place that lies in the centre of the city – the crowds stood and watched the rockets as they rose over the high walls of the palace half a mile away.

'The next day the Sultan asked me what I had thought of the display. I spoke of its beauty, and hinted at its waste. I mentioned the crowd in the square. "What did the people say?" asked the Sultan. "I didn't hear much," I replied; "but on several occasions someone would cry out, 'There goes another thousand dollars of our money.' "

'Moulay Abd El Aziz had expected to hear his own praises sung for having presented the brilliant spectacle to the people of his city, and my answer surprised him. It was, however, not without effect, or perhaps he was growing tired of coloured fires, for there was a great diminution in these displays, although the professional exhibitor remained for some time later at the palace.

'His afternoons in Marrakesh were given up to play. More than once, always accompanied by Menhebbi, the Minister of War, and some of his European employees, we rode in the immense wilderness of gardens of the Agdal Palace. At the edge of a great square tank we would dismount, and sometimes went for a row in one of the various boats that he kept there. On one occasion His Majesty and his Minister rowed – very badly indeed – while I, the only other occupant of the boat, steered. The Sultan, who rowed bow, caught several crabs, and splashed poor Menhebbi all over. The Minister of War rowed about one hundred short strokes to the minute, whilst the Sultan, struggling with his oars, rowed about ten extremely long ones. But both were hugely delighted with the performance, and our spirits were of the highest.

' "We are both boatmen, and you are the passenger. We are crossing a Moorish ferry," cried the Sultan.

'Entering into the Sultan's little joke, I replied "that they were the worst ferrymen I had ever seen, and that on landing I should complain to the authorities of their incapacity".

' "Oh, you will, will you?" replied Moulay Abd El Aziz. "Then all I can say is, we won't put you ashore until you pay us."

' "Then I'll stop here."

' "All right," replied the Sultan; and he promptly began to splash me with all his might and main, though poor Menhebbi was getting as wet as I was.

' "Will you pay?" asked His Majesty.

' "Willingly," I laughed. "How much?"

' "Half a peseta each" (about 4d.), answered the Sultan, and they duly pocketed their fee. It was the first time in my life I had tipped a Sultan and a Minister of War.

'Moulay Abd El Aziz was an expert bicyclist, and there were often great games of bicycle-polo of an afternoon in one of the courtyards of the palace. The only other Moor who played was Menhebbi, then at the height of his power and influence. The Sultan was a plucky but careful rider, seldom coming to grief, and handling his machine with the most perfect judgment. Menhebbi was equally plucky, but more excitable, and I have seen him, in pursuit of the ball, charge at full speed into the palace wall, to be rescued from what looked like a lot of broken umbrellas a minute later, as he shouted wildly for a new bicycle. As the Sultan was always supplied with the most expensive articles that could be purchased, most of his bicycles were of aluminium, and therefore not suited to bicycle-polo; but the more that were broken the more were required, and his commission agents reaped their harvest. The record,

I think, was taken by a young secretary of the British Legation, who successfully smashed six in one afternoon! But it was not at polo alone that Moulay Abd El Aziz was a skilful bicyclist, for he could perform a number of tricks that would almost have done honour to a professional. I have seen him myself ride up a steep plank laid against a packing-case, then along another plank forming a bridge to another packing-case, and down an incline at the end again. On one of these occasions he fell, and lodged on his head; but after being stunned for a minute or two, remounted his bicycle and successfully accomplished his object.

'All sorts of rumours and stories were current amongst the tribes as to what went on in the palace. For instance, the Sultan, finding the white walls of one of the interior courtyards too dazzling for his eyes, had them painted blue – an innovation unheard of at a Court where tradition ruled. Now the walls of this courtyard were visible from the hills above Fez, and the patch of bright blue soon attracted the attention of the tribesmen attending the local markets. To them, as it was contrary to Muslim tradition, it must be of Christian origin, and a story was soon being circulated that Moulay Abd El Aziz had lost his fortune playing cards with his Christian friends, and was now staking the various parts of his palace in lieu of money. He had lost this particular court, which the Christians had taken possession of and painted blue.'

The Sultan did not gamble; gambling is forbidden by the Muslim religion, and he was a strict observer of his faith. He did, however, surround himself with Europeans, a curious group of courtiers at whose heart was the comic-opera figure of *Caid* Maclean, with his tartan *bernous* and his English hunting boots. There can be no question but that *Caid* Maclean was feathering his own nest handsomely. He was the principal agent between the Sultan's Court and the world of European toys, receiving commission on an annual turnover that reached seven figures, and introducing ever more Europeans to the Sultan's circle. It is recorded that early in 1902, when the Sultan gave a banquet to celebrate the circumcision of one of his young brothers, more than forty Europeans were invited – a scandalous departure from tradition. More than one historian has remarked that had the Sultan dismissed the greater part of his European coterie he might by that one action have changed the history of Morocco.

'The Court had lost its prestige. The Sultan was openly scoffed at and despised, and anarchy reigned on every side.

'This final stage of the history of independent Morocco had begun and ended in the early years of this century, when the young Sultan, Moulay Abd El Aziz, entered upon that period of his reign which may be deservedly known as the years of the *commis voyageurs*. It was a pitiful period and one best forgotten, except that every now and again some incident would occur worth recording on account of its perfectly unintentional humour, which only rendered more pitiful still the depressing interludes. It was the last decadence of the decadent Moorish Court. The Treasury was fast being emptied, the revenues were being wasted, foreign loans were being raised, and the palaces of the Sultan were littered with packing-cases, the contents of which the British Press once seriously described as "evidences of Christian civilization at Fez". Everywhere it was packing-cases, and even today on some of the tracks from the coast to the interior lie the wrecked fragments of machinery and other rusty forsaken goods, which the weary camels could transport no longer.

'Of what did these "evidences of Christian civilization" consist? Grand pianos and kitchen-ranges; automobiles and immense cases of corsets; wild animals in cages, and boxes of strange theatrical uniforms; barrel-organs and hansom-cabs; a passenger lift capable of rising to dizzy altitudes, destined for a one-storied palace; false hair; cameras of gold and of silver with jewelled buttons; carved marble lions and living macaw parrots; jewels, real and false; steam-launches and fireworks; ladies' underclothing from Paris, and saddlery from Mexico; trees for gardens that were never planted, or, if planted, were never watered; printing-presses and fire-balloons – an infinity of all that was grotesque, useless, and in bad taste. As each packing-case gave forth its contents they were looked at, perhaps played with, and the majority speedily consigned to rust and rot in damp stores and damper cellars. It was, indeed, a glorious period for the *commis voyageurs*, but it was the "agony" of Morocco. Every incident in Europe was seized to push their wares. The coronation of King Edward VII brought crowns to the fore. The Sultan was told he must have a crown. He objected. It was contrary to his religion to put gold or jewels on his head. But escape was impossible. A coloured oleograph was spread out before him representing King Edward in his coronation robes, standing by a small table, with his index finger lightly resting on the summit of the Imperial Crown. This at least was a purpose to which the Sultan, without infringing the tenets of Islam, could put a crown. So the crown came.

'The crown, it was rumoured, came from Paris; but the State coach was British, and London's best, built by a famous coach-builder, and of fine workmanship. The afternoon that it arrived, transported in packing-cases carried on platforms, which in turn were slung between camels, the Sultan was playing bicycle-polo with some of his European suite, which included at this period an architect, a conjurer, a watchmaker, an American portrait-painter, two photographers, a German lion-tamer, a French soda-water manufacturer, a chauffeur, a firework expert, and a Scottish piper. All these enjoyed the personal friendship of His Majesty, and the *entrée* into the presence of the ruler who, with the exception perhaps of the Grand Lama of Tibet, should have been the most exclusive and the most secluded of sovereigns. It is no wonder that the tribesmen looked askance on the high palace walls.

'It was a gorgeous coach, of crimson lacquer, with gilded ornamentation. The inside was lined with rich green-brocaded silk, and the hammer-cloth was of scarlet and gold, and bore what were supposed to be the Royal Arms of Morocco – as a fact, non-existent. Like the coach itself, the purple harness, with its gilt fittings, was of the very best; and together they formed an ensemble as expensive as it was utterly useless, for there were no roads in Morocco.

'The bicycle-polo ceased, and the Sultan invited the Consul of a great foreign Power, who happened to be at the Court, and the writer, to come and inspect his newest purchase. In the centre of an immense field of swampy grass, surrounded by high crenellated walls, stood the scarlet carriage. In this field of many acres were opened all the packing-cases which were too large to pass through the gateways that led into the interior courts of the palace; it served also as a grazing-ground for His Majesty's menagerie. In a wide circle at some little distance from the State coach stood a ring of zebras, emus, wapiti, Hindu cattle, apes, antelope, and llamas, with a background of more timid flamingos and strange storks and cranes – one and all intent on examining, from a position of safety, the extraordinary scarlet addition to their numbers which had suddenly appeared among them.

'The Sultan was evidently pleased. As usual, he said little; but he called to one of his officers, and ordered four horses to be harnessed to the coach. It had to be explained to him that no horse in the Imperial stables had ever been in harness, for the Sultan's previous purchases of carriages and hansom-cabs lay rotting idle and neglected in stores and cellars. But His Majesty was not going to be deprived of the pleasure of seeing his coach in movement. Men – soldiers and slaves – were harnessed and told to pull. Slowly the lumbering, useless, expensive but glorious State coach began to move.

' "We will ride in it," said the Sultan; and, beckoning to the Consul of a Great Power to get up behind, he himself mounted to the scarlet-and-gold seat of honour on the box. The writer rode inside. When all were seated, the vehicle started on its first and last progress of State. The soldiers and slaves sweated and puffed as the wheels sank deeper and deeper into the swampy ground, and the "progress" was slow indeed. Slow, too, were the paces of the procession that followed us, for, doubting but fascinated, the whole menagerie was in our wake, led by an emu whose courage had already been proved by an unprovoked attack upon the Scottish piper, and by having danced a *pas-seul* on the prostrate form of the expert in fireworks a few days previously. Close behind the emu followed a wapiti – with the mange – and then in turn the zebras, the Hindu cattle, the apes, gazelles, and lastly, the timid llamas, with their great luminous eyes and outstretched necks. Away in the background half a dozen cranes were dancing and performing the most absurd antics.

'It rained that night, and the next day the little lake of water in which the State coach stood was purple from the dye of the harness, and the beautiful hammer-cloth of scarlet and gold flapped limp and ruined in the wind. Inside there was a pool of water on the green-brocaded seat.

'Few of the things that he bought gave him any pleasure. Photography amused him for a time; but even this was made a means of exploiting him. A camera of gold at £2,000 came from London; 10,000 francs' worth of photographic paper arrived in one day from Paris. His Majesty once informed me that his photographic materials, not including cameras and lenses, for one year cost him between

£6,000 and £7,000! He naturally did not know what was required, and left it to his commission agents to purchase the "necessary" materials. They did, with a vengeance.

'The Sultan's caterers were at their last resources. Fireworks were played out; bicycle tricks had led to bruises and sprains; and even photography had lost its pristine interest. At this critical moment came word of a belated circus at one of the coast towns. It must naturally have been a very poor circus ever to have found itself at that dreary little port, but its advent was welcomed as enthusiastically as if it had been Barnum's entire show. Imperial letters were directed to the local *Caids* and Governors, agents rushed wildly to and fro, and eventually the circus, bag and baggage, consisting of a dozen people and three or four horses, started out across the weary plains of Morocco to obey the royal command. It all took time, and meanwhile in Court circles it was the absorbing topic of conversation. One or two serious rebellions among the tribes, and an acute quarrel with the Government of a European Power, passed into temporary oblivion.

'Now, the proprietress of this circus was an extremely stout Spanish lady of uncertain age, on whose corpulent body the rough jogging on a mule for more than a hundred miles had left almost as painful an impression as the discomfort, heat, and worry of the journey had upon her temper. She herself took no active part in the performance, and it was on this account, to her intense indignation and wrath, that she was refused admittance to the court of the palace in which the Sultan was to witness the show. His Majesty's orders were that none but the actual performers should be allowed to enter.

'So the fat lady and one or two of the employees of the circus remained in an outer courtyard adjoining the enclosure in which the Sultan, seated under a gorgeous tent, was witnessing the performance. A wall some twenty feet in height separated these two courts; and in the outer one, where the fat lady found herself, the Sultan had been building some additions to the palace, and a pile of stone, mortar, and other material reached almost to the top of the wall. The lady was both angry and bored, nor were a herd of gazelle and a few fine specimens of moufflon – Barbary wild sheep – that roamed about the enclosure sufficient to keep her amused.

'To have received a royal command to come all that way to the

Moorish capital, and then to be deprived of the glory of seeing her own circus performing before a real Sultan, was more than she could bear, and she straightway began to climb the great heap of building material that lay piled against the wall. It was hard work, nor was her figure suited for such mountain-climbing; but she was to receive assistance from a source undreamed of. Affected, no doubt, by her slow progress in a sport of which he himself was so proficient, the old ram moufflon lightly bounded after her. Balancing himself for a moment on his hind-legs, he lunged forward and butted the fat lady so successfully from below that her ascent was materially assisted. In a series of repeated bounds, owing to no voluntary action on her own part, she found herself pantingly grasping the top of the thick wall.

'Meanwhile the performance of the circus was progressing to the Sultan's satisfaction. Suddenly, however, an expression of wrathful consternation became visible in his face, and, speechless, he pointed at the wall. There, far above, was the agonized and purple visage of the fat lady, peering down at the Sultan and his Court. In a moment the officers of the suite were shouting and gesticulating to her to retire. But the only reply they received was a sudden vision of a considerable portion of her immense body, as a playful moufflon, himself invisible, gave her another hoist up. At last all her body was on the wall, to which she clung for dear life with arms and legs, as she lay extended on its summit. It was at this moment that the moufflon appeared. With a majestic bound he leaped on to the summit, stood for a moment poised on his hind-legs, then suddenly dropped, and with a terrific prod from his wide horns, butted the fat lady at least a yard along the wall. He was evidently intent upon taking her round the entire circuit of the court-yard.

'For a few moments there was turmoil. The Sultan sat silent and amazed, while the Cabinet Ministers all shouted to the lady to dis-appear, which she was certainly most anxious to do. The slaves, more wisely, pelted the moufflon with stones, and drove him from his point of vantage. Then slowly the lady disappeared – the fat legs first, then the heaving mass of body, and finally even the purple face was seen no more.'

Despite these many episodes of farce, the story of Moulay Abd El Aziz is a tragedy. In the following incident told by Walter Harris the tinsel and the toys have gone, and only the realities of his reign are left.

'I spoke, perhaps, too warmly of the neglect with which the soldiers were treated, of their stolen pay, of their abject misery, and I failed to notice that the Sultan was not in a mood at that moment to listen to my complaint.

' "It isn't my fault," he said pettishly.

' "It is," I replied. "Your Majesty doesn't take the trouble to see that your orders are carried out."

'The blood rushed to the Sultan's face, and he drew himself up. "Remember," he said, "you are speaking to 'the Commander of the Faithful', " referring to his most coveted title.

' "I do," I replied, "remember it. It is your Majesty who forgets that these men are 'the Faithful'."

'Alas! as far as he is concerned, but few of them were any longer faithful.

'He bore me no grudge for what I said, and his look of anger passed into one of great sadness. For a little while he stood looking over the great plain that lay before us, then turned and said very gently, "You don't know how weary I am of being Sultan," and tears stood in his eyes.'

Palace courtyard

4

The Time and the Country

IN 1901, within a year of Bou Ahmed's death, the Glaoui brothers had completed at least the temporary subjugation of all their dissident neighbours. The last stronghold was no more than twenty miles from Telouet. The Oued Mellah winds its way down the arid valley of salt for perhaps eight miles until it takes a sharp right turn at a fantastic cluster of tall mud *kasbahs* called Anemetir, and begins a steeper descent towards the plain; its course forming the main caravan route from the southern oases to Marrakesh. Squarely on this route, on the lip of the river gorge, stood the gigantic fortress of Tamdacht, as imposing in its grandeur and the desolation of its surroundings as Telouet itself, and an infinitely more beautiful structure. Dissident tribes from all the region had united at this fortress under the leadership of one Ali n Ait Haddou, and their numbers were so great that they invited open war with the Glaoui. Ali closed the caravan route from the south, pillaging and murdering those who would not turn and go back the way they had come. 'Dues' from the caravans formed an important part of Madani El Glaoui's revenue, and he sent his young brother T'hami to take the fortress by storm. T'hami rode from Telouet at the head of a *harka* two thousand strong. His progress down the valley of salt was slow; three times the carriage of the Krupp cannon broke as it lumbered through the loose boulders behind the struggling mules, but on the afternoon of the second day it stood on a commanding eminence three hundred yards from the castle, and beyond the range of the defenders' flintlocks. T'hami opened with a bombardment of thirty rounds on the outer walls, built of *pisé*, some fifteen feet high and six feet thick. These had something of the effect that a sandbag has upon a rifle bullet; but the cannon did breach the wall in three places. However, the rifle fire from the castle – and from thousands of natural caves that honeycombed the high mud cliffs flanking the river – was so intense, and the breaches so narrow, that the besiegers lost many lives without ever reaching the main walls of the castle. Tamdacht might have withstood the siege had it not been for the presence of a traitor in the camp. During a lull in the attack Ali made a gesture of defiance by opening the great door of the castle and showing himself to the enemy. It was a fine gesture, but inadvisable, for when he turned to re-enter he found

Warrior with enemy head

the door closed and bolted behind him. Alone and without protection he tried to flee, but T'hami's men rode him down, hacked his head from his body and carried it back upon the point of a lance, while his mutilated body trailed at rope's end behind another horseman. At the sight of these things the garrison of Tamdacht surrendered, but many of them suffered the same fate as Ali, for T'hami had become annoyed by their prolonged resistance and the loss of Glaoua lives. For some years after this all resistance in the South disappeared.

There is very little surviving written record of T'hami during these early years when he was no more than his elder brother's lieutenant in barbaric tribal warfare, and for this reason – if not for others, equally obvious – it is worth quoting the diaries of an egregious English lady who contrived through the offices of *Caid* Maclean to visit Telouet during the height of the anarchy following the death of the Regent Bou Ahmed. This was a certain Lady Grove, wife of the first Bart, who in company with another English lady and three English gentlemen, escorted by soldiers of the Sultan, set out on mule-back from Tangier for a look at the interior of Morocco. Early in 1902 she published her memoirs of this expedition under the title of *Seventy-One Days' Camping in Morocco*. 'I venture modestly to hope that the hour or so given to the perusal of how we spent our seventy-one days will not be remorsefully regretted by those who chance upon it.'

No, indeed.

From the outset it was an arduous journey. ('We went over a typical Moorish house, which I should think must be a very depressing sort of house to live in.'), and once among the perilous mountain paths: 'I am not timid, but I found myself wondering – horrible thought! – whether, in a horse, the instinct of self-preservation would be strong enough, *supposing* something were to make him shy, to prevent his shying *a few inches too far!*'

'On 3rd June [1900] we arrived at Glaoui (Telouet). The Castle itself stands well, on a barren rock, but the country round, beyond possessing a certain rugged grandeur, is devoid of actual beauty. We were met by the *Khalifa* on horseback, brother [T'hami] of the *Caid* [Madani] and acting in his place during his absence at Tafilelt. We were first shown into the usual guest apartments, the square courtyard with three rooms facing the yard upon three sides. "But," we protested, "five human beings cannot live *here* for three or four nights; we are not sheep; we must have at least a room each and some place for our servants. Let us go and pitch our tents in some garden – we ask for nothing more; but to consent to be penned up here is impossible." We were told that to go outside the walls would never do; the *Caid* was responsible for our safety, and outside the walls at night he could not answer for it. I had made up my mind that if the worst came to the worst I could be fairly clean and comfortable in the one big room I had already taken possession of, and in which I had installed the "Señorita", who was taken suddenly ill with high fever and pains; when after about two hours the "Caballero" came back and said they had succeeded in getting other quarters. "Mizian,"[1] "Mizian besof,"[2] the soldiers told us with great glee. However, knowing the easily contented dispositions of even the highest Moors where their internal arrangements are concerned, I said, before moving our things and the sick child, I would go and see these wonderful apartments. So after threading a maze of dirty alleys we came to a huge doorway, and on this being opened I saw a dark, dirty-looking court. "Oh, I knew it would be no better," I said instantly; "I am going back." "Wait, we are not there yet," I was told; and indeed we emerged from the courtyard into a real garden. There were the crossed paths, the orange and lemon trees and the fountain; and wonder upon wonder – some truly palatial apartments! My room was about sixty feet long, with a large central doorway, over which was hung an embroidered curtain of Rabat work; on the floor were some beautiful rugs, which I longed to pack up and take away; the ceiling was really fine, harmonious, and resting to the eye. And opposite the door a large square mattress, and under the mattress – strange incongruity – a hideous piece of diapered pattern Manchester druggeting in flaring colours. But still more hideous and incongruous, on the wall two huge, cheap, tawdry, many-hued German clocks within a few feet of each other – neither of course going.

'After the other sheds that we had been offered this was luxury indeed. They were apartments reserved exclusively for the use of the *Caid*'s distinguished native guests, and were the rooms the Sultan himself would occupy if he paid a visit to Glaoui. The room corresponding to the one I occupied opposite was locked, but the men fitted up the "dry arches" all round with rugs and curtains, and made themselves very comfortable; and a large square covered-in space without doors served as the kitchen; and the invalid and I shared the big room, which we gathered was the withdrawing-room of the ladies. Nails all round the walls, which served us as pegs, showed that a *haiti* usually decorated the otherwise plain whitewashed walls. Our evident pleasure and gratitude at this pleasant and unlooked-for surprise seemed

[1] 'Good.'
[2] 'Very good.'

amply to reward the *Khalifa*, who beamed upon us and repeated "Maha babicum" (Welcome to our door) over and over again with the utmost geniality. "Señor Coronel," whose mules, strange to say, had gone astray, and who had gone in search of them, found us installed here on his return; much was his surprise and pleasure too. For on his previous visit he had of course had the usual guest-chamber where they at first wished us all to herd, and which for one man naturally did very well.

'Now for the moufflon or *oudad* hunt, the ostensible object of our visit. Everyone seemed to know perfectly well that they would never see an *oudad*.' (As early as 1893 Madani had been in the habit of organiz-ing large moufflon hunts, and this had done much both to deplete the stock and to drive the survivors into more inaccessible places.) 'How-ever, after a great deal of discussion, the day following the one after we had arrived, allowing one day for rest, we started off on a quasi-moufflon hunt. There were about fifty beaters, and as we all emerged beyond the Castle walls they burst into a kind of chant, the notes rising and falling as from one throat. It is the same chant with which they begin any operation of any kind – "There is no God but God, and Mohammed is His Prophet." Then wild shrieks and yells burst from them, and they rush about in an excited, inconsequent manner, meant to represent a mimic fight, the same kind of performance being gone through on horseback by the *Khalifa*, amid the delighted yells of his admiring followers. He would suddenly put his horse – a great big powerful black Barb, very much resembling a prize cart-horse – into a gallop, twist and turn about at full speed, and then without rhyme or reason fire off his gun, and with the same suddenness, and for as much reason as he started, bring his horse to a full stop. How long the horses stand this kind of treatment I do not know, but I believe a horse is considered rather old at seven or eight, and no wonder. We were all proceeding in a gingerly, careful manner for the most part up and down somewhat unpleasant-looking and precipitous places, and if we came to a place more precipitous and unpleasant-looking than the rest, these antics would begin again. Whether it was to exhibit the sure-footedness of his horse or his skill as a rider we did not know, but it struck us all as childish in the extreme, especially as it seemed to afford him and his followers an enormous amount of pleasure.

'After an hour or two of this sort of thing, and being no nearer to a

moufflon than we were before, or, according to one or two reliable
Moors we asked in confidence, were ever likely to be, I had had enough
of it, so I was given an escort home; and I was very glad to get back
and secure my rest and quiet, which I shared with the "Señorita" and
the "Coronel", both of whom were on the sick list, – the latter chiefly
from a very severe contusion he had suffered during a moufflon hunt;
but in this case the moufflon was the hunter, not the hunted, and it took
place in the Sultan's garden at Morocco City [Marrakesh]. The
aggressive moufflon was one of the two sent with the Mission to
England as a present to the King. The animal was walking about at
large, and the Sultan had begged for some of the "Coronel's" cigars,
about which the latter fancies himself very particular, wherewith to
feed it. The "Coronel" reluctantly gave up one of the best to the
moufflon, who having devoured it, was presumably so incensed at the
quality thereof that he straightway made for the owner and inflicted
some severe wounds on him, the worst having been on his hand, which
lasted some time.

'During our stay at Glaoui not a day passed but what some supplicant
for medicine made his or her appearance at my door. One lady
suffered from pains after eating. I diagnosed indigestion and recom-
mended "hot water". As, however, hot water alone would not have
appealed to them, I made up little packets of Eno's Fruit Salt, a pinch in
each, and folded them neatly into Seidlitz powder-looking kind of
arrangements. The *Khalifa* took us to see the lady in question, and we
walked through the same kind of dingy passages and yards, and found
"the ladies" sitting in a high walled-in courtyard. One of them
immediately proceeded to show me a "bad place", – thus momentarily
transporting one in imagination to the cottages in one's own villages
at home, – so having promised her something, I parted with some of
my precious Crême-Simon to her, and I hope it did her good. Others
came to see me: their husbands having first asked permission, which
having been graciously granted, they arrived. When asked what I
could do for them, my interpreter replied, "No quieren nada mas que
mirará la Señora,"[1] which was very gratifying, and a treat to which
they were quite welcome. Three were brought up at different times
for the same purpose; and then I began to think that I was no very great

[1] 'They only want to look at the Señora.'

success or there would have been more, as I accorded them all a very genial and smiling reception. I could do no more nor less.

'One other visitor we had was the *Caid*'s little daughter, and the "Señorita" presented her with a little silver knife on the back of her hand, which we had learnt was the only way to offer knives or pencils without giving offence. In return we were given bushel-loads of dates and almonds, and as a crowning gift one old lady brought me up a handful of henna, wherewith to stain my palms and nails.

'The next day I rode a donkey, accompanied by the lesser invalid, into the "Mellah"[1] or Jewish quarter, and made some purchases of Sous *selhams* – curious-looking garments made of camel's hair, with a large orange or red patch on the back. The other two went for a ride to the *Khalifa*'s Castle, and reported undreamt-of beauties and scenes of surpassing loveliness which we had missed.

'One evening after dinner, as we were all sitting under the portico of the garden, Sidi Mahommed, the man who carried the Sultan's letters, and is a sort of "king's messenger", a high official as we were informed, came and prostrated himself at the "Coronel's" feet, embracing his knees, kissing his clothes, and "carrying on" in a very strange and hysterical manner, and pouring out a kind of sobbing petition. After some minutes of this, it appeared to have been granted, for the high official rose with many reiterated "barakalaufics" and proceeded to embrace my garments too, and generally show many signs of deranged joy. When I was able to gather what it was all about, I was very much disappointed. I thought the "high official" had been misconducting himself in some way, had committed a murder at the least, and had come to beg the "Coronel" to intercede for him, and that he had consented to beg him off. But the actual fact was, that the *Khalifa* coveted the "Coronel's" gun, which, by the way, was the one he had been playfully toying with the day we were out with him, and had sent this ruffian to petition for it. Well, the poor "Coronel" had to part with his gun, which was a sixty-guinea one, and although not one with the very latest improvements, still a good serviceable gun in good working order. But "it is more blessed to give than to receive", and we may be sure the "Coronel" experienced the full delights of the

---

[1] '"Mellah" is the Arabic also for salt; but I do not know the connection between a Jewry and salt, unless it be an ironical allusion to the "salt of the earth".' Bless your innocent heart.

above maxim when he retired gunless to bed that night. The *Khalifa* himself made his appearance before we retired, and in a few dignified appropriate words acknowledged the gift; this, too, must have been very gratifying to the donor. He appeared an insatiable person, however, this *Khalifa*, for the next day he asked the "Señor Baron" for his gun, and offered to give him a mule in exchange. We thought this was so good a hint to be gone, that we decided to leave next day before we were despoiled of all our possessions. So we packed up our goods and departed.

'The morning we left the *Khalifa* came and toyed with an orange-sprig while I was having my breakfast alone, the others having finished. "He wishes to present me with a flower, I am sure," I thought, and not knowing how else to help him, being ignorant of more than a few words of his language, I merely smiled at him encouragingly. He smiled back, it is true, but shifted his feet uneasily and looked anxiously towards the entrance. This went on for some time, and the "situation was becoming strained". One reads of situations getting into this condition, and I now realized what it meant. However, the *dénoûement* was at hand: the high official appeared, and with him a slave carrying – bearing I should say – a rug. This was placed at my feet, "for the Señora" I was told. And then my face did I hope express the genuine pleasure the gift afforded me. "Barakalaufic,"[1] I repeated several times, and fingering the rug I exclaimed, "Mizian – mizian besof."[2] The "Coronel", I hasten to add, had also been presented with a little bag that we had admired on the *Khalifa*'s person. And I felt a qualm or two in having admired the rugs so much, as I had honestly not intended it for a hint, but merely as a polite expression of gratification at the commodious comfort of our lodgings. It had not occurred to me that to admire a thing necessarily conveyed a desire to possess it with the Moors. . . . But if I had thought any amount of hints would have procured the one carpet I most admired of all I have seen in this country, then I brazenly confess that none would have been spared. The one I did get, however, was very attractive: square in shape, which is rather uncommon, and the colouring and pattern both good.

'When we were all ready to start the *Khalifa* rode with us to the

---

1 'Thank you.'
2 'Good – very good.'

outskirts of the Castle, then he drew up between two soldiers and solemnly bade us farewell one by one.'

Though this tells us little enough about T'hami El Glaoui at the age of twenty-one, it paints a picture of gauche high spirits in startling contrast to the icy majesty of his middle age when he ruled all the south from his palace in Marrakesh, and when men said of him, 'The words of the Glaoui break the stones.' Yet even as an old man, when he had deposed his Sultan and supplanted him in all but name, one nagging ambition remained. Though he had received the Croix de Guerre and the Médaille Militaire, he was not an English knight. It had all begun with the coronation of King Edward VII in August 1902. The Sultan Moulay Abd El Aziz had sent as his representative his Minister of War, Mehdi El Menhebbi, accompanied by *Caid* Maclean, and Menhebbi had returned (in a hurry, because his absence had created a vacant post) as an English knight, the only Moroccan gentleman ever to be ennobled by a British sovereign. And so, fifty-two years after Lady Grove cast a tolerantly amused eye upon T'hami El Glaoui's equestrian exhibitionism, we may see him bearing to the coronation in London of Queen

Moroccan dagger and sheath

Elizabeth II a great crown of gold and emeralds for Her Majesty, and a golden dagger for Prince Philip. Both were refused, and an ambition just fifty years old had failed for ever.

By 1902 the imperial coffers of Morocco had been drained to the last dregs to pay for the Sultan's toys and the multiple commissions on them that amounted to almost five hundred per cent. As a result the viziers had obtained gigantic loans from European powers, loans that precluded possibility of any independent Morocco in the future. The proud *Mahgreb* was mortgaged to the hilt and far beyond it.

The time was ripe for revolution; indeed it was strange that during the two years since the death of the Regent Bou Ahmed there had been no serious *rogui* (pretender; since 1862 all pretenders were called *roguis*, after a notable but short-lived pretender of that date) to a throne that was for all practical purposes vacant. In previous times of hardship, famine, or tribal disaster it had been the wont of the people who belonged to the *bled el mahkzen* to explain it by saying, 'The Sultan does not know. May Allah bless and guide the Sultan.' Now they said openly, 'The Sultan does not care,' or 'There is no Sultan; he who was Sultan has sold the *Mahgreb* to the infidel Christians.' This dictum, though ill-informed, was in practical terms remarkably close to the truth, and numerous minor incidents were held to confirm it. In 1903, for example, a mounted tribal warrior decapitated an English doctor, Dr Cooper, in the centre of Fez, and immediately took sanctuary in the tomb of Moulay Idriss. This, by custom, should have given the assassin complete asylum. With utter disregard for established rights, however, Moulay Abd El Aziz had the victim dragged from his refuge, flogged, and finally shot.

'The rumours of Christian influence spread fast, and were soon taken advantage of. The Moors are essentially opportunists, and one, Omar Ez Zarhouni, was more opportunist than the rest. He was an educated man who had been a scribe at Court, but a forgery had put an end to his career in the precincts of the palace.' (More than one, the most impudent being a perfect copy of the Imperial Seal.) 'For a time, he was a sort of secretary to Hammou El Hassen, the Berber *Caid* of the Beni Mtir tribe, when I knew him. In 1901 he left the *Caid* and disappeared into the country. Amongst other useful attainments he knew a certain number of rather ordinary conjuring tricks.' (This attainment was of much greater significance than might appear, for the whole life of the Moroccan people was bound up with belief in magic, spells, djinns, and supernatural powers of all kinds. Walter Harris does not specify his conjuring tricks, but they are well documented in some of the more elusive literature. A Moroccan card trick, little known at that time but basically the same as the 'three card trick' was the most innocuous of his repertoire. The most spectacular and convincing, however, required the death of a slave or a captive, and Zarhouni went through this particular miracle routine many hundreds of times. Away from all onlookers, the slave was buried alive lying face upward. Between his lips he held a hollow bamboo connecting him to the air three feet above; through this he could breathe, and even produce some semblance of speech. A further hollow reed led from one ear to the surface. When all these preparations were completed to Zarhouni's satisfaction he would summon his audience – often numbering thousands – and begin to harangue them. In the course of his opening speech he would mention the miraculous powers bestowed upon him by Allah, and offer supernatural protection to the families of any who would join him. The speech was followed by a few harmless conjuring tricks, and when the audience expressed their wonder and amazement he would say contemptuously that these things were nothing, that he had showed them but the outermost fringe of his powers, that were it required of him he could even hold audible converse with the dead. There was usually among the multitude who were listening to him at least one sceptic who challenged him to a demonstration of this claim, and then the murder was under way. Zarhouni would begin with a show of reluctance, saying that such things called for a great drain upon spiritual energy, that he was tired, that this small occasion did not warrant the taxing of his strength. The more excuses he could make, the more he could appear to be trying to evade putting his words to the test, the greater the stupefaction of the people when at last, appearing angry with them for their insulting incredulity, he performed his miracle.

'Because of these holy and mighty powers that you worthless people dare to doubt,' he would declaim, 'I can feel that a man not long dead is buried somewhere within the circle that you form about me.' Raising his voice as though he were calling to someone far off, he shouted, 'Oh dead man, speak to me if you are a believer in the true faith!' Hollowly, from under the ground, came the voice of the buried slave, 'I am here. What do you want of me, Sidna?' (Sidna is the form of address used only to a Sultan, the supreme spiritual leader of his people.) 'I want nothing of you but to tell me whether your earthly name was Abd El Wahed' (or whatever name had been decided upon), and the voice from the grave would reply, 'That was my name, Sidna.' 'Then sleep in peace,' Zarhouni would rejoin, and, stepping over to the grave he would plant his heel firmly upon the reed that served as breathing tube. He would then hold his audience by other means until the body of the suffocated slave had time to grow cold, and exhume the corpse for their verification. (The slave, presumably, had not been told of any sequel to the faked conversation with a dead man.)

'Omar Ez Zarhouni possessed as well a most fluent tongue. By the aid of these accomplishments he was able to make a living, travelling from tribe to tribe on a she-donkey, from which fact he became known along the countryside as "Bou Hamara" – literally, the "Father of the she-donkey".' (Walter Harris offers no further explanation of the name, though in Islamic mythology Bou Hamara is the equivalent of the Christian anti-Christ. He comes at the end of the world, riding a she-donkey. He finds famine, misery and starvation, and brings with him riches and plenty and feasting and dancers for all mankind. The faithful are not deceived, for they can read on his forehead the words *Naalah allah*, 'The Accursed of Allah', but the unbelievers welcome him, partake of his seductions, and are cast into eternal flames.) 'It was amongst the simple tribesmen of the Rif that he met with his principal success. Starting with the idea of merely earning a livelihood, he soon saw the possibilities of a career on a larger scale. His conjuring tricks, his wily tongue, and his forgeries – to say nothing of the she-donkey – encircled him with a sort of religious prestige; and one day he suddenly declared himself to be Moulay Mohammed' (who had been captured by Bou Ahmed and confined to the palace after the Rehamna tribe had declared him Sultan), 'the first-born son of the late Sultan Moulay Hassan, and therefore the elder brother of the then reigning sovereign, Moulay Abd El Aziz. For a time he did not discard his donkey, and the humility of this means of transit added attractions to his prestige in the eyes of the devout.'

Bou Hamara was roughly of an age with Moulay Mohammed whom he impersonated – a little under forty – and he made the most of a slight superficial resemblance of feature. Moulay Mohammed had been called Le Borgne, the one-eyed, because his left eyelid habitually drooped; Bou Hamara cultivated this perpetual wink until it became natural to him. Even the wildest of his inventions found ready belief among the tribespeople whom he recruited. The ruling Sultan, Abd El Aziz, was, he said – and who should know better than he, who had been brought up at the court of Moulay Hassan? – not a Moroccan at all, but an Englishman, who had been substituted for the rightful princeling, son of the Turkish lady Lalla R'kkia, at birth. The real Abd El Aziz, he asserted, was a prisoner in London.

'The vicinity of Bou Hamara's jurisdiction to the Spanish port of Melilla, on the Rif coast, had seriously inconvenienced the Spanish authorities and inhabitants of that town; and at length, in order to obtain supplies for the population, the Spaniards had been obliged to negotiate and to enter into direct relations with him. A mining-engineer told me that he had once accompanied some Spanish capitalists on a visit to Bou Hamara's headquarters at Selouan. They all went with a certain fear and trembling, but the stake was a big one. They wanted to obtain a concession for the working of some valuable iron-mines in the neighbourhood. The Pretender received them cordially enough, and invited them to sit down with him on a large carpet spread in the shadow of a tree. The discussion of the terms of the concession pro-ceeded, and Bou Hamara's demands became more and more exacting. The capitalists hesitated and protested, but were brought to acceptance by the fact that while the conversation was still in progress a number of the Pretender's soldiers arrived carrying the recently-severed heads of a dozen or so of his enemies, which they arranged round the edge of the carpet. At the end of the interview the three or four very pale capitalists had accepted in their entirety the Pretender's propositions, and were thanking him for his cordial reception, surrounded by the ghastly exhibition that had not a little influenced their decision.'

It took ten years and a different Sultan to defeat and capture Bou Hamara, and no Sultan ever defeated or captured the second thorn in the Chereefian flesh, the great brigand Raisul, who held *Caid* Maclean, and later Walter Harris himself, to ransom.

'He is by birth sprung from one of the most aristocratic families in Morocco, and is a *Chereef*, or direct descendant of the Prophet, through Moulay Idriss, who founded the Mohammedan Empire of Morocco, and was the first sovereign of the Idrisite Dynasty. The children of Moulay Idriss were established in various parts of the country, and it is from Moulay Abd es-Salam, whose tomb in the Beni Aros tribe is a place of great sanctity, that the famous brigand is directly descended – his family, and he himself, still holding a share in the lands, the rights and privileges which were enjoyed by their renowned ancestor. A branch of the family settled in Tetuan, where a fine mosque forms a mausoleum for his more recent ancestors, and is venerated as a place of pilgrimage.

'Possibly it was this holy ancestry that turned Raisul from the paths of virtue, for after having received an excellent education in religion and religious law at Tetuan, he took to the adventurous, lucrative, and in Morocco by no means despised, profession of a cattle robber. It is a risky business, and requires courage. You may just as likely be shot yourself as shoot any one else; but prestige tells in favour of the head of the band, and a reign of terror of the young Raisul ensued. He became celebrated. He was a youth of great courage, of the most prepossessing looks. I confess that his personality was almost fascinating. Tall, remarkably handsome, with the whitest of skins, a short dark beard and moustache, and black eyes, with profile Greek rather than Semitic, and eyebrows that formed a straight line across his forehead, Moulay Ahmed er-Raisuli was a typical and ideal bandit. His manner was quiet, his voice soft and low, and his expression particularly sad. He smiled sometimes, but seldom, and even though I knew him much better later on, I never heard him laugh. With his followers he was cold and haughty, and they treated him with all the respect due to his birth.

'At length his acts became insupportable. The whole country round lived in terror of his raids. The late Sultan ordered his arrest. His greatest friend betrayed him; he was seized, and sent to prison in the dreaded dungeons of Mogador. When, in 1903, I was Raisul's prisoner at Zinat, he narrated more than once to me the history of those four or five years spent in prison. He showed me the marks of the chains on his ankles, wrists, and neck; he told me of the filth and the cold; of the introduction of a file in a loaf of bread; of five months' patient work at night; and of a delayed flight. He escaped, but for a very few hours. He did not know his way about the town, and he had forgotten that the chains would almost prevent his walking. He entered a street that had had no outlet, and was recaptured. Fresh chains were heaped upon him, and it was not till two years later that he was released on the petition of Hadj Mohammed Torres, the Sultan's representative at Tangier. He came back to his home, meaning to live a quiet and peaceful life, but he found that his friend who had betrayed him had become Governor of Tangier, and confiscated all his property. He applied for its return, but could not obtain it. He threatened, but they laughed at him – and then he took to his old profession and became a brigand.'

Raisul raised £20,000 on *Caid* Maclean, but this was as nothing to the rewards that accrued to the kidnapping of a Greek-American resident in Tangier. This Mr Perdicaris's life was bought in exchange for $75,000 and Raisul's official appointment by the Sultan as Governor of Tangier and its provinces. We might now seem to be in the realm of pure burlesque were it not for Walter Harris's sobering account of one of Raisul's victims.

'It was a ghastly sight. The summer heat had already caused the corpse to discolour and swell. An apple had been stuck in the man's mouth, and both his eyes had been gouged out. The naked body was shockingly mutilated, and the finger-tips had been cut off, to be worn, the tribesmen told me, as charms by their women. The hands were pegged to the ground by sticks driven through the palms, about a yard in length, bearing little flags. A wreath of wild flowers was twined round the miserable man's head, and the village dogs had already gnawed away a portion of the flesh of one of the legs. I was jokingly informed that that was probably what I should look like during the course of the next few days.'

Throughout the ten years of Bou Hamara's rebellion he was in friendly contact with Raisul. Walter Harris, while he was held hostage, discovered a document signed with Bou Hamara's alias, Mohammed

Ben Hassan, and franked with the forged steel Seal of State, appointing Raisul Governor of the north-west mountain tribes.

'In the late autumn of 1902 Moulay Abd El Aziz left Fez for Rabat. His departure had been delayed on account of this incipient rebellion of Bou Hamara's; but affairs seemed to have quieted down, and the departure of the Court took place in November. An army had been meanwhile sent in the direction of Taza to put down the rebellion. The choice of a Commander-in-Chief for this army was typical of Morocco of those days. The situation was critical, and the future depended largely upon the success of His Majesty's troops. The Sultan was leaving North Morocco, and by this fact alone his position would be weakened; but the tradition of corruption – accepted and permitted – was too great. I asked the Sultan, for I was at Fez with him at that time, whom he had chosen as Commander-in-Chief. To my astonishment he replied, "My brother, Moulay El Kebir." "But he is still a boy," I replied, "and has never been a soldier." "True," replied the Sultan, "but my other brothers have all commanded expeditions. It is Moulay El Kebir's turn. He has never had a chance of making a little money." The making of a little money was, of course, the abstraction of the soldiers' pay and extortion everywhere. I accompanied the Sultan when he left Fez in November. The Court proceeded, with all its pomp and majesty, to Meknès, where we stayed a few days, and then on into the Zemmour country, where rebellion was rife. It is impossible to say of how many people the rabble which accompanied the Sultan consisted, but we were probably 18,000 or 20,000 in camp, with at least half perfectly useless for warfare. A number of Fez merchants, who followed the Court from capital to capital, accompanied the Sultan, and each had his family and retainers with him. Amongst other strange groups were hundreds of beggars, for the most part blind, who also migrated with the Court.

'There was some fighting in the Zemmour country, but still more in the Sultan's camp. The incidents which occurred were typical of the time and country. The Zemmour tribesmen decided to resist the Sultan's progress at a deep ravine which crossed the plains at right angles to our line of march. This ravine was perhaps 400 feet in depth, a few yards wide only at the bottom, where a little river flowed, and half a mile across at its summit. Aware that the army was likely to meet with resistance at this spot, a halt was called on the edge of the valley. Half-way up the steep slope on the opposite side was an open ledge of green grass, on which was a group of black tents and thatch huts of the Zemmour villagers. From the thick brushwood opposite a few rebel shots were fired at the army. The Sultan's artillery and machine-guns were brought up to the edge of the ravine, and began firing pro-miscuously into the brushwood. It was soon clear that the valley was not strongly held. The Zemmour tribesmen are horsemen, and their attack was more likely to be made on the plain across the ravine, at the moment when the army was extricating itself from the precipices and brushwood.

'A regiment – the Doukkalas – was ordered to clear the valley in preparation for an advance, and started down the steep hillside with much noise and singing. A few shots were fired at them as they descended. The river crossed, they began the ascent, and soon reached the little deserted village. Here temptation was too strong, and instead of mounting higher they began to loot. The villagers had carried off all their movable property, but their stores of grain remained, and grain is valuable in the Sultan's camp. The question was how to transport it. The Moorish soldier is not easily foiled, and the brave Doukkala regiment was quite up to the occasion. In the presence of the Sultan and of the whole army they laid down their rifles, took off their baggy uniform breeches of bright blue cotton, tied up the holes through which the legs ordinarily protruded with string, and filled the rest with wheat. This done, they loaded up their booty on their backs, picked up their rifles, and started to return to the army.

'Nothing would make them go on: bugles were blown, signals made, orders shouted; but the Doukkalas felt that their day's work was done, and steadily climbed homewards. In exasperation the Abda regiment, equally famous and equally brave, was sent to support them, and to see if they couldn't be persuaded to turn once more in the direction of the enemy and abandon their loot.

'With music and singing the Abda regiment set out. They met the Doukkalas struggling up under their heavy loads near the river-bed. A collision was inevitable, and the Abda charged. The Doukkalas threw down their loads and commenced firing, and in a few minutes a little battle was raging far down below us in the ravine between the two

loyal regiments. A ceasing of the firing bespoke a compromise. The
two bodies of troops fraternized, the Doukkalas temporarily abandoned
their breeches' loads of grain on the river-bank, and returned bare-
legged to the Zemmour village with their comrades the Abdas. Once
there it was the latter's turn to step out of their nether garments, and
the Doukkalas assisted them to load up the remaining grain. This done,
the two regiments, except for a few killed and wounded, returned
together, every man bearing on his back his voluminous baggy blue
breeches stuffed to bursting-point with wheat and barley. I shall never
forget the sight of these troops struggling up the steep slope, puffing
and perspiring, dressed in the scarlet "zouave" coats, with just a fringe
of shirt encircling their waists – and nothing else, – and on the summit
the enraged Sultan and his Court and the rest of the army, impotent
to change the course of events. The afternoon was well over, and all
thought of crossing the ravine that night was out of the question, so
the camp was pitched on the side we were on.

The Doukkala and the stolen grain

'I have passed many strange disturbed nights in Morocco, but this
one was perhaps unique, for the Doukkalas and Abda regiments
quarrelled over the division of the spoil, and fought on and off all the
night through. Bullets were flying in every direction, and one had to
lie as low to ground as possible. Eventually things quieted down, and
one of my servants came and announced to me that "it is all right. The
army is now being flogged," – which was a fact, for the energetic
Minister of War had managed to arrest the survivors of the two
regiments concerned, and was having them individually severely

flogged one after the other by soldiers of other regiments and slaves and volunteers.

'We never crossed that ravine. The next day the news reached the Sultan that the army under his brother had been defeated by Bou Hamara near Taza. In all haste we turned back, and proceeded once more to Fez.'

Madani El Glaoui had been for too long out of direct contact with the Sultan for his liking. His wars of repression and consolidation had taken him far to the south and the east of the Atlas; too far from the throne, he felt, to receive his rightful share of Imperial favours. He knew that the *harka* led by the Sultan's boy brother against Bou Hamara was weak, no more than twenty thousand men, for what Chereefian troops could be mustered were widely dispersed in repression of other dissidents in the south. Dreaming, no doubt, of the rout of Bou Hamara and the largesse of the grateful Sultan, he rallied a force of southern tribesmen and with his brother T'hami marched to join the Imperial column.

It was one of the few enterprises of his life that ended in total failure. Besieged for four months in the enemy territory of Taza, wounded three times and with his route of retreat effectively blocked, he and some remnants of the column took refuge across the Algerian frontier. There he was received by Lieutenant Louis Mougin, head of the French Mission, who arranged for their re-entry into Morocco by cargo boat from Oran to Tangier. T'hami, who had nominally commanded his brother's army on this expedition, had fought a rearguard action and made good his escape to the south. He then made the pilgrimage to Mecca, and did not return to Morocco for three years, with the coveted title of Hadj.

By the rout of the Sultan's army at Taza, Bou Hamara gained not only a major victory but also one of the magic cannons and the Sultan's Master Armourer, one Bensalem Fasla. Bou Hamara immediately set him to work upon the manufacture of imperial regalia – lances of damascened steel, a replica of the Imperial parasol, and a new gun-carriage for the cannon.

Madani had been wounded not only physically but in his self-esteem, and when after his return from Algeria he at last reached Fez he expected both recognition and remuneration. These he might well have received from the Sultan Moulay Abd El Aziz, but to have followed the Sultan's career thus far is to realize that he was always under somebody's thumb, and at this time it was the thumb of his Grand Vizier Omar Tazi, who directed all affairs of State, and was also the Sultan's personal confidant.

The relationship between Madani El Glaoui and Omar Tazi began with mutual dislike and ended in deadly hatred. All that they had in common was egoism and ambition; for the rest it would have been hard to find two Moroccans as dissimilar either in mentality or appearance. Madani was tall and thin, with a sombre, ascetic dignity of voice and gesture, a skin the colour of dark terra cotta, and black eyes that were described as 'burning like coals'. In all contemporary descriptions of him exists a curious paradox; he gave the impression of a savage and implacable warrior of almost brutal ugliness, yet he affected an almost epicene grace and delicacy of movement.

Omar Tazi was red-haired, white-skinned, with small malicious eyes shaded by colourless lashes. He was so fat that he waddled, and he was complacent, cunning and sensual. He regarded Madani as a mongrel upstart from the uncivilized mountain tribes, and he treated him accordingly.

Madani stayed with the Court at Fez for five months, and his rancour and desire for vengeance grew every day. He had been used to power and pomp and vassals who ran to kiss his knee; now, rarely received in

Old Berber daggers

audience by the Sultan, he was forced to submit to such slights and indignities as Tazi saw fit to impose, inhabiting bleak and draughty quarters in Tazi's palace adjacent to those of the slaves. This, had Tazi understood it, might have been compared to baiting a panther. When Madani left Fez for Marrakesh he had already vowed to depose the Sultan and to destitute Tazi.

5

The Defeat of Abd El Aziz

THE exact sequence of events that led to the invasion of Morocco by France concerns only indirectly the story of Madani and T'hami El Glaoui, and it was in any case so extremely complex as to be of interest to none but the pure historian. Since, however, some general background is necessary to understand succeeding events, I present the barest outline, in the hope, like Lady Grove, that it will 'not be remorsefully regretted by those who chance upon it'.

By 1900 the French had been in formal occupation of Morocco's neighbour, Algeria, for seventy years, and of Tunisia, adjoining Algeria, for sixteen years. Naturally enough for a colonial power, France wanted Morocco too, and encouraged incidents on the Algerian frontier. A long series of rapacious secret agreements with the other European colonial powers ended by their ceding to the French the right to 'protect' Morocco. In return, Britain was given carte blanche in Egypt; Italy the same in Tripolitania; and Spain, whose influence int he country went back for centuries, received chunks of Morocco which included the Mediterranean ports. Germany's attempts at intervention were unsuccessful.

The follies of Abd El Aziz had placed his country deeply in debt to European international syndicates. In order to become Morocco's principal creditor, France made him enormous loans to clear these debts (fourteen million francs by 1909); then still further sums for arms – provided that these were bought from France. These arms were necessary to keep the various pretenders and other rebels from taking over the country, and it is more than likely that these enemies of the Sultan received every possible encouragement from France.

When Madani El Glaoui returned from Fez to Marrakesh with the determination to depose the Sultan Moulay Abd El Aziz, the whole French plan was already laid, and it was only a question of how peacefully the penetration could be achieved.

Moulay Abd El Aziz's *khalifa* in Marrakesh was his elder brother Moulay Hafid, nicknamed Scurvy – doubly appropriate as a contemporary writer pointed out, because he both was scurvy and had scurvy. By nature he was mean, sadistic and ruthless, greedy for power and bitterly jealous of his younger brother's luxuries and extravagances. By comparison with Madani he was a pauper, and his prestige was limited to a narrow circle of intellectuals; for he was a remarkable scholar, and despite his essentially evil and venomous personality, a Koranic theologian of great learning. He inhabited a dilapidated and ramshackle palace in Marrakesh, from which, with the aid of his Jewish Vizier Ischoua Corcos, he fostered such dissension among the local tribes as his limited influence would allow. The most significant of these tribes, recurring throughout this story, was the Rehamna, a tribe claiming Arab origin, inhabiting the plains west of Marrakesh. Their then *Caid*, El Ayadi, was a swashbuckling soldier of fortune, and professional brigand and highwayman. Moulay Hafid kept him

Caid *El Ayadi of the Rehamna*

supplied with information vital to these activities, and in return requested present propaganda and future armed support. This was granted
on two conditions – the release of all Rehamna tribesmen imprisoned
in Marrakesh, and the expulsion of all Europeans resident in the town.

In Moulay Hafid Madani saw the perfect instrument for his aims;
here was a violent and unscrupulous cadet of the royal house, needing
nothing but an army behind him to march on Fez and unseat the
Sultan, who had by now ordered the arrest of Madani El Glaoui.

Moulay Hafid was not, however, a wholly co-operative conspirator,
and the prolonged intrigue between the two was interrupted by
constant quarrels and flares of temper. These concerned, almost
invariably, the question of money. Hafid believed Madani's wealth to
be inexhaustible, and month by month his own personal demands, the
price of collaboration, became more and more outrageous. After such
a quarrel Madani would leave Marrakesh for his *kasbah* at Iminzat, in
the foothills of the mountains, and in due course Hafid would send
Corcos the Jew to make peace. Corcos, besides being a bland ambassador, was a man of immense personal riches, and he hit on the happy
idea of lending Madani the money to meet Hafid's demands. This he
did against the pledge of next year's harvest of oranges or olives in
such and such a district of Madani's wide domains. The arrangement
suited all parties, each according to his nature – Hafid in his greed,
Corcos in his traditional role of usurer, and Madani in his single-
minded ambition.

There is every indication that Madani was aware by this time that
Morocco's future lay in other hands than those of her own people. He
followed contemporary events in Europe closely, and had translations
made for him of all French Parliamentary debates that touched upon
the question of Morocco. He cannot have had factual knowledge of the
various secret agreements between European powers, but with his agile
mind and his profound familiarity with intrigue he may have guessed
much.

The plan which he set before Hafid was admirable in its clear
thinking. A rebellion in the South could only succeed if backed by a
strong army with undivided loyalty. Such an army could be achieved
only by the unification and alliance of the tribal warlords, and more
especially of the Lords of the Atlas – the Goundafi, the M'touggi and

the Glaoui. When this had been achieved as far as it might be possible (and it would not be easy, for it was less than a year since the Glaoui-M'touggi faction had sacked and pillaged the Goundafi's *kasbahs*) Hafid was to trust Madani's knowledge of world affairs to choose the right moment for declaration of rebellion.

In May 1906 a Frenchman named Charbonnier was murdered in broad daylight in the streets of Tangier. On 19 March 1907 a French doctor and philanthropist, Dr Mauchamp, was murdered in Marrakesh. All surviving accounts agree that this man was of a saintly disposition and uninterested in the politics of colonialism. The German contingent in Marrakesh, however, put about a rumour that he was, in fact, an officer of the French Military Intelligence in disguise, preparing the way for French invasion of Morocco. These rumours quieted as a result of the doctor's obvious detachment from all sources of political information, but the chief German Secret Service agent in Marrakesh, a certain Holtzmann, needed a French death. Moroccans, always deeply imbued with fear of magic, at that time cherished a peculiar horror of wireless sets, which had been among Abd El Aziz's toys, and believed that they contained an evil magic fluid capable of summoning to them instantly all the instruments of power – armies, cannon, munitions, even un-thought-of weapons beyond any of these. Mauchamp, unsuspecting, had bought a great carpet as a present for Hafid, in order to acquire approval for his medical projects. Holtzmann disseminated the report that this seemingly innocuous but enormous bundle contained, in fact, the masts and antennae of a gigantic radio set. It was never delivered to Hafid. Holtzmann pointed to some long bamboo poles supporting an awning on Mauchamp's terrace; these, he said, were still further aerials for the diabolical engine. The same evening a mob whose motive was nothing but fear hacked the unfortunate doctor into quite small pieces, and burned, without further inspection, his packaged carpet and his bamboo poles.

As a result of this second incident a French column under General Lyautey crossed the frontier from Algeria and occupied Oujda in the north-east. In accordance with a Franco-Moroccan agreement of 1902, Oujda already had a French mission, under the same Mougin as had

assisted Madani's escape from Morocco and re-entry; by this time he
had been promoted to Captain. Still Madani waited.

At the end of July of the same year nine European workers were
massacred by an excited mob at the then small and insignificant fishing
port of Casablanca, with a population of some twenty-five thousand
Moroccans. Under an agreement of 1901 a European concern had been
granted the right to build a harbour at Casablanca, and had recently
begun work in a small way. Three of the dead were French, the others
Spanish and Italian. A week later the French cruisers *Galilée* and *Du
Chayla* and the battleship *Forbin*, together with the Spanish gunboat
Don Alvar de Bazau, bombarded the town before landing troops for the
protection of the European population.

'Scenes of the wildest confusion ensued, for not only was the town
under the fire of the cannon of the warship, but the tribes from the
interior had taken advantage of the panic to invade and pillage the
place. Every sort of atrocity and horror was perpetrated, and Casablanca was a prey to loot and every kind of crime. The European force
was sufficient to protect the Consulates, and the greater part of the
Christian population escaped murder. When order was restored the
town presented a pitiful aspect. I saw it a very few days after the
bombardment, and the scene was indescribable – a confusion of dead
people and horses, while the contents of almost every house seemed to
have been hurled into the streets and destroyed. The looting was
incomplete: piles of cotton goods, cases of foodstuffs – in fact, every
class of merchandise still lay strewn about the roads. Many of the houses
had been burned and gutted. Out of dark cellars, Moors and Jews,
hidden since the first day of the bombardment, many of them wounded,
were creeping, pale and terrified. Some had to be dug out of the ruins
of their abodes. Over all this mass of destruction horses and men had
galloped and fought. Blood was everywhere. In what had once been
the poorer quarter of the town, where the houses, mostly thatched in
straw, had been burned, I only met one living soul – a mad woman,
dishevelled, dirty, but smiling – who kept calling, "Ayesha, my little
daughter; my little son Ahmed, where are you: I am calling you."
Turning to me she asked, "You haven't seen my little children, have
you? – a little girl and a tiny boy, almost a baby." She didn't wait for
an answer, but passed on, still calling Ayesha and Ahmed.'

The first French troops to be landed at Casablanca were commanded by General Drude, and numbered about 3,000 men, supported by six 75 mm guns. The soldiers were for the most part colonial, mainly Senegalese and Algerian, with units of the French Foreign Legion and Spahis. At first their sorties were limited to a range of some ten miles from Casablanca, for they were closely surrounded by tribes who, while suffering consistent local defeat, were unconquered. The French would send up a balloon from which to establish the position of the enemy and mount an attack accordingly. They retained no prisoners; all captives – pathetically ill-armed and often little more than children – were roped together and shot in the back. There exist some peculiarly unpleasant accounts of this the Moors' first view of a Christian civilization in armed action.

For four months General Drude held Casablanca as a bridgehead, his military operations confined to the maintenance of an empty no-man's-land extending in a half circle round the landward side of the town. At the New Year of 1908 he was replaced by General d'Amade, and the number of troops increased to 8,000. With these d'Amade extended the range of operations to a radius of fifty miles, and took and destroyed the important town of Settat, lying on the main route to Marrakesh.

It was the beginning of the French occupation of Morocco – but not, as Walter Harris wrote ingenuously in 1920, 'the final end of centuries of cruelty, corruption, and extortion'. It was the beginning of an era during which these things were kept decently out of sight by an industrious horde of French crossing-sweepers.

Madani was at Iminzat. As soon as the news of the French landings at Casablanca reached him (there was still neither road nor railway in all the country) he and Hafid arranged to meet at a gazelle hunt, so that their conference might appear to have no connection with events out-side Marrakesh. Even in the tension of the moment the party contrived to kill sixty-two gazelles, and at the banquet that followed the hunt Madani told Hafid that 'today he recognized the hour of destiny'.

Two days later, on 16 August, they summoned every southern notable whom they felt that they could trust – *Caids*, tribal chieftains, and religious savants – (the *oulemas*, without whose consent no Sultan may rightfully ascend the throne) – to Hafid's palace. To this assembly, suspicious, whispering, each thinking of his own future, Corcos read with great emotion a series of letters purporting to emanate from the region of Casablanca. Every one of these letters, whether in fact they originated from Marrakesh or Casa, called upon Moulay Hafid to rid the land of the infidel Christians, to whom his frivolous brother had sold the Chereefian Empire of Morocco. Then Madani rose, saying that only Moulay Hafid could, by his learning and by the might of the united South, restore to Islam this pitifully mortgaged heritage. He concluded with words that his younger brother T'hami used of another reigning monarch forty-six years later, saying that Moulay Abd El Aziz was 'no more than the shadow of a Sultan'.

For some minutes there was absolute silence in the gathering; Madani had not foreseen, in his own single-mindedness, a reluctance to admit yet a third and simultaneous Sultan of Morocco. Abd El Aziz was Sultan in Fez; in Tadla the people had proclaimed Bou Hamara as lawful Sultan and prayed to Allah in his name every Friday. Yet a third Sultan was a concept difficult for the individuals of this meeting to accept. The question was, very simply, which party was going to win. To be on the losing side meant destitution, torture, imprisonment and a slow, painful death.

After a long silence a *Caid* pointed out that the election of a Sultan was the responsibility of the religious fraternity, the *oulemas*. This body passed the buck to the *cadis*, small-time arbitrators in Islamic law. They, in turn, disclaimed all authority in so grave a matter.

The meeting had already lasted for two hours, and Madani was becoming impatient. He turned to where his own tribesmen thronged the palace courtyard and made a quick sign. With the precision of a well-drilled regiment every man faced Moulay Hafid with a great shout of 'Long live our Lord!' – the greeting that is given only to a Sultan.

After this reminder of force there remained only one dissenting voice. Moulay Moustaffa, brother-in-law of Aziz and Hafid, refused to sign any declaration of Aziz's dethronement, pointing out forcibly that such an action was against all religious law, and that it was blasphemy to depose a reigning *Imam*. Shouting with rage, Madani declaimed that Moustaffa was in league with the Christians, and that if he would not sign he would be killed on the spot. Three of the conspirators seized Moustaffa and raised their daggers, but before they could strike he struggled free and threw his arms around Moulay Hafid, both to confuse their aim and so that, if the steel should enter his body, his blood would stain Hafid's robes.

At this precise moment the call to prayer echoed through the room from every minaret in Marrakesh. The scene dissolved, and like obedient children the entire assembly trooped off to pray at the Berrima Mosque. Like a naughty child, however, Madani raised the symbol of sultanate, the crimson parasol, above Hafid's head as he left the mosque. The brief revolution, farcical but wholly successful, had begun.

Inside a mosque

There ensued a lapse of nearly three months before Madani and Hafid
were prepared to launch their offensive against the unfortunate Sultan
Abd El Aziz in Fez. This was due not so much to administrative preparations as to shortage of men and a profound mistrust of the situation
that they would leave behind them in the South; for in Morocco the
worst danger in launching an expeditionary force had always been the
risk of finding, on return, a stranger insolently occupying one's palace.
Thus the delay, which in the light of the hilariously comic campaign
that followed it, an historian might be tempted to ascribe to intrigue
with the enemy, was almost certainly devoted to the enrolment of
deserters from the opposing side and the elimination of treachery at
home.

In November Madani and Hafid marched on Fez with forty
thousand mounted warriors of the Berber tribes under Madani's
domination. Almost exactly simultaneously – a curious circumstance
after so protracted a period of inaction – the Sultan Moulay Abd El Aziz
marched on Marrakesh with an even stronger army, several pieces of
heavy artillery, and French instructors versed in their use. In their
efforts to avoid contact with the enemy both armies had chosen so
unusual a route that there seemed every chance of a bloodless exchange
of cities. As soon, however, as Aziz's superiority became known to
Hafid, he justifiably conceived the battle lost before it was joined, and
dispatched Madani to discuss peace terms with Aziz, whom he still
referred to not as the Sultan but as 'my little brother'.

The reasons for the farce of the ensuing twenty-four hours are
historically obscure, at all events to the present writer, but the facts
remain incontestable. Madani, carrying his flag of truce, and presumably with bitter despair at his heart, was still on his way to treat
with the enemy when he learned of their magic dispersal after a purely
token exchange of shots. Aziz had left his camp to stage, and to watch as
one of the diverting spectacles to which he was accustomed, the
bombardment of an outlying detachment of Madani's cavalry who had
come closer to Aziz's army than either Sultan had foreseen. He and his
Viziers and his French instructors, equipped with the latest European
telescopes and prismatics, were grouped in anticipation behind the
artillery when, without any order being given, several columns of his
own cavalry charged as if to encircle and outflank the enemy tents. A

few desultory shots were exchanged; Aziz, vaguely perturbed, sent runners to report upon the situation. They returned with the incomprehensible statement that Aziz's cavalry had been defeated and were in rout. Aziz protested that this was impossible because there had been no engagement. But the words were hardly off his tongue before his cavalry returned at the gallop, disbanded and in flight, and enemy bullets began to whistle about his ears. His Viziers fled on horseback or on muleback, and he was left alone with a personal retinue of black slaves and a few badly scared French instructors.

At this moment he displayed a coolness, a detachment from his private situation, that suggests what he might have become had it not been for the skilful and patient seduction by his Viziers during his adolescence. 'We have been betrayed,' he remarked with no hint of emotion, and he gave orders to fall back upon his camp. Surrounded to a distance of several hundred yards by the ranks of his slaves, he rode for the distant imperial tents, changing horses at the gallop when the first showed signs of tiring; by the time he reached the camp, nevertheless, his cloak had been pierced by six bullets, though he remained miraculously unharmed.

His headquarters were the scene of wild disorder. His disbanded troops had begun to loot and pillage, breaking open cases of ammunition, slitting with their daggers the Viziers' tents to carry off whatever was portable. He assembled his women (for like most Sultans he had journeyed into battle with half his harem) and, still accompanied by his French instructors, he sought hiding in the countryside. At nightfall his retinue erected for him and his women some sort of shelter composed of saddles; when this had been completed to his satisfaction he drew aside one of the French officers, and, sitting at the foot of a fig tree under the open stars, said calmly – almost, perhaps, with relief, for he was weary of being Sultan – 'This morning I was the Sultan, and it was I who appointed the *Caids*. This evening I am a man like any other man. It is the will of Allah.' What dignity he had lost at the hands of his Viziers he regained as they departed in flight.

There is no reliable or contemporary account of the true circumstances that led to the rout of Abd El Aziz's army. All that is recorded historically is that it was the tribesmen of the Rehamna, under El Ayadi the highwayman, and of the Glaoua under Madani, who gave the coup de grâce to the section of the Imperial *harka* that had not already deserted to their side.

Moulay Abd El Aziz survived to live in gentlemanly retirement at Tangier.

Madani and Hafid had won the day. Madani was rewarded for his bizarre victory by the posts first of Minister of War and then of Grand Vizier to the new Sultan Moulay Hafid; in this capacity, comparable to that of an administrative dictator, he ruled all Morocco under the Sultan. He immediately filled every post of *Caid* in the South with his relations, building for each of them a fortress of a type still recognizable today wherever they or their ruins stand.

To his son-in-law Si Hammou, husband of his daughter Lalla Halima, he gave the *caidat* of Telouet, Tinerhir, Ouazarzat and Zagora, and the command of all the South beyond the Atlas, thereby making Hammou one of the most powerful figures in the whole country.

To his jolly coal-black eldest son Mohammed El Arbi, aged just eighteen, he confided the Ministry of War. His brother, T'hami, he made Pasha of Marrakesh, the most important single office in southern Morocco. That he did not entirely trust him is evidenced by a letter dated 11 December 1910 from the French Consul at Fez to the French Chargé d'Affaires at Tangier. The Sultan Moulay Hafid was preparing to move south to Marrakesh. 'The Sultan's decision is based, above all, upon financial considerations [collection of taxes]. For the rest he wants to make his authority felt over El Hadj T'hami El Glaoui, who is enriching himself too quickly, and is following too personal a policy. While on this subject, I would mention that during a recent conversation the Grand Vizier [Madani] replied to a remark about his brother's lack of goodwill by saying, "If you want anything in Marrakesh, ask me and not my brother. You will see that you have more to gain with the *mahkzen* than with El Hadj T'hami." '

To his brother Hassi, Madani gave the post of Pasha of the *Kasbah* of Marrakesh. The *kasbah* included the palace of the Government, the arsenal, a quarter occupied by familiars of the Court, and the State prisons. (There was a separate prison where women who caused their husbands annoyance were incarcerated by order of the Pasha. The inmates were fed by their families, but owing to the high incidence of poisoning it had become the custom for special guards to prepare the food and to make the donors taste it before feeding the prisoners.) All Government troops in the South came under the command of the Pasha of the *Kasbah*, and in the absence of the Sultan he was especially charged with the surveillance of the palace and all its slaves. He also appointed his own numerous administrators.

The Glaoui empire was established. It was just fourteen years since the dying Sultan Moulay Hassan had passed by Telouet and left the petty chieftain a bronze cannon.

The other two Lords of the Atlas, the Goundafi and the M'touggi, could hardly be said to have shared the Glaoui's fortune. In 1906 Madani and the M'touggi had profited by the Goundafi's absence at the Court of Fez to sack and pillage his extending lands. He returned to what was left of them in a huff, and refused to support Madani's movement to depose Abd El Aziz. When Hafid was proclaimed Sultan, Madani persuaded the Goundafi to come to Marrakesh, and, in an effort to repair past quarrels, offered him the Ministry of War; but the Goundafi refused, saying it was not his métier. He did not care for the look of the new régime, and found Marrakesh 'full of unpleasant strangers from the Pre-Sahara'. He went back to his mountains and did not emerge for several years.

The M'touggi had agreed to support Moulay Hafid – in return for the rights of conquest over vast new tracts of tribal land, and the post of Minister of Justice. He accompanied Hafid's victorious march on Fez – for part of the way. When he learned of the strength of Abd El Aziz's army, and the fact that Madani was going ahead to plead truce, he deserted in the middle of the night, leaving his tents pitched so as to arouse no suspicion. He sped back to Marrakesh to open its gates to the conquering Abd El Aziz. Learning the truth, he tried once more to attach himself to Hafid, but for the next few years it is difficult to follow his figure through the swirling sandstorms of tribal warfare that enveloped him. T'hami in his new position of Pasha of Marrakesh, confiscated the property of all who had supported Abd El Aziz, and these patently included the M'touggi, who was not, however, prepared to accept destitution without battle. He formed new allies, took the offensive, and after a series of bloody victories over the armies of the new régime, at the end of 1908 laid siege to Marrakesh itself. The Government forces could not get out, and the M'touggi could not get in; in this position of stalemate the M'touggi consented to negotiation. The results were a formal reconciliation between himself and T'hami, a solemn State entry into Marrakesh, and the restitution of the great quantity of Government weapons and ammunition that he had captured during his campaigns. These, including several cannon, Madani El Glaoui directed to be sent to Telouet, to be held by his son-in-law Hammou. The image of Telouet as a great arsenal had now become a reality.

Sultan Moulay Hafid, 1907–12

6

Madani's Sultan - Moulay Hafid

THE northern capital, Fez, had accepted Moulay Hafid as Sultan on the distinct condition that the city was to be exempted from all taxation.

'This His Majesty solemnly promised – and he kept his promise for a few weeks, until, in fact, he was strong enough to break it – and then he collected taxes, legal and illegal, with gusto never before experienced.

'His ability to act thus was owing to his having meanwhile collected a little army. Naturally the Treasury was empty, and no tribesmen presented themselves as desiring to take military service, as no pay was forthcoming. The situation was precarious. Without troops Moulay Hafid could do nothing, not even collect the taxes he had promised to forgo; and without the taxes he couldn't live. At all costs he must have an army.

'So one morning the public criers announced in the streets and market-places that the Sultan was on a certain day giving a great feast at the palace to the adepts of the sect of the "Gennaoua". Now the confraternity of the "Gennaoua" is very popular in Morocco, though limited almost entirely to the Southerners, who are largely of Negro extraction, and form a class by themselves of labourers and water-carriers – it is looked upon as unorthodox by the more educated Moors." (The word derives from Guinea, where the Negro founders of the sect had their origin.) 'The Sultan even hinted that he himself had leanings towards their particular doctrine.

'On the day in question the "Gennaoua", washed and in their best clothes, flocked to the palace, and entered its great walled courts, surrounded by frowning towers. With every sign of holiday-making and joy, they manifested their pleasure at the honour of being invited to the Sultan's religious-garden-party – and sought refreshments. Alas! there were none – nothing but high walls and closed gates – and the next day a sad but resigned army was being drilled on the palace parade-ground.'

With these unfortunates he was able to enforce a certain amount of tax collection and to indulge in a certain amount of plunder, but despite this he found himself under the necessity of contracting still further loans from foreign powers. The letters requesting these were couched in characteristically Moorish style, such as 'His Imperial Chereefian Majesty the Sultan of Morocco, Commander of the Faithful (may God increase his power and make the glorious sun and moon glitter in the firmament of his felicity!) has authorized his humble, incorruptible and honoured slave so-and-so to contract in the name of the Treasury (may Heaven fill it!) a loan from his friends (may God help them and prolong their days!) for the sum of such-and-such (may God return it to the lenders increased a thousandfold!).'[1]

---

[1] A further example of contemporary literary style may be found in Appendix III.

The reign of Moulay Hafid, as the last independent Sultan of Morocco for half a century, was exceedingly 'traditional', characterized by tyranny, cruelty almost comparable to that of Moulay Ismael, perpetual and widespread rebellion, and the uprising of new pretenders to the throne. In addition to these things French columns under the Supreme Command of General Lyautey, 'the architect of Morocco', were advancing deep into the country, for the true invasion had now begun. While in no way mitigating the rapacity and cynicism of the French colonial policy, it is incontestably true that it would have been difficult to conceive of a new régime as barbarous or as bad as that which it replaced.

Madani returned from Fez to Marrakesh soon after Moulay Hafid had been formally invested as Sultan, for he had his own empire to consolidate. He installed himself at the Bahya palace which the Negro Grand Vizier Bou Ahmed had completed for himself before his death in 1900, and there for a few months he lived in pomp as great as any Sultan had achieved. By now his personal domains extended to nearly a third of all Morocco, and it is at least probable that at this period he considered establishing a new State independent of the Sultan's rule. This thought must certainly have crossed Moulay Hafid's mind too, for not only was his Grand Vizier installed in the southern capital, but also his Minister of Foreign Affairs, Aissa Ben Omar; and − most disquieting of all − his own younger brother Mohammed El Kebir, who at the age of sixteen had led the Imperial army to defeat by the *rogui* Bou Hamara. What Madani had done once he could do again.

Hafid began to press Madani to return to Fez, but Madani showed no haste to obey the Imperial command. When he did at length travel north he did so with the full retinue of a Sultan; and, savouring his vengeance to the full, took up residence in the palace which − among much else − he had confiscated from the ex-Grand Vizier Tazi.

The majority of his children, numbering at that date a little over eighty, he left in the South, for every male over the age of sixteen or seventeen he needed to administer his vast southern territories, but he brought to Fez a few young sons whom he thought might benefit in some way by a sojourn at the Imperial Court.

'Amongst these few was a favourite son by a black slave woman. He was about twelve years of age, very dark, but of a remarkable vivacity and intelligence, and most amusing. Unfortunately this temperament had its disadvantages, and his conduct for his age was disgraceful. He had already indulged in the wildest life. His father had sent him to the French school, but it was only on the rarest occasions that he ever turned up there. No matter how many of the Vizier's retainers took him to the door, he invariably by some means or other escaped, and spent his days in far less eligible society elsewhere. At last things became so bad that the schoolmaster insisted on complaining personally to his father. The boy was summoned into his presence, and was asked why he played truant. He denied it, to the surprise of both. He insisted that he attended school regularly, and that it was only because the school-master disliked him that this accusation was made against him. The schoolmaster continued naturally to contradict the boy, who at last said, "Well, I can prove it. If I hadn't attended school I couldn't speak French. Examine me." Hurriedly one of the Vizier's Algerian retinue was called and asked to address the boy in French. He did so, and the black imp replied with the facility almost of a Parisian, but it wasn't the French that schoolboys ought to learn. The expressions and words he used made the schoolmaster's hair stand on end, but undoubtedly he spoke French, and with a fluency that was appalling. It was not in a school for the "sons of gentlemen" that he had learned it – nor in a school for the "daughters of ladies" either – but in a French *café chantant*, as it called itself, which had recently been installed in the Jews' quarter of the city.'

For the time being, now that he had Madani under his eye, Hafid decided upon strengthening his alliance with what was by now the most powerful single figure in all Morocco. He took Madani's daughter Rabiaa as his principal wife and Madani in turn married one of the Sultan's daughters – an ugly one, marked by the scars of smallpox, but a Sultan's daughter. Madani's brother T'hami, Pasha of Marrakesh, exchanged daughters with El Mokri, then Minister of Finance, and representing one of the oldest and noblest families in the country. (El Mokri was remarkable in that he had filled the same office under the defeated Sultan Abd El Aziz; his wisdom and learning were indispens-able to any Sultan.) The alliance between the Glaoui brothers and the *mahkzen* would have appeared stable enough, but nothing in Morocco was ever stable.

'The Moor is a gambler. He staked under that old régime not only his fortune but his life. Often he lost both; but sometimes he won, and it was the lives of others that were sacrificed and their properties that accrued till a great estate was built up, till palaces were built in all the capitals, till his slaves were legion and his women buzzed like a swarm of bees – and then one day the end came. If fate was kind he died in possession of his estates – and they were confiscated on the day of his death; but more often he died in prison while his family starved. Meanwhile nothing could be imagined more pitiable than was the lot of the country people, victims of robbery of every kind, for, from the Sultan to the village *sheikh*, the whole *mahkzen* pillaged and lived on the poor.'

In March 1909 occurred an event whose full and massive repercussions were not felt for a further forty-four years. There were at the time some ten notable religious sects in Morocco, of which one, the Kittaniyine, with headquarters in Fez, was headed by a young *Chereef* (descendant of the Prophet), Mohammed El Kittani.

'People spoke much of him; his popularity and reputation were great. From the precincts of the palace the Sultan followed his every movement, and spies reported his every word, but no excuse could be found for his arrest. But Moulay Hafid was determined that he must be got rid of. He let the young *Chereef* understand that he was in danger, that the Sultan meant to arrest him, and, influenced by a spy, the young man was persuaded to abandon Fez. He fled by night – straight into the trap. He was allowed to reach the Beni Mtir tribe-lands, and there he was arrested. Meanwhile the report was spread that he had tried to get himself proclaimed Sultan, and evidence to this effect was easily produced. He was brought back to Fez – I saw him brought a prisoner into the palace – and in the presence of Moulay Hafid he was flogged. Blow after blow from knotted leathern cords was rained upon his back and legs, till, life almost extinct, he was carried away and thrown into a prison in the palace. He was not even allowed to have his wounds tended. He lived for a few days only, and the slaves who washed his dead body for burial told me that the linen of his shirt had been beaten so deeply into his flesh, which had closed in hideous sores over it, that they had merely cut the more exposed parts of the evil blood-stained rags away and left the rest.'

As a result of this bestial execution Kittani's younger brother Abd El Hay Kittani – who had been arrested, but his life spared to show that Hafid had reason for murdering his brother – swore vengeance against the Alaouite dynasty and against every Alaouite Sultan who should ever mount the imperial throne. At the time of writing (1965) it is no more than twelve years since that vow came to its late fruition.

In September of the same year the Pretender Bou Hamara was captured after seven years of armed rebellion.

Hafid had already tried to discredit him by producing before the people of Fez the real Moulay Mohammed whom Bou Hamara was impersonating, but this had produced unfortunate side effects. Moulay Mohammed was not, in fact, a prisoner; but lived in voluntary retirement deep in the heart of the Imperial Palace. Once a week he accompanied the reigning Sultan to the mosque, and but for these brief public appearances he lived the life of a total recluse, granted certain facilities for his sexual pleasures. Twenty years in the position of under-dog had stripped him of all ambition; by now he detested the power vested in his lineage, and he lived in fear that some dissident would once more try to proclaim him Sultan. This in fact did take place during the closing years of Moulay Hafid's reign. Because Moulay Mohammed stood in such obvious contrast of demeanour to any of their recent masters, or perhaps because he seemed a potential instrument of vengeance upon these, the people accorded to him an especial reverence, and believed above all that he had great power of *baraka*, or blessing, that plays so large a part in the mysticism of Moroccan Islam.

So it was that, dragged from retirement to call attention to his continued existence, he stole the Sultan's thunder and received a spontaneous ovation that could never have been accorded to Hafid. The processional route was from the Imperial Palace to the tomb of Moulay Idriss, patron saint of Fez. Preceded by his standard bearers and flanked by a double rank of the Black Guard, Hafid led the procession beneath the crimson parasol, and behind him rode the humble figure of Moulay Mohammed.

His appearance had an utterly unexpected effect. The narrow streets of Fez were choked by crowds so dense that the procession could hardly force a passage. Men, women and children fought and scrambled to touch any part of Moulay Mohammed's person. Risking death by breaking through the ranks of the Black Guard, they clung to his stirrup and kissed his feet, imploring his benediction; even his horse was held to be holy, and lost an uncountable number of hairs from its tail. The Sultan himself was completely ignored; for all the attention he commanded he might have been one of his own slaves. It was with difficulty that the furious Hafid and his profoundly embarrassed brother regained the Palace. Moulay Mohammed was restored quickly to obscurity, and the experiment was not repeated; if it had undermined the prestige of Bou Hamara it had done the same for Hafid.

At the moment of his defeat, Bou Hamara was far from his base, and separated from it by tribes who had re-established their independence. This represented an axiom of Moroccan internal politics – as soon as any war lord or a pretender left a certain district he was ignored and forgotten, and this had been responsible for the peripatetic existence of a long line of Sultans. Together with the principle of pillaging and killing the vanquished, this form of amnesia was basic to the whole Moroccan mentality, and more especially to that of the Berbers.

A marabout, tomb of a local saint

It was Bou Hamara's misfortune that there was no senior European officer at the head of the *harka* that captured him; European officers were noticeably squeamish, but at the time they had their hands full elsewhere. The two French non-commissioned officers who were in charge of the Imperial artillery were too horrified to intervene, and the soldiers of the Sultan were enraged by this campaign conducted in the shattering heat of summer.

Bou Hamara's troops fled at the first assault, and, left without armed support, he and four others – of whom one was a woman – took refuge in the tomb of a saint, a *marabout*. There, according to the custom of the country, he should have had absolute asylum against any human enemy. But Hafid, who was fundamentally opposed to the cult of local saints, both because of his religious erudition and because they tended to undermine his central authority, had instructed the *Caids* in command of the *harka* that no religious asylum should be respected.

The rank and file of the *harka* itself was for the moment given up to indiscriminate massacre and plunder of the whole region, including the tribes who had blocked Bou Hamara's retreat. The two French non-commissioned officers wanted nothing but to rest, but chose to do so in a position from which they could repel possible counter-action; they had seen enough of Moroccan warfare to know that nothing was more precarious than a government victory, however seemingly decisive, in the *bled es siba*.

The *Caids* advanced on the *marabout*, but were driven off by the enraged people of the district, who insisted that the tomb of their saint should be respected, and themselves placed a guard about the sanctuary.

The *Caids* returned to the French artillery emplacement, and demanded that the two non-commissioned officers open a bombardment on the *marabout*. They hesitated, but they were influenced by three facts – they were nominally under orders of the Sultan; they had been outraged to find that the enemy had been using French ammunition; and the white dome of the *marabout* offered a tempting target on the bare plain.

The first two shells put the local guard to flight; the third struck the cupola of the refuge itself, killing two of the occupants. Bou Hamara fled from the ruins, but fell stunned by the explosion of the next shell, and was made captive.

The two Frenchmen went to look at him when he was brought in to the camp. He had been stripped of all clothing but his cotton trousers worn under the *djellabah*; these his captors had left, for it was among the customs of the country that no living man be made quite naked. He appeared as one in epileptic seizure, his lips drawn back from the pure white teeth and foam thrown out from them by heavily labouring breath, staring eyes wandering from face to face of his captors. As the Frenchmen turned away, having seen too much too quickly, he suddenly called after them:

'O infidels! If you are of any use to anyone, kill me now!'

But they went, in conformity with army regulations, to see to the cleaning of their cannon.

It was to the cannon, however, that Bou Hamara was dragged, bleeding and almost unconscious now, to make his act of submission; and to the cannon that four hundred of his men, chained neck to neck with iron collars, were made to bow down. It was to the cannon, too, that the returning pillagers began to bring in the heads of those whom they had slaughtered. Holding a head aloft, its bearer would cry 'May Allah bless our Lord Sultan!', and a *Caid* would throw him five silver *douros* as the head was laid on the cannon or upon the growing piles around them. It was the regular tariff for an enemy head.

The night passed in feasting and revelry, and the harem of women and boys – '*éphèbes réguliers*' – that had, as was customary, accompanied the *harka* into battle, danced until dawn, while the army experimented with the captured children of the tribes.

A whole book has been written about the death of Bou Hamara; it is instructive, but not edifying. While Walter Harris's account is a three-hundredth part of its length, and omits many of the disgusting details of the monograph, it is enough.

'Confined in a cage carried on the back of a camel, the famous Pretender was brought into the Sultan's presence. The interview was protracted. For several days Bou Hamara, squatting in the small space of his cage, was exposed to public view in the great court of the palace where the Sultan held his receptions – and the Sovereign who held the throne and the Pretender who had so long threatened it were face to face. Eventually the prisoner of State was put into the lions' cage in the presence of the Sultan, while the ladies of the Court lined the roof of the palace to witness the execution. The lions, however, too well fed, refused to eat him, but mangled one of his arms. After waiting for some time longer to see if the kings of beasts would change their minds, the Sultan ordered the Pretender to be shot, and he was despatched by the slaves. His body was afterwards burnt, to deprive him of any pos-

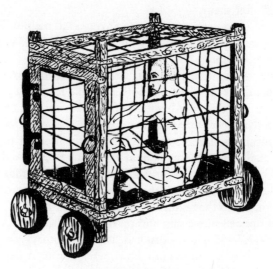

Bou Hamara caged

sibility – for the Moors believe in a corporeal resurrection – of going to heaven. Terrible as was his end, Bou Hamara himself had been guilty of every kind of atrocity, and had regularly burnt, after sprinkling them with petroleum, any of the Sultan's soldiers that he had been able to capture during his campaigns.'

To this account it should perhaps be added that Bou Hamara, trapped and tortured, looked down from his cage with disdain upon Hafid; that never once did he show fear or weakness; and that before he was shot he pronounced the *chahada*, the Muslim affirmation of faith.

'While Moulay Hafid was Sultan, from 1908 to 1912, in which year he abdicated, the palace was the scene of constant barbarity and torture. The Sultan himself, neurasthenic, and addicted, it is said, to drugs, had his good and his bad days. There was no doubt that at first he meant to reform his country – or perhaps, more correctly, to save it from the encroaching intervention of France. He was possessed of a certain cunning intelligence, and had some idea of government, but disappointment met him. Things had gone too far. Morocco was doomed. Finding all his attempts to preserve his country's independence futile, he gave way to temptations, and became cruel and avaricious.

'Rebels taken in the war – many, no doubt, were harmless tribesmen – had their hands and feet cut off. Twenty-six were thus tortured at Fez in one day. Twenty-five succumbed, mostly to gangrene; for though the European doctors in Fez implored the Sultan to be allowed to attend them, Moulay Hafid refused. Publicly the butchers cut and hacked from each of these unfortunate men a hand and a foot, treating the stumps with pitch. The one survivor of that particular batch is living today.

'Perhaps the most tragic of the tortures perpetrated by Moulay Hafid were upon the family of the Pasha Hadj Ben Aissa, the Governor of Fez, a man whose reputation was certainly no worse than that of the majority of Moorish officials, and very much better than that of many.

'Believing that he was very rich, Moulay Hafid had the Governor arrested and thrown into prison, with several members of his family. The usual floggings and privations took place, and Hadj Ben Aissa surrendered all his properties to the Sultan. But Moulay Hafid was not satisfied. He believed in the existence of a great fortune in money. As a matter of fact, the Governor of Fez had been a keen agriculturist, and had invested all his gains – licit and illicit – in land, but nothing could persuade the Sultan that this was the fact. He gave orders that the fortune was to be found; and thus fresh privations and more floggings ensued, but all to no avail. Then the women were arrested, amongst them the aristocratic wife of the Governor of Fez, a lady of good family and high position. It was thought that she would know, and disclose the hidden treasure. She was tortured, but disclosed nothing, because there was nothing to disclose.

'The whole of this story came to my knowledge, and the barbarity of the Sultan's proceedings determined me to let the world know what was passing. *The Times* opened its columns unreservedly to these wrongs, as that great paper had never failed to do whenever there has been a wrong to redress. It was not so much the torturing of the wife of the Governor of Fez – terrible though that was – as the fact that these things were still happening in Morocco – and must cease. The evidence I had was legally slight, but I determined to see it through. The Sultan denied, threatened, and denied again, but the repeated efforts of *The Times* were sufficient even to move the Foreign Office, and it was decided that some action must be taken. The late Sir Reginald Lister was British Minister at that time, and his encouragement and help assisted me in my campaign. At long length the British Government decided to ask the Sultan to produce the lady, as no other proof would be sufficient to persuade them that great cruelties had not been perpetrated. The French Government stood side by side with our own in the interests of humanity. The Sultan agreed willingly, but failed to produce the lady. The energy of Mr McLeod, the British Consul at Fez, was untiring. He was determined to see the matter through. At length, driven by the force of circumstances, the Sultan allowed the Pasha's wife to be visited by two English lady medical missionaries, accompanied by the wife of a French doctor. They saw her in the recesses of the palace, and, in spite of protestations and threats on the part of the slaves, they insisted on examining her. Her crippled body, and the terrible scars of recent wounds, amply justified *The Times*' action. The Sultan had lied throughout. The woman had been cruelly tortured.

'Two years afterwards, when circumstances had brought Moulay Hafid and myself together again, I asked him to explain his action. He told me that he knew the woman had been tortured – she was not the only one – but that he personally had not intended it. He said that when he had been informed that Hadj Ben Aissa's fortune could not be found, he had ordered the arrest of his womenkind. A little later he was told the women "wouldn't speak", and he acknowledged that he had replied, "They must be made to speak." Such words from such a source were taken to mean one thing, and one thing alone – torture; and they were tortured.'

At this point it must be emphasized again that all these savageries, while they became periodically more flagrant and more frequent under the reigns of such Sultans as Moulay Ismael and Moulay Hafid, were not in any way a departure from tradition that was many centuries old. They were unjust, they were terrible; but, a learned Moroccan pointed out to me, they could not be compared in scope or numbers to the atrocities of the Holy Wars of France during the crusading days, or of the Spanish Inquisition. I protested that he was going back centuries to find parallels, but he replied, 'Consider, my friend; you are speaking of Moulay Hafid. His reign ended two years before the First World War, when an unthinkable number of Europeans died in circumstances of horror. Then, only twenty-one years later, came the Second World War, the famous concentration camps, and the new refinements of torture invented by Germans, Russians – and, for all I know, Englishmen and Frenchmen. And then the Algerian War, in which the French tried hard to surpass the most terrible acts that any nation, Eastern or Western, had ever committed. The Algerians tried to rival them, but without success. No, my friend, be reasonable; these things were not only the tradition of North Africa, they are the tradition of all mankind. They may change; *inshallah*, they will change – but not yet.'

But Moulay Hafid was undoubtedly a sadist, and a contemporary writer described the revolting look of satisfaction and enjoyment on his face as he witnessed suffering – even that of a sheep thrust alive into a tiger's cage.

Hafid watched Madani, who was now not only his Grand Vizier but twice his brother-in-law by the double alliance, with a bitter and venomous jealousy. Because Madani was himself a mountain tribesman, he understood the complex politics of the South as no other courtier of Fez could hope to. Because he had installed his own family in every possible governing position throughout the High Atlas and the Pre-Sahara; and because he relied for his information service not upon them alone but upon poor and weary travellers whom he would feast and entertain as though they were ambassadors of some great power, his intelligence service was such as no Grand Vizier before him had ever possessed. Because he made it customary for distant tribes against whom it was impracticable to send tax-collecting *harkas*, to submit a double tribute (the *hediya* sent in cash and in kind on feast days) to himself and to the Sultan, his riches were said to exceed those of His Imperial Majesty himself.

'May Allah break this ladder upon which I have climbed to power!'

Moulay Hafid was not the first Sultan to express this emotion, and, like his predecessors, he felt that Allah might appreciate a little judicious assistance in the matter.

The campaign began with calumny and quarrels, Hafid accusing his Grand Vizier of appropriating funds that should go to the Sultan. In an attempt to placate him Madani turned the screw still further upon the northern tribes, until they revolted and Fez was under siege. The French were already nearby; Hafid, who had long been in open negotiation with Germany, now called upon the French for protection, and, led by General Moinier, their column entered the city on 21 May 1911. The throne was rocking; Hafid needed a scapegoat, and his jealousy of Madani admitted no choice.

The *dénouement* took place in May 1911 as the notables of the *mahkzen* left the palace in procession for Friday prayers. One of the Sultan's slaves came abreast of Madani as he walked, and murmured that he brought a message from His Majesty. It was the imperial command that Madani should not attend the mosque.

Madani stopped, and turned to the slave, his great eyes smouldering with rage.

'He has abandoned me! May Allah abandon him for ever!'

The greater part of Madani's régime fell with him. Not all of it, because his immense power beyond the Atlas could not be challenged except in word, and no *harka* Moulay Hafid could raise could risk assault on Telouet, where the sinister figure of *Caid* Hammou brooded over his fabled arsenal. The more accessible members of Madani's vast family were, however, formally dismissed and destituted. The nineteen-year-old black Minister for War, Mohammed El Arbi, was banished to the distant Pre-Saharan oasis of Ouazarzat; Madani's brother T'hami was divested of his mighty position as Pasha of Marrakesh and became a private citizen; from all the *kasbahs* on the north face of the Atlas the

Glaoua *Caids* scuttled for safety before their replacements could arrive. It was a measure of Hafid's weakness that no one was put into a spiked cage, no one was sawn longitudinally in half or thrown to the lions, very few were beheaded, and only a slightly greater number were chained in dungeons.

But it was the M'touggi's hour. Nominated by Hafid as ruler of all the South, he was master of Marrakesh and its plains, and it was his men who found the mint tea still warm in the empty *kasbahs* of the Glaoua *Caids*.

Kettle and charcoal brazier

7

The Hostages

THE French occupation of Fez moved Germany to an act of protest, for she had not been signatory to the secret European agreements by which France had been given a free hand in the country. Protest took the form of a warship, *The Panther*, sent to protect a few German residents in the little port of Agadir, far down the Moroccan Atlantic coast. *The Panther* represented no more than the threat of force behind simultaneous Franco-German negotiations in Paris, negotiations which ended in France ceding to Germany some hundred thousand square miles of the Congo in exchange for complete freedom of action in Morocco. 'Morocco,' said the German Foreign Minister, 'shall be yours.' The French thus 'legalized' with the last dissenting European power her role of would-be conqueror of Morocco.

A few months later, early in 1912, Moulay Hafid signed the Treaty of Fez, which, in a thousand well chosen words handed over his country to France – or rather he handed over what little of it he governed. Under Article 2 he gave the right to conquer the *bled es siba*; under Article 5 he surrendered the right to all foreign representation; under Article 8 he pledged himself to contract no loans except from France. He had risen against his brother Moulay Abd El Aziz with the slogan that Morocco was being sold to the Christians; he himself now gave it away to them without the formality of payment.

To do him justice, he had at least made a show of refusal. When the French Minister presented him with this rapacious treaty he exclaimed that he would rather abdicate than accept the domination of France and Spain. He maintained this intransigent attitude for a whole week, while the French persuaded him that they would make it worth his while. He signed on 30 March, and in doing so he unwittingly signed away his own throne besides his country's independence.

The news of the Sultan's action roused to a pitch of fury the people of Fez and the surrounding districts. Already bled white by the Sultan's remorseless taxation, they now learned that he had sold Morocco to the French in exchange for a palace and a kingdom overseas. On 17 April, in the temporary absence of occupying troops, revolution broke out within the town itself. The whole European population of some eighty persons was massacred, and the fearfully mutilated bodies displayed before the palace. The Sultan's army of Gennaoua, enlisted by the curious trick that Hafid had played upon them four years before, joined the rebellion, barricading the seven gates of the town and manning twelve miles of its ramparts against relief. Four hundred French troops arrived at the gallop, but when they had broken down the barricades they found themselves in a city whose every window and house-top poured down a storm of bullets. The following day heavy reinforcements arrived from Meknès, bombarded and occupied the town, and declared a state of martial law. Hafid was removed to Rabat under escort.

'Before leaving Fez he had already begun to secure his future comfort in life. He had informed all the royal ladies of his palace – and they were legion – the widows of former Sultans and a host of female relations – that they must all accompany him to Rabat. He gave them stringent orders as to their luggage. All their jewels and valuables were to be packed in small cases, their clothes and less costly belongings in trunks. They strictly followed these injunctions, but on the day of the Sultan's departure the ladies and the trunks were left behind. They are still in Fez; the jewels, there is reason to believe, are in Europe. Moulay Hafid always prided himself on his business qualities.

'The last weeks of his reign were one continual period of wrangling with the French authorities. He was still Sultan and therefore dangerous, and the question of his successor had not been settled, so he yet held some trump cards, which he played successfully. Even when everything was arranged, and the letters for the proclamation of his younger half-brother, Moulay Youssef, the reigning Sultan, had been despatched to the interior, Moulay Hafid changed his mind. On reconsideration, he stated, he thought he wouldn't abdicate or leave the country, as had been decided. He had already obtained the most generous terms from the French Government, but the situation was desperate. Instructions had already been circulated in the interior to proclaim the new Sovereign, and the reigning one refused to abdicate! Then Moulay Hafid said that possibly he might be persuaded again to change his mind. He was; but it cost another £40,000, which was given him in a cheque as he left the quay at Rabat for the French cruiser that was to take him on a visit to France. In exchange, he handed to the French Resident-General the final document of his abdication. The mutual confidence between these two personages was such that for a spell they stood each holding an end of the two documents, and each afraid to let go of his lest the other paper should not be delivered.

'The night before the signing of his official abdication Moulay Hafid destroyed the sacred emblems of the Sultanate of Morocco – for he realized that he was the last independent Sovereign of that country, and was determined that with its independence these historical emblems should disappear too. He burnt the crimson parasol which on occasions of State had been borne over his head. The palanquin he hewed in pieces and consigned also to the flames, together with the two cases in which certain holy books were carried. The books themselves he spared. The family jewels he took with him.'

(Walter Harris's anecdotes end, alas, at this date. His subsequent dealings with Moulay Hafid, in the role of mediator between the French and the ex-Sultan's extravagant financial claims, are not relevant to the House of Glaoua, but his account of them is such delightful reading that I have preserved it in Appendix II to this book.)

While this tragicomedy was being played out in the North, things were far from quiet in the South. At such a crisis in Moroccan history it would have been unthinkable for there to have been no new Pretender to the throne, and there was, in fact, the most spectacular of all their long procession – El Hiba.

Ahmed El Hiba was a 'blue man' from Mauretania in the far south, the land of mirage and illusion. (The blue men are so called because they are, literally, blue. Delighted long ago by the stains produced by an unfast dye in the cotton material they imported, it has been manufactured especially for them ever since.) He was the son of a well-known *marabout* or saintly personage named Ma El Ainin, and he was pro-

claimed Sultan at Tiznit on 10 May 1912, forty days after Hafid had
signed the Treaty of Fez. His slogan was the same as Hafid's had been –
to rid the country of the *roumis*[1] (Christians) and to re-establish pure
Islam in Morocco. All the tribes of the region rallied to him, and on

El Hiba

15 July he left the town at the head of a mighty *harka* to march on
Marrakesh. Between cavalry and infantry he led more than twelve
thousand warriors, and with them trundled no less than eight archaic
Portuguese cannons, taken from the walls of Tiznit. He crossed the
Atlas by the M'touggi's pass. The M'touggi, in his new role of Master

[1] Derived from 'Romans', and come to mean any intruder.

of the South, had given Fez absolute assurance that this could not and
would not take place; when eventually he had to explain the dis-
crepancy between this promise and the facts, it was not, fortunately for
him, to Moulay Hafid but to the French. It would have been impossible,
he said, to have gone against the local current of feeling – it would have
been suicidal. So would this explanation, to a Sultan; but the French
had other plans for the M'touggi, and they forgave him his treachery
as a peccadillo.

Just one month later, on 15 August, El Hiba entered Marrakesh
unopposed and with the full majesty of a Sultan. Nearly all the great
Caids of the South had already gone forth from the city to pay him
homage.

Perhaps more than at any other moment in all Morocco's long history
of storm and bloodshed it must have seemed almost impossible to
choose a course of action that would not lead to death or dungeon;
more impossible still to select one that would lead to certain power.
Since the Treaty of Fez, the Sultan Hafid was no longer a power; all
his functions had been assumed by the French. His abdication appeared
imminent; the French would therefore require a new Sultan. If they
chose to make terms with El Hiba and put him on the throne it would
be suicidal to resist El Hiba now. If, on the other hand, they chose to
fight El Hiba it might well prove suicidal to be one of his followers.
Safety could lie only in an agile and perilous sword dance which kept a
foot in both camps, and one's head from decorating the walls of
Marrakesh. Only by a full appreciation of this fact is it possible to assess
the happenings of the next few days. The present writer can detect
neither absolute villain nor absolute hero, only varying degrees of
agility.

The M'touggi, ruler of the South, believed that Madani El Glaoui
was better informed than he; believed, and rightly, that Madani had
been in contact with the French for a very long time. Madani's post of
Grand Vizier had brought him into constant contact with French
representatives, and the *Documents Diplomatiques Français* of the period
are illuminating, revealing duplicity and intrigue in many high places.
It was, however, hardly an easy moment to ask for Madani's advice.
M'touggi had replaced T'hami El Glaoui, as Pasha of Marrakesh, by
one of his own followers, Driss Mennou; and T'hami's brother Hassi,

as Pasha of the *Kasbah* of Marrakesh, by another of his own men, *Caid* Mbarek. This last had caused to be kidnapped three young boys who had been part of the Glaoua ménage, and whom either he or one of his colleagues coveted as bed companions. In return, six M'tougga boys disappeared; one of them, from Amizmiz, had 'eyes like stars, and at fifteen was as great a warrior as he was a lover'. There had been further incidents. A minstrel in the Place Dj'mma El F'naa, the great perpetual funfair of Marrakesh, had composed a song in praise of the disgraced ex-Pasha T'hami, and had been shot dead by one of the M'touggi's men while singing it. (The bullet passed through his body and killed an eight-year-old child in the little circle of audience.) The Glaoua faction had slit what M'tougga throats they could, and had been repaid in kind. Relations between the two ex-allies were exceedingly strained.

When the M'touggi learned in late July of El Hiba's impending march on the southern capital he ordered his Pasha of Marrakesh, Driss Mennou, to send a messenger to the Sultan asking for Government instructions as to what he should do. Possibly the letter never reached Fez; it could not in any case have reached the Sultan or his Grand Vizier, for the French in the person of General Lyautey, Resident-General and incorporating the Ministries of War and Foreign Affairs, were by then in control. In either case there was no reply, and El Hiba was at the gates. It is probable that, like Madani, Driss Mennou believed the future of Morocco to lie with the French. What is factually certain is that he advised the European Consuls of his inability to defend the city, and offered them and the tiny European population safe conduct to Safi on the Atlantic coast. The Consuls expressed their gratitude and the desire to be informed when the Pretender's army reached Imi-n-tanout, seventy-five miles from Marrakesh, so that they might depart in good order. They were duly informed of this fact on 11 August. They met at one of Marrakesh's seven gates, Bab Doukkala, and under a guard of four hundred warriors they left for Safi. They included all foreign nationals except the French. The French Consul, M. Maigret, had received explicit instructions from General Lyautey to remain where he was, and to retain with him the handful of Frenchmen resident in Marrakesh. These were: Commander Verlet-Hanus, just arrived, rather too late, with a mission from General Lyautey to unite the great *Caids* of the South against El Hiba; M. Alicot,

Chancellor to the Consulate; Dr Guichard, Sergeant Fiori, brother of the Algerian Deputy, and M. Cuadit.

M. Maigret, however, thought it preferable to answer to General Lyautey for insubordination than to El Hiba for being a Christian. He went to see the ex-Pasha T'hami El Glaoui, who offered him and his party a small escort of mounted Glaoua tribesmen to accompany him to the coast. They left after dark, but had not travelled more than some ten miles before they were ambushed by a party of Rehamna tribesmen and fled back to Marrakesh and the protection of T'hami El Glaoui.

That same night El Hiba pitched his tents outside the city wall. That same night Colonel Mangin, commanding the French troops at Safi, received a characteristic despatch from General Lyautey. 'Get there quickly. Save our compatriots. Support our friends. Drive out the enemy. Unite discretion with whatever force may be necessary. Allow neither check nor delay, and do not start until fully equipped and munitioned.' The situation in which the Lords of the Atlas found themselves certainly called for agility, and indeed they were so agile that it is difficult for an historian to follow their movements.

The following morning El Hiba summoned the Pasha Driss Mennou to his camp outside the ramparts. Learning that El Hiba bore him no ill will, he went; and found his master the M'touggi with El Hiba. El Hiba demanded that all Europeans in Marrakesh should be handed over to him at once. Driss Mennou, who had learned of Maigret's departure but not of his return, replied that there was no Christian left in all the city. El Hiba said he had information to the contrary, for the M'touggi had told him the whole story, and had added that he represented T'hami El Glaoui in a plea for pardon for having sheltered the Christians. This was too agile for Driss Mennou, who protested that be knew nothing of these developments.

El Hiba sent for both Madani and T'hami. Keeping a foot firmly planted in both camps, Madani sent T'hami and stayed at home himself. Nothing is known of what took place at the interview, but two days later, on 23 August, the M'touggi, acting in the name of the Pasha Driss Mennou, requested T'hami to hand over the Christians in return for a receipt exonerating him from all blame in the matter. T'hami refused, and the following night he handed over five out of the six to El Hiba, saying that there were no more. Either at Madani's suggestion or on his own initiative, he insisted on sharing their captivity.[1] Sergeant Fiori he kept hidden in his house, from where he communicated regularly with Mangin's advancing column. Thus T'hami, too, by remarkable agility, had contrived to place a foot in both camps.

The half-dozen Frenchmen were by now worth at least their weight in gold. Colonel Mangin's column was drawing daily nearer, and whoever was in a position to hand them over to him intact when he reached Marrakesh would be certain of fame and fortune for the rest of his life. El Ayadi of the Rehamna tribe offered El Hiba one hundred thousand *douros* in Spanish gold for the five he had; but El Hiba believed that possession of the hostages was enough by itself to make the French call off the whole campaign, and he would not sell.

Driss Mennou received a despatch from Colonel Mangin's advancing column, urging him to save the hostages in El Hiba's hands, and adding that he would not find the *mahkzen* ungrateful. (The *mahkzen* now meant both the Sultan and the French, and Mangin had the Sultan's *khalifa*, El Omrani, attached to his expeditionary force.)

Driss Mennou certainly did his best, although there is not a shred of evidence to suggest that his motives differed in any way from those of his competitors. While professing loyalty to El Hiba, like everyone else, he sent every scrap of information that he could lay hands on to Colonel Mangin. He was able to lay his hands on a considerable amount, for many old friends from the South were with El Hiba's army; in particular he learned that the guard at the prison door had orders to shoot the hostages in the event of El Hiba's retreat. Driss Mennou relayed this information to Colonel Mangin, requesting that the French column should fire two cannon salvoes when they reached a point some five miles from Marrakesh. At this signal he would attempt to liberate the prisoners.

El Hiba led his *harka* forward to meet the French column, and the two armies clashed at Sidi Bou Othmann, twenty miles north-west of Marrakesh, on 6 September. No one in El Hiba's forces had ever seen European troops in action; accustomed in their own traditional warfare to charge, fire their ivory-inlaid muskets at the gallop, wheel about,

[1] Food, with messages concealed in it, was brought to him and the prisoners by Madani's black slave Idder, who in the later days of T'hami's power became both his Chamberlain and his closest confidant and adviser. Return messages from the prisoners went out concealed in the empty cooking utensils.

retreat, reload from their moufflon-horn powder-flasks, and fire again, they found themselves helpless before the machine-guns, mortars and magazine-rifles of the French. The engagement was a massacre, and the *harka* fell back on Marrakesh in rout. Colonel Mangin's losses were two dead and twenty-five wounded.

'Nothing ever came from the Sous,' says a contemporary ballad commemorating the battle, 'but oil and lies and locusts.' El Hiba's revolt had been, in the Berber phrase, like the spate of a mountain river in spring, one day a roaring foaming torrent, the next day a dry and arid river-bed. His sojourn in the southern capital had lasted no more than two weeks.

Learning of El Hiba's defeat, Driss Mennou did not wait for the pre-arranged signal of cannon salvoes to put his plan into action. He sent

El Hiba

thirty tried warriors to overpower the guards of blue men on the prison door, with instructions that when they had done so they were to barricade themselves inside the prison with the hostages, and withstand all siege until relief arrived. This relief he would lead himself, the instant a chosen one of the thirty reported to him that the first part of the plan had succeeded.

It did. Brandishing their daggers and with their white robes crimson with blood, Driss Mennou's men burst in on the terrified Frenchmen, yelling, 'You are free! You are free!' As, however, they spoke in Berber and not in Arabic, they were not at first understood; two of the French tried to break out and escape from their rescuers, and had to be manhandled back before the door could be barricaded from inside.

Driss Mennou, meanwhile, with two hundred mounted warriors, was awaiting word and awaiting it impatiently, for the advance guard of El Hiba's defeated army was already approaching the city walls. When the messenger did arrive, he did so at a most inopportune moment. Driss Mennou and his cavalry rode straight for the prison at the gallop, and clashed head-on with El Hiba himself, on his way to organize his headquarters for flight. El Hiba had been told of the death of his prison guards and of who had planned it, but he had not enough martial force surrounding him to challenge physically Driss Mennou's two hundred armed cavalry. Words flew, but no bullets.

The argument was at its height when Colonel Mangin's column fired the two salvoes announcing to Driss Mennou that he was within five miles of the city. The salvoes were very loud. El Hiba and all his commanders panicked. They had been nurtured on the belief that what Moroccans knew about torture and atrocity was but a pale shadow of the Christian tradition, which could inflict and prolong pain into infinite degrees and ages. They fled instantly, many of them leaving behind them all their possessions in the great mediaeval encampment of El Hiba's army – their wealth, their booty, even their harems of women and boys. Driss Mennou rode on at leisure to liberate the hostages before Colonel Mangin should enter the city.

At this stage it must certainly have appeared to him that he had won the battle of agility. As I have said, his motives were in all likelihood no different from those of any other intelligent Berber – enlightened self-interest, but at that moment he had every right to congratulate himself; at exactly the correct moment he had both feet in the winning camp. It is not surprising that he was dismayed, hurt, bewildered, when within twenty-four hours his enemies received all the credit that he had earned so hardly. But the fact was that they were even more agile than he was; and, after all, agility is an important attribute of a statesman.

The statesmen, in this as in many other cases, were the Glaoui brothers Madani and T'hami. They had remained off-stage during the week preceding El Hiba's flight, and at any time that they were off-stage it would have been wise to assume an impending *coup d'état*.

M. Maigret received Driss Mennou as his saviour, making a moving speech of undying gratitude, and even theatrically wiping the sweat from the Pasha's forehead. Driss Mennou led them to a secluded place, where at three o'clock in the morning they were joined by the two Glaoui brothers and the M'touggi, each arriving separately. The conversation was probably limited to assuring the hostages that at no time had any of their visitors supported El Hiba. It did not, in any case, progress far. Hearing desultory shooting, Driss Mennou feared a bombardment, and begged Verlet-Hanus to send a despatch to Colonel Mangin's column explaining the full circumstances. This he did, adding that the hostages owed their safety to Driss Mennou.

T'hami El Glaoui left bearing the despatch and escorted by a small escort of cavalry carrying the tricolour flag. Less than a mile outside the town his party was attacked by a band of Rehamna tribesmen and he turned back, his despatch undelivered.

Led by Driss Mennou's guides, the freed hostages went to T'hami El Glaoui's house, where they had first sheltered, to collect the belongings that they had left there with Sergeant Fiori. An hour later an officer of Mangin's forces, Commandant Simon, arrived at Government House asking Driss Mennou their whereabouts, and demanding to see them immediately. Driss Mennou, uncomfortably no doubt, gave him directions. It was, after all, T'hami El Glaoui who was finally in a position to hand over the goods, and in a position to talk privately with Commandant Simon. Moreover it was from T'hami's house that Sergeant Fiori had kept constant contact with the advancing French column. T'hami held a royal straight flush.

In the late afternoon Colonel Mangin reached the range of little hills called the Gueliz, which later gave their name to the French town of Marrakesh, little more than a mile outside the old city walls. Here he summoned his six compatriots and all the *Caids* and notables of the city. Having greeted them all, he withdrew for a moment's private conversation with Commandant Simon and M. Maigret, who had changed his mind about several things.

He then addressed the assembly through his interpreter. It was late in the day, he said; he and his staff were tired, and all matters of detail could wait. For the moment he had only one order to give – to recognize Si Hadj T'hami El Glaoui as Pasha of Marrakesh, and to obey him.

M. Maigret then presented the new Pasha to the Colonel, and in a moving speech stated that if it had not been for him the six Frenchmen would by now be dead.

The Glaoui star was back in the sky to burn for a further forty-two years before its spectacular extinction.

8

The Beginning of the Great Caid Era

THE French knew as well as any Marrakshi that nearly all the great lords of the South had flirted with El Hiba. Madani El Glaoui had pondered El Hiba's offer to become his Grand Vizier, before rejecting it in favour of agility. The M'touggi could scarcely be said even to have kept a foot in both camps, and both he and Madani had in various ways assisted El Hiba's retreat. Only two could be said to be, if not above suspicion, at least out of reach of flagrant proof – El Ayadi of the Rehamna, who had joined the French troops against Hiba in the battle of Sidi Bou Othmann, and the Goundafi, who had never left his mountain stronghold during all the recent events. True, El Hiba had retreated through the Goundafi pass of Tiz-n-Test, and had been in no way hindered, but when reproached with this fact the Goundafi replied that he could neither play host nor butcher to every Sultan who passed his way.

T'hami El Glaoui, restored as Pasha of Marrakesh, did exactly what any Moroccan of the period would have done. It is, in fact, strange that it should be necessary to emphasize that fact; but when, many years later, T'hami started deposing Sultans and influencing world politics, there were such hysterical outbursts of calumny and eulogy that it is desirable at this point to refocus the customs and traditions of his country, or at least those of any part of it holding power.

It was, above everything, the custom that the winner took all – and 'all' included life, unless there were some excellent reason for sparing it. This was no new departure, no evidence of a peculiarly diabolic nature; it was simply an accepted rule of the game, like paying poker stakes when a hand is seen and loses. In conformity with the accepted pattern, T'hami destituted and imprisoned those who had been against him during his fall from power. The destitution was, naturally, complete – sacking of houses, confiscation of harems, imprisonment in chains of the chiefs of the houses concerned. Most of them died in dungeons. If he had been the loser and they the victors they would have done the same to him.[1]

The French literature on the subject written during T'hami's long lifetime is for the most part almost incredible, the praise so fulsome as to suggest clumsy sarcasm; T'hami was a knight like Sir Galahad, a saint like Saint George, a sage like Solomon, he was all that was noble, brave, kind, unselfish, statesmanlike, and faithful to his word. The other, minority picture, is of all the devils of the human mind in one incarnate form; a monster of avarice, cruelty, treachery and lust, whose appetite for gold and for human flesh was insatiable. In fact, he was a thirty-four-year-old Moroccan from the mountains, with Arab, Berber and Ethiopian blood in his veins, clever and ambitious, who found himself in a position to exercise the traditional duty of vengeance with little hindrance and little to fear by doing so.

General Lyautey himself arrived in Marrakesh, and in the gracious gardens of Agdal, with the orange trees and cypresses as foreground to the great ramparts of the mountains, he received the official submission of the Lords of the Atlas, pardoning those who had gone astray. It was strangely unlike the submissions they themselves had received in the past; no black bulls were brought to be sacrificed before the conqueror, no slaves or sheep flocks were demanded. Everything was words and bits of paper.

The Goundafi arrived a few days after the others, certain that they had already conducted a campaign of calumny against him. He was agreeably surprised by the apparent goodwill and cordiality of the General, who promised to restore to him all the possessions he had from time to time lost to the Glaoui and to the M'touggi. He introduced to

---

[1] The ex-Pasha Driss Mennou fared better than might have been expected. The French themselves asked for his resignation, but gave him permission to reside in Marrakesh. T'hami objected, saying that Marrakesh was not large enough to hold both of them, and Driss Mennou was banished to Settat, more than a hundred miles away. This achieved, it was the French, not T'hami who confiscated his property, including the site of the famous Mamounia Hotel, and the site of the Mauchamp Hospital. He died in 1956, outliving T'hami by a few weeks.

him the French staff. 'This,' he said, indicating Colonel Mangin, 'is my *khalifa*. He could not without my personal permission so much as remove one thread of this carpet on which we sit. You have nothing to fear from him – on the contrary he will always be your ally.' Lyautey then questioned him closely but courteously upon all matters concerning local politics and territorial claims, while the General's *aide de camp* Colonel Beriau transcribed his replies into a ledger.

The Goundafi was a sceptic, and he kept an open mind about future benefits, but a few weeks later he received the first proof in the form of a letter from French headquarters in Marrakesh.

'From Colonel Mangin, commanding the region of Marrakesh, – may God help him – to the honoured *Caid* Si Tayeb El Goundafi. Greetings, and may God have mercy on you. Before leaving for Mogador with my *mehellah* (government army) it gives me great pleasure to inform you that I give you the command of Amizmiz and of Aguergour. It is my desire that you exercise justice and goodwill. In friendship and greeting. 15 October 1912.'

Thus, under the new masters of Morocco, the Goundafi gained by a single letter incontestable rights to the lands he had conquered, lost, and reconquered so often in the past.

To Madani El Glaoui Colonel Mangin restored command of all the lands and tribes he had lost at his fall from Hafid's grace two years before, thereby making him king of the South in all but name.

Lyautey's policy, however impossible of realization it might appear in view of the past history of the war lords, was to unite them into a single striking force with which to subdue the whole southern *bled es siba* under France. The lands they conquered would be apportioned between them; they would become vast feudal barons with the implied might of the French army at their backs; and they would therefore give their full support to the occupying power. They would receive French honours and decorations, and they would feel themselves to be a part of France. They would have free hands provided that they did not fight amongst each other. If they did that they would receive a sharp rap on the *kasbah* from French heavy artillery.

It was, basically, the instability of the situation in Europe, and the increasing likelihood of war with Germany that dictated this cat's-paw policy on Lyautey's part. It was impossible to commit French forces to large-scale repressive operations south of the Atlas; indeed Lyautey was freely criticized in the French press for having penetrated as far south as Marrakesh. As he himself wrote, in a letter to Colonel Lamothe, who succeeded Mangin as commander of Marrakesh and the South: 'Action of *harkas* in the Sous must consist essentially of intervention by native troops only, acting on behalf of the Sultan Moulay Youssef, to the absolute exclusion of direct armed intervention on our part, so as to give no further pretext for a holy war against the Christians. We must, therefore do nothing to compromise the success of the Great *Caids*, or to be compromised by their lack of it.'

These *harkas* were nominally under the command of Moulay Zin, brother of the Sultan, but in fact under that of T'hami El Glaoui, Pasha of Marrakesh, and his first mission was to drive out El Hiba from the stronghold of Taroudant to which he had retreated down the giddy descents from Tiz-n-Test, where the track clung to the edge of precipices with thousands of feet of sheer fall at their lips; down through the shrub slopes of juniper and myrtle; on across the red-earthed plain where the gnarled, spiky argan trees grew like some endless olive grove; leaving behind him the white ramparts of the Atlas and, at his right, the single towering mountain of Jebel Alouime that formed the sentinel peak of the southern High Atlas. The Goundafi, ambitious to shine in the eyes of the French, opened his pass as the main supply route to the south, and T'hami's munition caravans passed almost unescorted through the territory of the man who had been until lately his deadliest enemy. The ancient rivalry now took a new form, to be first at Taroudant and claim the *grand prix* for the defeat of El Hiba. The Glaoui and Goundafi *harkas* were to form easterly and westerly half-circles round the city walls; T'hami, delayed by a strong guerrilla action on the way, covered the remaining seven days' march in three, and arrived simultaneously with the Goundafi. The city yielded on 24 May 1913, after a three-day siege, and El Hiba fled still further southwards. The French policy of the Great *Caids* was paying off, and when rivalries looked like becoming traditional, Madani played the peacemaker, a role in which he had always excelled.

Meanwhile the M'touggi, who had shown a distaste for fighting south of the Atlas since a crushing defeat in the Sous two years earlier, was laying about him merrily in the plains between Marrakesh and the sea, concentrating on the tribes who had blocked his horizon in the past. It was the old cry *'Allons chez les rebelles, couper les têtes et travailler pour nos maisons!'*, but now it had the fullest possible sanction. Old scores were settled by the hundred, heads rolled by the thousand but to the disappointment of the Great *Caids* the French would not allow them to be exhibited on the walls of Marrakesh.

Colonel Lamothe was fully aware of the less desirable aspects of the policy. He wrote in his report:

'It is easy not to appreciate the real fruits of the so-called Great *Caid* policy, and to see only its drawbacks and its abuses, which seem the

Kasbah *of Skoura*

more glaring to our twentieth-century French mentality. These, even seen in perspective, are very real and very terrible. But they cannot be compared with the advantages and facilities that the existence of these Great *Caids* has procured us. These notables have mutually exclusive interests in the Sous; there was an intransigent rivalry between them that precluded any serious action against El Hiba. United under our protection and our rewards they will become our right hand. The overriding principle of our policy has remained to avoid at all costs involvement in the Sous. No further military occupation south of Marrakesh, no military action south of the Atlas.'

Madani controlled; T'hami was no more in those days than his adjutant, jealous of his elder brother's vast power, but obeying his orders. In the course of the campaign against El Hiba tribe after tribe fell into their hands, some conquered years earlier but become insurgent once more during their masters' destitution and the stimulus of El Hiba. By the end of 1913 six more tribes had been added to the Glaoua empire.

The social structure of the Berber communities thus reduced had been exceedingly complex. Between tribe and tribe, and between fraction and fraction of different tribes, there had existed a system of alliances called '*leffs*' which produced a pattern closely enough knit to preclude by an exact balance of opposing forces any serious inter-tribal warfare. (This system had never been adopted by the Arab tribes of the plains.) Each community consisted, in fact, of a tiny Berber republic, each with its own customs and its traditions of democracy or of oligarchy, strongly allied to a number of other such republics who were not necessarily its neighbours. A dozen or so villages formed a 'fraction', to which the French gave the name *canton*, and anything between three and ten *cantons* formed a tribe. Tribes in turn grouped together to form 'confederations'. (The whole terminology is French, words used to define new ideas, as they are in the development of a new science. The Berbers had no exact words for any of their social units; indicating, for example, a confederation by attaching a prefix to the tribal name. They had no written language.) This structure, and the hierarchy within it, was flexible enough to allow for the very widely varying living conditions of, say, a community at 10,000 feet in the barren High Atlas and one inhabiting a fertile oasis in the desert.

Beginning with the smallest unit, a village in the High Atlas would consist of twenty or thirty houses, built of mud, either upon the steep slope of a valley or upon some rocky outcrop, and peopled by two or three family groups. Monogamy was a strict rule, despite the nominal religion of Islam which permitted four wives, and there was a saying, 'May the locusts eat the crops of him who has two wives.' Women went unveiled, ate in the presence of their menfolk, and, in great contrast with the Arabs, played roles of considerable importance in village life. The village would carry either the name of one of its families, or, as in European countries, a word describing its position. Two or three such villages close together formed a 'sub-fraction', whose characteristics were the possession of a communal fortified grain-store (*agadir*) and an assembly point for males capable of bearing arms.

Several of these 'sub-fractions' – four or five on the northern slopes of the Atlas, and usually three on the southern – formed a 'fraction' or a *'canton'*. This was the little republic. A council of the heads of all established families composing the *canton* was responsible for all legislation and administration, its president being chosen by annual election. The council punished crime – theft, in particular, very harshly – imposed fines, adjudicated in dispute, eliminated quickly and surely any member of the *canton* who displayed ambitions against the general interest.

It was a major concern of the council that its lands should never be swallowed by any war lord, and that its people should never be governed by any other authority. Liberty was all. They chose their own representative of the central Government (*sheikh* or *amghar*), who had no power, except to transmit the demands of the *Caid* under whose authority the village nominally rested. These were for the most part negligible; if heavy taxes were demanded, the village refused, and waited – sometimes for years – for a punitive government raid.

The frontiers of a *canton* tended to be stable, established by long tradition. It was this sense of territory that created the general social bond within a *canton*. If a *canton* became unwieldily big it simply divided by binary fission and became two smaller *cantons*. In the same way a bellicose *canton* that tried to conquer a whole valley tended immediately to split into small units that became individual republics. There appears to exist in the Berber make-up some basic inhibition against the forming of large groups.

Each *canton* had a strictly individual flag by which, in times of war or local trouble, its warriors could be recognized; the flag represented the territory rather than the people, its loss in battle was shameful, and its capture a subject for corresponding triumph. Inter-*canton* warfare was, however, rarely prolonged and almost invariably ended in mediation, so that, in the traditional phrase, 'the tribe should not be weakened'.

Whereas a minimum of two or three *cantons* theoretically composed a tribe, many of them never united for any practical purpose, and each remained a little republic on its own, enjoying complete political and administrative autonomy. Only in times of exceptional emergency would the somewhat nebulous unit of the tribe take firm shape, emergency such as the invasion of a Sultan's army. It is therefore clear that the Lords of the Atlas – owing their power to control of the mountain passes – in their constant efforts to conquer and unite the *cantons* under their own rule, were attempting a transformation that could succeed only by means of complete destitution. As long as the means of life were there, the small independent groups would continue to reform. Thus the Glaoui, M'touggi and Goundafi were in no sense trying to perpetuate a mediaeval feudal state; they were trying to create one. They had begun to do so long before the arrival of the French, but it was the French who assured their success, substituting an un-limited despotism for the little Berber republics. It was a complete and absolute social revolution in reverse, and a cynical one for the French, of all people, to support.

The method of subjection had always followed two distinct and parallel lines. When the fertile plain lands were the target of conquest, the policy had been immediate exploitation of the conquered *canton* in such a way as to extract the greatest possible plunder by force of arms and in the shortest possible time, for in the past the danger of re-conquest had always been acute. If the object was the incorporation into feudal territory of mountain *cantons* contiguous to it, the campaign was one of intrigue and the maximum manipulation of local politics. In either case, however, the final state of servitude to a feudal overlord was identical. This extension of the overlord's power carried with it a snowball of extortion. To equip an army whose necessary size increased with every extension of territory, to buy the complicity of local *canton* leaders, to give the right presents at the right moment to the Sultan and his courtiers, necessitated destitution of the people by taxation, whether or not this had been an original part of the plan. Cultivable lands left vacant by ruined *cantons* were worked by slaves bought solely for this purpose; the remaining Berbers who still owned their lands pledged their unripe crops, almond trees still in flower, lambs unborn. When these pledges were accepted, an entirely new hierarchy grew into being to ensure their fulfilment – tax collectors who pocketed half the taxes and enriched their relations, *khalifas* who had to be bribed. Every minor person of importance now felt the necessity to ally himself with others, and for this reason the strict monogamy of the Berbers began rapidly to disappear in the new class. Daughters were given away as wives or concubines, so that the officials of the new régime were soon in possession of large harems. To accommodate these they built themselves new houses, and as befitted the residences of important people, these were *tighremt* – the tall castellated buildings of the rich. The almost unbelievably corrupt régime of the old *mahkzen* had penetrated at last, not by punitive raid but by assimilation of principal, into the social structure of the southern Berbers. It was a gift from the young twentieth century.

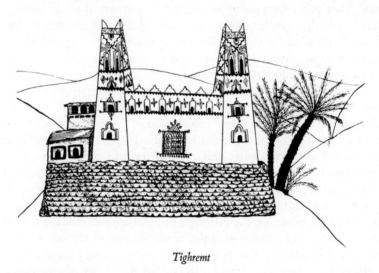

Tighremt

The campaign was essentially one of destruction. Every *agadir* (the fortified communal grain-stores of the *canton*) was destroyed and the grain impounded; every powerful *amghar* was dismissed and replaced by a new local whose only real function was to collect the taxes imposed by the new *Caid*.

It is impossible to escape the conclusion that this was colonialism in its very worst form. The new *kasbahs*, built in a recognizable *mahkzen* style, uncompromising and with little ornamentation, were occupied by *Caids* or *khalifas* of the Glaoui, and a guard of Glaoua warriors, whose function was to keep order and to transmit to the *amghar* the demands of the occupying power. These demands never varied – they were for the maximum possible sums in cash or in kind. The *Caids* or *khalifas* lived their own lives in the garrisoned *kasbahs*, with their own slaves and their own harems, to which they added the most beautiful village girls of the region under their command. The families of these girls were often exempted from all taxes thereafter, and became a new privileged class, imitating their masters in the acquisition of harems and castellated dwellings. The *Caids* were utterly indifferent to the internal life of the *cantons*, their past or their customs. They accepted their sojourn, isolated among hostile tribes, because of the riches they might amass during their period of office.

In this same year, 1913, T'hami El Glaoui had his first flight in an aeroplane. The M'touggi described it to a Frenchman. 'I was there – I saw it, at the Fête de la Menera – the thing was flying about the sky! Fantastic! The French certainly know a thing or two. They explained the workings of it to Hadj T'hami, and he said he understood. And it's true that he wasn't a bit afraid. He fastened his *bernous* with a cord round the waist, and got in beside the French officer, between the wings. And then brr-brr and lo and behold they're flying across the sky as far as the Gueliz and back like the prophet's horse Bourak! When the Grand Vizier's *khalifa* Hadj Ben Chaib, saw it he cried out "A Chleuch in an aeroplane! – And me, an Arab, still on the ground!" But when his turn came to fly he was trembling and he said he had a fever. But I saw him saying his prayers!'

While Lyautey's colonization was thus being effected for him by the Lords of the Atlas in the South, his own French troops were engaged in bitter fighting along the whole line of the Middle Atlas Massif, where they had penetrated deeply into the mountains. To them the mounted Berber warriors offered the same tigerish resistance as they had shown to early invaders. Neither the Romans nor the Arabs had ever truly conquered them; they knew no masters but their own elders. They seemed unafraid of guns; the sound of firing drew them as to a natural rallying point, and they would gallop straight at the stammering mouths of the machine-guns. To the French they were terrible enemies, long practised in the arts of ambush and swift, savage raid. In the mighty forests of the Middle Atlas where the cedars do not grow below the 4,500 foot line and stand with the snow always at their feet, the guerrilla armies harassed every mile of the French advance, and out on the bare mountains the Berbers' almost miraculous use of every vestige of cover imperilled the passage of every supply column. To the Berbers pillage and plunder was half the point of war, even when, as in this case, it was a defensive war. In the space of a few months their own muzzle-loading muskets, inlaid with gold and silver, ivory and mother of pearl, had become almost things of the past – they were armed now with European magazine rifles, the French Lebel '74 and '88, Winchesters, Martinis, and Mausers. They would come in the dark into the encampment of a French brigade and creep under the tents to steal the Lebel rifles, naked and with a knife between the teeth they would crawl through barbed wire entanglements to stab the sentries on arms dumps and lead in the looters. Nor were they entirely dependent upon their own efforts in the matter of arms and munitions, for German agents, well established in the Spanish zone, supplied these as well as funds. Usually preoccupied by local disputes and the quarrels of a *canton* or of a fraction, the Berbers had succeeded temporarily in uniting against the invader, and all along the Atlas huge gatherings of their tribes were ranged against the forces of the French.

However, it was not everywhere as simple and direct a war as it seemed. The Moors were essentially opportunists, essentially intriguers, and Lyautey had learnt from General Galliéni in the Madagascar campaign that words could be as active in warfare as bullets. Whom he could buy, whom he could bribe with promises of power or revenge upon ancestral enemies, were as much Lyautey's concern as the strategic handling of the battlefield. With one eye on the increasingly ominous situation in Europe, he wanted above all a quick campaign and a quick consolidation. Besides the fear of a French war with Germany, he was faced with discontent among his own troops. Life for them was much as it must have been for the Roman legions encamped against the Berbers two thousand years before – a shortage of food and water; an absolute absence of roads; boulders and more boulders; marches over scorching desert alternating with exhausting marches in the snow-covered mountains; roasting days and freezing nights; fever and dysentery; and, above all, the homesickness that comes to a soldier when all communication with his country has gone. They could not know how soon they were to forsake this comparative paradise for the glutinous hell of warfare in their own land.

On 2 August 1914 General Lamothe, commanding the Marrakesh region, and Colonel Mangin brought together the Lords of the Atlas and their numerous nepotic *Caids* to tell them of the declaration of war between France and Germany. This was done on the orders of General Lyautey who, not for the first time, had decided to defy the orders he himself had received from Paris on 29 July. He had been instructed to withdraw all troops from the interior of Morocco and to quarter them in the coastal towns where they would be readily available for shipment to France; to send twenty battalions home at once, and to maintain nothing more than communication lines to Algeria. In effect, the Moroccan campaign was to be abandoned. To Lyautey, whose whole heart was in Morocco, who loved the country with a passion that saw her future not as a colony of France but as a noble friend unified and exalted by his hand, this was like death itself. He knew, too, that the revolt that would inevitably follow a French withdrawal to the coast might not be confined to Morocco, that the whole of French North Africa might rise in rebellion. In his own eyes he had no alternative but direct insubordination. He had created the policy of the Great *Caids*; they were now the only instrument that could save his dreams from utter annihilation. He was in the hands of these powers whom he had forged. The Protectorate of Morocco was only two years old; German agents were everywhere at work to stir up rebellion; at Marrakesh the French had only a tiny garrison. They were surrounded by hostile tribes in an unmapped country – tribes loyal to the Lords of the Atlas, whose real attitude to their European masters was, to say the least of it, uncertain. If they were to declare against France, they would do so in the knowledge that there could now be no reprisals, and Morocco would have to be abandoned.

Mangin spoke. For several minutes after his interpreter had finished there was complete silence in the white-robed company who sat before them. Among the listeners were many whom Madani El Glaoui had forced into submission or agreement before; now they were

General Lyautey

hesitant and uncertain, waiting for their master to speak. Just as he had been the first to declare against Aziz, he was the first to speak now.

He was not ignorant of the European situation, for he had had translations made of all the important European newspapers; he had a clear idea of the forces opposed to France, and of her risk of being conquered in the coming war (and indeed Mangin had not minimized this risk in his speech); he knew that such a conquest would result in the occupation of Morocco by Germany, and in the destitution of those who had befriended France. It is, in fact, difficult to ascribe the spirit of his reply to any motive other than that of loyalty.

He said that in signing the Protectorate Morocco had linked her fortunes with those of France, and that the hour had now come to honour the word of that signature. It was not, he said, a question of forecasting the victor in the coming struggle between France and Germany; 'We are the friends of France, and to the very end we shall share her fortune, be it good or bad. That is my sworn word.'

He pronounced his brief speech with such force and vehemence that not one *Caid* dared to express a contrary view; each in turn swore to support France and to complete the work that had been begun. Later the same day, Madani summoned together all the members of his own family, and announced to them his resolution, as head of the House of Glaoua, to remain faithful to France. He said that if there were any among them who had anything to say on this subject it must be said now. After some deliberation his brother T'hami put forward a characteristic suggestion – that it might perhaps be possible to ask some substantial recognition of services in advance. Madani did not trouble to discuss the pros and cons of such a course of action, replying curtly that if any member of his family had doubts or reservations there were dungeons at Telouet from which, once entered, no prisoner had ever emerged either alive or dead.

There was no further dissent.

Lyautey had been ordered to supply twenty battalions immediately: half, that is to say, of all his forces in Morocco. By his agreement with the Lords of the Atlas and with their counterparts to the north he was able to comply with his instructions immediately, but at the same time he refused to yield one inch of conquered ground. By this inspired piece of insubordination, swiftly forgiven him by his country, he was able to continue the Moroccan campaign right through the First World War. Later, he was able to supply his home front with a highly trained division of Moroccan soldiers, many recruited from the Sous.

The Lords of the Atlas also continued their campaign. Madani was by now by far the greatest single figure in Morocco, and he combined the pomp of mediaeval splendour with such modern luxuries as splendid limousines for use on what few roads the French had as yet contrived to build. His elegance of clothing, the vastness and splendour of his retinues, the ritual of majesty with which he surrounded himself, equalled that of any Sultan. The members of French missions, medical and others, who visited Morocco were impressed by these things, but even more profoundly impressed by his personality and by his interests outside Morocco. They found that he followed with absorption, and with a remarkable grasp of major strategy, the four years of world holocaust that were the last four years of his life.

Madani was fifty-two at the outbreak of war, and fifty-six when he died in July 1918. He died, it is said, of a broken heart. There must, no doubt, have been some more directly somatic reason for his death, but he had no more will to live. He was engaged at the time on a punitive expedition against tribes lying to the southward, with the support of General Lamothe.

At that date Madani had something over sixty-four surviving children; thirty-six of these were sons and the majority were minors. The eldest was still under thirty years of age. Eight of these sons were of fair skin, and lived for the great part of the time in the Glaoui palace at Marrakesh; the rest, of various hues ranging to pure negroid, were dispersed among all the *kasbahs* of his territory on both sides of the Atlas. Amongst all these he had one favourite son, Abd El Malek, whom he had early chosen as his successor, and whom he had made *Caid* of Demnat – his most prized possession – when the boy was not yet seventeen years old. For Abd El Malek Madani nourished a devotion so profound that had he possessed no other outstanding quality this love alone would have separated and elevated him from his mountain compeers. Abd El Malek has been described by several French contemporaries, and he would appear at least to have been a youth of singular charm and beauty. Doctor Paul Chatinières, head of an early medical mission, met him first in 1913, 'a boy of slightly feminine features and manner'. The doctor had arrived at Demnat in a blinding sandstorm and suffocating heat, to be led into the cool and sheltered gardens of the *kasbah*. '*Combien m'avait paru alors séduisant le doux et fin sourire du tout jeune et aimable Abd El Malek m'accueillant dans cette oasis de montagne!*' The Tharaud brothers, officers of the French command, wrote of him at the year of his death, 'One eyelid a little fallen, and his long shining blue-black curls gave to his charming young face something equivocal, something disturbing. The magnificent rifle in his hands, with its butt resting on the saddle, could not disguise some feminine characteristic whose sweetness contrasted with the rough faces grouped around him. One could see that none of the harshness of life had touched this beautiful adolescent, whose life had been passed among cushions and carpets and an entourage of servants and women.'

Abd El Malek was in command of the advance guard when it was engaged fiercely by the enemy, troops of Sidi M'ha at Bou Yahia. 'It is a sight that is always the same, always moving,' the Tharauds wrote, ' – a warrior ballet perhaps, or some new image of the ancient tilting match. The combatants are face to face; one of them, following his standard bearers, hurls his horse towards the enemy, fires his rifle, and wheels about with all his flags flying. Then the other charges in his turn, fires, turns on his tracks pursued at the gallop by an enemy who has by now reloaded his rifle and fires only to wheel about again. It was the first time that Abd El Malek had been into battle like this.'

The Tharaud brothers watched him from afar, watched him charge and drop his reins and fire at the gallop from the back of his black stallion, always the first to charge and always the last to retreat; they wondered whether this was indeed the indolent, effeminate adolescent whom they had seen the day before at Madani's camp, holding hands with one of his intimates.

In the course of one of these heraldic charges Abd El Malek was fatally wounded, a bullet passing through his stomach from side to side and liberating the entrails. He died before his litter-bearers reached General Lamothe's headquarters at Tanant; the French doctor had ordered his attendants to refuse him water, but they disobeyed, and Abd El Malek died.

Before his own people Madani remained aloof, and unmoved; in the presence of the French officer he wept bitterly, saying, 'Now nothing matters any longer.' On two prowlers from the enemy camp he took savage vengeance. Beaten and stoned and dragged to the edge of a precipice from which they were hurled into the ravine below, their broken bodies still remained for many hours a target for bullets and stones.

Madani left his army as soon as he had certain news that Abd El Malek was dead. He was driven in one of his great limousines to Demnat, where his son had been buried that day. When he had visited the tomb he left at once for his palace of Dar El Glaoui in Marrakesh. He retired to his sleeping-chamber, and in less than forty-eight hours he died. A serving-woman of his palace was carrying on her head a great brass tray loaded with silver and china when she learned of her master's death; she hurled her burden to the ground and herself collapsed dead amid the debris.

Madani was buried, according to the tradition of his family, in the precincts of the tomb of the saint Sidi Ben Slimane in Marrakesh.

All his power and his immense riches passed to his younger brother, T'hami El Glaoui, Pasha of Marrakesh, the second king-maker.

Moroccan daggers

BOOK TWO
T'hami El Glaoui

9

The Golden Years

NOT even T'hami El Glaoui's most intransigent supporter has ever claimed for him that he possessed the qualities of his elder brother Madani, in whose character one is tempted to trace some true elements of greatness.

Madani's egoism and nepotism must be regarded as characteristics typical of the Great *Caids*; not personal idiosyncrasies, but in the tradition of his country. Moreover it would have been impossible for one only twenty-seven years old when presented with a Krupp cannon to escape the role of warlord to which he had been environmentally conditioned. He had shown, it is clear, an extraordinary political ability, great personal bravery, and a certain fidelity which appeared in its most crystalline form where his son Abd El Malek was concerned. He was of harder fibre than the tortuous El M'touggi, more flexible and subtle than the unbending feudal warrior El Goundafi. In principle, he had trusted none of his compatriots or co-religionists; he had, however, placed a reserved trust in the French, which may well have been due to their apparent unity in contrast with the perpetual inter-tribal warfare that composed his own background.

His younger brother T'hami, certainly, he had trusted but little, recognizing with jealousy an ability only slightly inferior to his own, the curious deep jealousy that can exist only between brothers in their mutual rise to power. '*Vous verrez*', it will be remembered that Madani had said to the French Consul at Fez while he was Grand Vizier to Hafid, '*que vous aurez plus à gagner avec le* mahkzen *qu'avec El Hadj T'hami*'; and that the Consul wrote of this to the French Chargé d'Affaires in Tangiers, explaining it by the comment that T'hami had 'enriched himself too quickly, and followed too personal a policy'. On more than one occasion Madani had asked the French to approach him rather than T'hami, for anything that they required. 'You do not know my brother; he is a dagger one might use, but which one must afterwards discard.' During the last six years of his life he had watched with growing perturbation T'hami's influence with the French Protectorate. It was to keep T'hami out of political mischief that Madani had entrusted him with the command of the *harkas* against the tribes of the South and the East, and T'hami in his turn feared and resented the domination of Madani, in whose footsteps he had trod, and whose ghostly trail he continued to follow, compulsively it may seem, until his death in disgrace thirty-seven years later – a disgrace that Madani would surely have foreseen and forestalled.

During those thirty-seven years he became a myth in Europe, an image of oriental splendour and romance unrivalled even by the most gorgeous of the Indian maharajahs. It may be said that by the time that T'hami El Glaoui succeeded his brother, the Glaoui family enjoyed, potentially even if not in those early days actually, greater power than the Sultan himself, who, under the conventions of the Protectorate, was deprived of all his ministers except for his Grand Vizier, a Minister of Islamic Law, and a third whose functions lay in the administration of religious charities (*habous*). He had no representation abroad, and the signature to French decrees was no more than a formality. The Glaoui family, on the other hand, enjoyed almost total freedom of action in the South, provided that they continued the work of pacification at which they had proved themselves conspicuously, if not wholly disinterestedly, successful.

This was Lyautey's policy towards unification of the country, a goal at which no previous ruler of Morocco had arrived. This policy had to some extent been forced upon him by the outbreak of the First World War, and the necessity to delegate his armed authority, but it is difficult to see how a long-term policy of an enfeebled Sultan in the North and a feudal dictatorship in the South could have led to anything but disaster. It led, in fact, to the ignominious ejection of the French thirty-seven years later, for Morocco could only have been unified under a powerful Sultan acting in concert with the so-called Protectorate. As improbable a mixture of fur and feather as can be imagined; it was not found then or later.

It may be as well at this point to review two earlier French documents. The first is a letter from the French Chargé d'Affaires in Tangiers to the French Foreign Minister, dated 9 May 1911, describing an interview he had had with Moulay Abd El Aziz. 'I told him that the French Government had no intention of occupying the country, but of favouring a new Government which would avoid the mistakes [crushing taxation] of Madani El Glaoui, and so keep the tribes contented.' The second was written on the very day of Madani's fall from the post of Grand Vizier, 26 May 1911, by the French Foreign Minister. 'Collaboration with the Glaoui, Aissa Ben Omar [a powerful *Caid* in the plain of Abda, behind Safi] and the M'touggi may appear necessary for a certain time, but whatever the changes that may be adopted the Sultan can deal with immediate difficulties if he exercises his personal authority, and if he understands that he should take advice from our agents and keep in constant communication with them.' Collaboration with the Glaoui certainly lasted 'for a certain time' – forty-five years, to be precise.

The responsibility for the fantastic history of T'hami El Glaoui after the death of Madani must remain with the French who had armed these tribal overlords with modern weapons and put it into their power to rule as despots, perpetuating the corruption and oppression that the Europeans had nominally come to purge, bolstering the mores of destruction that were there before they came. Twentieth-century Europeans have accepted as necessary in war many courses of action that would be condemned in peace-time; southern Morocco had, in that sense, always been at war, and the mores had formed accordingly. The Glaoui myth rests upon these equivocal foundations. There were few Moroccans who, placed in his position, would not have acted much as he did; to present him, against his background, as either a monster of evil or as a benign saviour of his country would be ludicrous. He did not, as had the 'great' Sultan Moulay Ismael, cut off heads for daily pleasure; he did not, as had Moulay Hafid but seven years earlier, cut off the hands and feet of captured rebel tribesmen; nor, except to a very small fraction of the people of Morocco, did his long rule bring any particular benefit (though it might be said, perhaps, that he helped the French to occupy his country for long enough to build roads and railways and to exploit its natural resources for their own ends). Certainly he caused a number of people to die violently for one reason or another, or to starve to death in dungeons, but then so had every potentate in Morocco before him; certainly the external circumstances of his life were spectacular, but it was the custom of the country for every ruler to live in pomp, and he would have been despised had he not. It was the European limelight that made of his qualities and his position a theatrical image isolated from a context in which they would have been comparatively inconspicuous; the European limelight, too, that cast shadows about him deeper than could the Moroccan sun.

On Madani's death T'hami El Glaoui was nominated by General Lyautey as head of the Glaoui family, by-passing by absolute decree the claims of Madani's sons. All the vast ramifications of Madani's family became, therefore, T'hami's potential rivals. It was the custom of the country to deal with such a situation swiftly and simply, by depriving the rivals both of money and of position. This T'hami did, but there is no evidence that he carried out the programme with unusual severity or cruelty. There was an immediate attempt by one of Madani's sons, Mohammed El Kebir, to remove valuables from Madani's palace: the attempt failed and T'hami forbade any of Madani's family further entrance. He placed a strong guard over the premises, and set about dealing with the rest of Madani's clan systematically, deposing (with the collaboration of the French and the helpless Sultan) his nephews from the *caidats* of Madani's wide domains, and substituting his own sons. Those of his nephews who did not hold official position he simply relieved of all property, portable goods or real estate, that he considered surplus to their absolute requirements. All this was traditional. The best documented instance is that of Mohammed El Kebir, who had been a lieutenant in the French army during the First World War. He had been wounded and married his French hospital nurse, a certain Mademoiselle Jehane Sabey, daughter of a French general, at Damas in 1918. He was thus to a large extent Europeanized, and, after his destitution, wrote a petition to the French Resident-General.

'All our troubles, my brothers' and mine, date from our father's death. In fact according to the law of the Chraa [religious law] we had a natural and legal guardian in the person of my eldest brother [the black Mohammed El Arbi whom Madani had when Grand Vizier to Hafid made Minister for War when he was only seventeen]. General Lyautey, with an authoritative – and, if I may say so, arbitrary – gesture, declared our uncle El Hadj T'hami to be the head of our family and our trustee. The Resident-General of France thereby violated not only the Muslim law but the moral law of which France has always appeared the guardian and guarantor in the eyes of the world, and more particularly in the countries of which she has made herself the protector. Thus we found ourselves, my brothers and I, delivered body and soul with our not inconsiderable heritage, to our uncle Hadj T'hami – dependent on his goodwill and his whim.

'The result of this arbitrary act is that the members of my paternal family, who number more than *three hundred persons*, find themselves at the Pasha's mercy, homeless, landless, and penniless. More than fifty million francs' worth of goods, land, jewels, real estate, grain, various harvests and livestock, have fallen into the hands of our uncle. And not only are we poor and ruined, but the Pasha is intending to claim from us nearly another two million francs as the price of our keep while we were minors under his charge.

'We ask firstly for the restitution of our personal heritage as it was at the death of our father, and for reinstatement, in so far as we may be found worthy of that mark of confidence, in the offices and functions of our lamented father. Concerning our heritage, I would request the formation of an *oulema* [council], composed of persons of competence and integrity, to examine the facts and judge of the legitimacy of our claims. We desire that this council should include one or two high officials of the French Protectorate, free and independent Frenchmen, because we are aware that by reason of his authority, his great riches, and his political connections, our uncle is all-powerful.

'We place our cause, Monsieur le Résident-Général, in your hands, in the hands of France the Protector, and in the hands of God.'

It remained in the hands of that able trinity for about three years, after which the Resident-General, Monsieur Théodore Steeg, arrived at a form of compromise which certainly achieved some reconciliation, for six or seven years later T'hami spent large sums in obtaining Mohammed El Kebir's divorce from Jehane Sabey. The other members of Madani's family had not found it prudent to associate themselves with this letter of protest.

The women of Madani's harem T'hami absorbed into his own, with the exception of those who had sons of mature age, for these were considered dangerous, and potential conspirators. To his own harem of ninety-six he added fifty-four of Madani's, and strengthened his position with the imperial palace by marrying one of Madani's widows, Lalla Zineb, daughter of the Grand Vizier El Mokri. By Madani she had had one son, Mohammed, and two daughters; to T'hami she bore two sons, Abdessadek, now a lawyer in Rabat, and Hassan, a talented painter who lives in France.

Despite his vast riches, his position of power as Pasha of Marrakesh, and the full support of the occupying power, T'hami El Glaoui began his long reign with a handicap that he did not shed until 1934, sixteen years later. There was a skeleton in his cupboard, not a simply physical skeleton such as could have been found in any one of the dungeons of his numerous *kasbahs*, but an active, living, and extremely malign skeleton at Telouet itself. This was his nephew by marriage, Si Hammou, who had married Madani's daughter Lalla Halima, and whom Madani on his own appointment as Grand Vizier to Hafid had made *Caid* of Telouet, Ouazarzat, Tinerhir and Zagora, appointing him ruler of all the lands beyond the Atlas. The arsenal of Telouet, constantly reinforced by Madani during the height of his power, was now Hammou's, and, by virtue of the great extent of the areas over which he held jurisdiction, he could raise four times the fighting men that T'hami could. It is difficult to understand why Madani had ever placed so great a faith in this ogre, and it is possible that his appointments were in deference to his wife, for Lalla Halima was one of Madani's favourite daughters. Hammou was a man of enormous wealth, for in addition to his wide sources of irregular revenue, he had extended the salt mines, and had discovered silver mines at Bouaza Imini. He cannot by any standards have been an attractive personality: he was ugly, uncouth, ill-mannered, debauched, self-centred and exceedingly cruel. In his approach to the tribal problems of the South and East he envisaged only his own military steamroller and the policy of absolute destruction. He

T'hami El Glaoui, Pasha of Marrakesh, in the early years after Madani's death

Hadj Idder, T'hami El Glaoui's Chamberlain and confidant

The ramparts of Marrakesh, with the High Atlas in the background

Marrakesh: the Koutoubia Mosque and the High Atlas beyond

Marrakesh: the Place Dj'mma El F'naa— 'a sort of perpetual fun fair'

(Courtesy René Bertrand)

Tribal reception for El Glaoui; the *achwash* dance

Mounted warriors at a tribal reception

The *kasbah* of *Caïd* Omar El Glaoui at Taliouine

Telouet: the *kasbah* of *Caid* Brahim El Glaoui, the 'palace of 1,001 nights'

Telouet: the *kasbah* of *Caid* Brahim during the golden years

(Courtesy René Bertrand)

Telouet: the *kasbah* of *Caid* Hammou (left), the village, and the *kasbah* of *Caid* Brahim (right)

Men of the Glaoua tribe

Telouet interiors

T'hami El Glaoui (left center) with his son *Caid* Brahim (right center) at Telouet

Telouet: the *kasbah* of *Caid* Hammou in 1961

(Courtesy René Bertrand)

Telouet: the *kasbah* of *Caid* Hammou from the *kasbah* of *Caid* Brahim, 1961

T'hami El Glaoui during the height of his power

did, indeed, burn down the *kasbah* of a dissident fraction in the region of Telouet, roasting alive every living thing that was in it, including the women and children. His political adhesions – or rather his total lack of them – did not become apparent until after Madani's death, but when they did so they were acutely embarrassing to T'hami. Hammou was obstinately anti-French, and cherished the notion of a Berber revolt against the occupying power. For many years now he had been hoarding and smuggling arms for this purpose. If Madani had died during the period of French reverses in the First World War, Hammou would have made this dream reality; now T'hami was able (though until Hammou was actually dead he was never entirely certain that he had succeeded in doing so) to persuade him of the inadvisability of this course. As late as three years before his death – that is to say in 1931 – Hammou gave a practical demonstration of his convictions. He arranged a huge banquet at Telouet, to which he invited the great personalities of the country, both French and Moroccans. After the feast had begun the guests were alarmed by the sound of fusillade upon fusillade of shots at very close quarters and from every point of the compass. Hammou had caused his *kasbah* to be totally surrounded by several thousand of his mounted warriors, and now, as they began their demonstration, he announced with passion that he wished to see every Frenchman in the country dead.

He also indicated the same wish commercially. In 1927 he contracted to the Marseilles firm of Rippert and Nicolet the supply of one hundred thousand kilos of Moroccan olive oil, receiving a pre-payment of 500,000 French francs. The oil was never delivered. The firm brought a civil action for recovery of this sum and the case was found in their favour. There was however no very obvious way of implementing the decree, and at length, 'to save the name of Glaoui from dishonour' T'hami gave the French his own personal guarantee for the amount owing.

The existence of Hammou delayed the full establishment of the Protectorate for a further sixteen years. The French had no representation of any sort beyond the foothills of the High Atlas, and neither they nor T'hami could run the risk of further civil war that might snowball to their disadvantage. For this reason the 'pacification', of the South was delayed until after Hammou's death in 1934; and for this reason, too, the pass of Tiz-n-Tishka was constructed by a more difficult, adjacent, route that avoided Hammou's stronghold.

Hammou was the epitome of the force that had kept every Moroccan potentate in power in the past – they were hated but they were feared even more than they were hated. Since they were hated anyway, the more sadistic their behaviour the greater the fear they inspired. This resulted in a sort of random cruelty that was the more terrifying for its utter unpredictability. Hammou had brought this to a fine art; he was a specialist in dungeons, and he chose their occupants as one might select names from a telephone directory with closed eyes and the stab of a pin. The following tale is representative of many that are still current about him.

The Sheikh of a dissident fraction, the Ait Affan, came to Telouet to make his ritual act of submission, the slaughter of a beast before the gates of the *kasbah*. Hammou accepted the submission, and in token of acceptance presented the Sheikh with a silver-inlaid rifle. The Sheikh hurried home and sent his son to Hammou with the gift of a superb black stallion. Hammou took the stallion, but threw the boy into a dungeon. He would listen to no appeal from the father, merely remarking that his son would never see the light again. Two years later, he had an ambush laid for the Sheikh's brother, and he too joined the sightless company of those chained deep underground.

There is every reason to believe that Hammou earned to the full his nickname of The Vulture.

For the first two years after succeeding Madani, T'hami was still an active army commander, quelling the hydra-headed aftermath of a second appearance on the southern horizon of the pretender El Hiba. There was revolution everywhere in the Pre-Sahara, and in July 1920 T'hami led an army, with his nephew Hammou as second in command (for Hammou's fortunes also depended upon subjection of the tribes beyond the Atlas) to pacify the region of the now touristically famous Todghra gorges. By the time of their triumphant return (with some rebel leaders for Hammou's Telouet dungeons) T'hami's strictly military career was over.

Within the vexatious limits imposed by Hammou's impregnable existence, T'hami's career developed much as might have been expected. Above all he cultivated the grand manner towards Europeans – vast banquets; hospitality that included the bestowal of almost priceless gifts; a delicately handled air of omnipotence. Despite the pomp and splendour there was no vulgarity; his manners had become exquisite, his clothes a refinement of tradition, for he would wear nothing that was not woven to his order by the women of his own tribe. He knew, even then, that his status as a second Sultan in the South depended upon the French, and he knew that the French had no alternative but to depend utterly upon him. (As powers to be reckoned with, the Goundafi and the M'touggi had gone. The Goundafi fief came to pieces in 1924, and he himself died three years later; the M'touggi lands were swallowed – though not wholly digested – in 1928.) To European guests T'hami gave, literally, whatever they wanted, whether it might be a diamond ring, a present of money in gold, or a Berber girl or boy from the High Atlas. Nothing was impossible, for he was already at work on building his own myth. In the 1920s T'hami had become, among many Europeans, a fashion, like American jazz, or the Charleston dance, or the new art form of cubism. To be aware of 'The Glaoui', and to be able to speak of him with familiarity, was equivalent to what was known forty years later as being 'with it'. It was fashionable to quote his *bons mots*, as, for example, his comment upon M. Daladier, at that time the French Minister of War: 'He is like a dog without a tail – there's no way of telling what he is thinking.' Or his reply to his Chamberlain who asked him whether he should eject from a great banquet an inveterate parasite who had gate-crashed it: 'Certainly not – treat him, on the contrary, with the greatest consideration, since he has taken all the trouble to come without even being invited.'

T'hami journeyed often to Europe, always with a gigantic retinue and a portion of his harem, and gradually created what came to be known as 'the Glaoua tribe on the Oued Seine' – that is to say a strong and clannish body of metropolitan French supporters who regarded him as little less than a god.

He was extremely easily offended, and it sometimes called for great dexterity to avoid this, as in the case of the American visitor who

offered him a fifty dollar bill as a souvenir. The incident had begun by
the American remarking, during the course of dinner, that the United
States held sixty-five per cent of the world's gold reserves, but that the
country was not the richest in the world, on account of her export
difficulties. 'If you have too much gold,' began T'hami, 'you could
perhaps . . .' He was interrupted by a representative of the Residency,
M. Tranchant de Lunel, who explained that America's gold reserves
were not currency, but a sort of guarantee of the value of her bank
notes. To illustrate this the American produced a fifty dollar bill and
handed it to T'hami for inspection. T'hami examined it with interest
and passed it back. The American waved it away, saying, 'Keep it –
I've got plenty more where that came from.' T'hami's face clouded
with anger, and he held the note as though it were burning his fingers.
M. Tranchant de Lunel came brilliantly to the rescue. Snatching the
offending piece of paper from T'hami's hand, he tore it across twice so
as to leave intact only the portrait of President Wilson. This he handed
back to T'hami, saying, 'The American gentleman did not want to
leave Your Excellency's table without presenting you as a souvenir a
portrait of one of his country's greatest men!'

Not all the visiting French were favourably impressed by the fantastic
pomp of his palaces; it was, after all, little more than a century since
they had overthrown their own monarchy and condemned the
splendours of Versailles. Madame Barthou, the aged mother of the
French Minister for War, expressed her disapproval with a pungent
sarcasm that must have wounded T'hami deeply. In those early years of
the French Protectorate the greater number of important administrative
posts were held by the military, and Madame Barthou was therefore
treated with especial consideration by all the authorities, who had
received instructions from France to make her visit to Morocco a
memorable one. Her short stay in Marrakesh was therefore naturally to
include a banquet given in her honour by the Pasha of Marrakesh at
his palace. The guests, largely made up of high-ranking French officers
and their wives, assembled in one of the huge and magnificent reception
rooms, all of them paying court to the old lady, who, though obviously
tired, insisted on remaining standing and was no more talkative than
bare courtesy demanded. The Glaoui greeted each of his guests, and
awaited some signal from Madame Barthou that the meal might begin.

Moroccan tile work

The splendidly robed black slaves who were stationed in pairs at every door to the room likewise waited for the guests to take their places at the numerous low round tables that they had placed in readiness. Many more slaves laden with silver dishes were visible in the corridors outside. At length the Glaoui requested one of the French officers to ask Madame Barthou whether she would now take her place at the table of honour. Her lassitude and boredom immediately deserted her, and she replied loudly and with great emphasis, 'But I couldn't possibly sit down before His Majesty does!'

T'hami's greatest fault as a politician, manifest even in these early days, was a certain arrogant intolerance that precluded his listening to the advice or the viewpoint of another, and this stemmed, without doubt, from the positions of military command with which his brother Madani had always entrusted him. Complementary to this intransigence of viewpoint was a refusal to be deterred by any obstacle to his personal desires, more especially when a woman was concerned. His talent scouts were everywhere, both in his own country and in France, and when they found something that he wanted nothing in the world could stand in his way. At Casablanca, Rabat, and Tangier he had organized agents who frequented the railway stations to spot any attractive un-accompanied European female who was travelling south. Alerted by telegram or telephone, their opposite numbers in Marrakesh would greet the tourist as 'guides', and arrange a visit to the Glaoui's palace. If he was taken by the looks of the visitor he would make an accidental appearance, and courteously invite the tourist to dine with him, a dinner that was often the prelude to a mutually profitable association. (He had one or two shocks, as the following anecdote illustrates. A face in Paris had caught his fancy, and he issued orders accordingly. Two nights later the girl, quite overcome by the magnitude of the gift she had already received, was ushered discreetly into his bedroom. The secretary who had brought her departed, and his guards stood posted before the door. After a few minutes it burst open, and a distraught Glaoui shot out yelling, 'Take her away! Take her away! She wants to eat me!' There is one form of love-making that does not appear on Morocco's otherwise comprehensive menu.)

Nor was he invariably successful with women who were not of his own people, but even in case of defeat he was at pains to preserve the grand manner. In 1932 a troupe of Egyptian musicians visited Mar-rakesh, and he gave a huge banquet in their honour. During the course of it he became enamoured of one of the principal singers, and before the party left he showed her his fantastic collection of precious stones, hidden in secret and well-guarded rooms, inviting her at the same time to return on the following day to his private apartments. She accepted, but when the time came she sent instead another extremely beautiful singer, bearing a letter. 'Your Excellency, I much regret that I feel unable to accept the invitation you extended to me yesterday evening, and I am really sorry not to be able to satisfy your ardent feelings. But I have, as you know, a husband, and I love him, so I am sending you someone else, who will be happy to do anything you ask her.' The substitute was entirely satisfactory, and she received rich rewards, but T'hami sent the more princely gifts to the singer herself, and they were accompanied by a courteously understanding letter.

In his own country there was no possibility of – nor will to – dissent. If he or one of his agents saw a desirable girl, her parents were requested to send her to the palace, where she would be assured of work and of being brought up in security. In exchange, the parents would receive a gift, and the girl became one of the Glaoui's concubines. As a rule this arrangement was agreeable to all parties, but there could not, in any case, be the slightest question of refusal, and once the doors of the harem closed behind a new acquisition she knew that she would never again leave the women's quarters of her master until she was carried out to the cemetery. From then on she was a woman of the harem, her life bounded by its jealousies and rivalries and petty squabbles and household breakages that were judged and punished by the Glaoui himself; her conversation limited to the endless sexual gossip of her fellow concubines; her sexual life limited to her necessarily infrequent turn in her master's bed and the sometimes passionate solace of her own sex. She would never again see any other man than T'hami face to face, for not even his own sons were permitted to enter the harem after they had reached puberty.

The Glaoui's extravagance in the matter of sexual partners and all other matters (a single trip to Paris or Vichy or the Côte d'Azur would cost a fortune) demanded an enormous income, in the region of seven million old French francs a year, and to maintain his great pomp and boundless hospitality he was perpetually in search of money. Deprived of the great revenues from beyond the Atlas, which were the per-quisite of his odious nephew Hammou, he showed himself an able and ruthless businessman, cornering the southern markets and achieving a monopoly in hemp, olives, oranges and other valuable commodities. (Drugs he used but little himself, contenting himself with occasional indulgence in opium, but hashish was a feature of his hospitality for those who wished to experiment.) This endless quest for money led him later, in 1936, to defy even the Islamic conventions; learning from his *khalifa* El Byaz that there was treasure in the tomb of a female saint, Lalla R'kkia, in Marrakesh, he took personal charge of operations. The

Jewelled haik *pin*

tomb in question adjoined a quarter occupied by Europeans, and on rising one morning the inhabitants of an apartment were astonished to see from their balcony the Pasha of Marrakesh squatting at the edge of a newly-dug deep ditch, directing the operation of a digging squad, while one of his Jewish advisers was sprawled against the inner wall of the shrine itself. Seeing himself observed, the Pasha and his party retired, but the following day work was resumed behind a discreet screen of reed matting. After a few days rumours were silenced by the announcement that the Pasha had been horrified to learn of the ruinous condition of this holy place, and had decided to rebuild it. In fact, so strong did this rumour become that T'hami felt obliged to put it into effect, the cost was but a fraction of the treasure he had acquired by rifling the tomb.

Much of the revenues of Marrakesh itself escaped him, for the many taxes payable on cafés, on the dispensary of prophylactics, on the various trades, and on prostitution (which was in those days one of the principal industries of Marrakesh) were payable to his *khalifa*, who in turn had to disgorge a large proportion to the French. This *khalifa* was, for the earlier part of T'hami's reign, a person – one might almost say a growth – of incredible malignity named El Byaz, who for all practical purposes governed the whole town of Marrakesh. El Byaz had worked for the Sultan Hafid's Vizier, Ben Slimane, and had 'run at his mule's tail'. It was in fact the French who were responsible for the appointment of El Byaz as *khalifa* of the Pasha of Marrakesh, succeeding in 1913 Mohammed ou Toughza, and he was to all intents and purposes a spy for the occupying power. (*Caids* and Pashas were nominated by the Sultans by *dahirs*, or Imperial decrees, while *khalifas* were nominated by decree of the Grand Vizier. In practice this had little effect since both Sultan and Vizier were securely under French orders.) El Byaz counted not a single friend, even among his own family, and in 1937 he imprisoned his own brother on suspicion of anti-French activities. His loyalty to the French was an affair of personal opportunism, and while he abused his power by every kind of extortion and corruption, always pretending to act under the orders of the Glaoui, he made his master very considerable gifts on feast days in order to ensure that he remained in T'hami's good graces. T'hami had few direct dealings with his *khalifa*; he was wont to employ intermediaries. The first was Hadj Mohammed El Mokri, then successively T'hami's eldest son Brahim, and Madani's daughter R'kkia, who had married a rich Marrakesh merchant named Boubker Ben Bachir El Ghandjaoui. El Byaz's trickeries and extortions continued until T'hami was apprised of certain facts by one Ben Zaara, and obtained from the Sultan the order first for his removal to a lesser post and then for his exile to Agadir.

Despite his enormous greed for money, T'hami remained characteristically generous, whether from a psychological need to feed his image as a *grand seigneur* or as a more calculated question of policy it is difficult to say; but few who sought his aid were refused it, and it is factually certain that this attribute saved many from ruin. He loved to give alms, not because their giving is one of the five pillars of the Islamic faith, but because he desired the worship of the poor; during the month of Ramadan or at the approach of Aid El Kebir (the 'sheep festival') there were few who did not bless the name of the Glaoui for his lavish distribution of food.[1]

For the Aid El Kebir his Chamberlain Hadj Idder held a gigantic list of names to whom he sent a sheep every year. One year, while on a pilgrimage to Mecca, T'hami left this distribution to his son Brahim, who, at that time anyway, appears to have lacked his father's open-handedness, for he erased many names from the list and sent a fraction of the usual number of sheep. T'hami's return was always the occasion of a great reception, and at the ceremony of hand-kissing he was amazed to hear those who had waited in vain for their sheep whisper to him, 'May Allah keep you with us here among your people!' As this was not a traditional form of greeting, T'hami asked what was wrong, and received the reply, 'Sire, this year we could not keep the feast of Aid El Kebir because you were not here with us.' T'hami understood the situation immediately but said nothing in reply, nor did he address himself immediately to Brahim. He waited until a day when he was dispensing justice, and asked Brahim to attend so that he might learn how to act when some day he should succeed his father. Each plaintiff was ushered in by the Chamberlain, who explained his petition, at the same time handing a sealed envelope to T'hami, who placed it unopened upon his table. As soon as each request had been read he despatched two officials with the plaintiff, to see that justice was done. Some came before him only to ask alms; to each of these T'hami handed one of the sealed envelopes, without even looking to see how much money it contained. At the end of the session he asked Brahim to open the remainder and count the receipts. When Brahim had done this and announced the total, T'hami said, 'Look, Brahim – Allah has sent us this fortune today, and Allah sent a fortune to those poor men to whom I gave an envelope containing money to buy food. One must not be too greedy. You ought to have done the same thing with the distribution of sheep which I entrusted to you. We receive

[1] Aid El Kebir (literally, The Great Feast) commemorates Abraham's sacrifice of a ram in place of his intended sacrifice of his son Isaac. At Aid El Kebir every orthodox Muslim of Morocco must sacrifice a sheep, and generally contrives to come by one, by hook or by crook.

presents (*hediya*) of enormous numbers of sheep for the feast, and those which we give away lose us nothing, because we have the blessing of those who receive them.'

That story was told to me by an eye-witness; the following, in support of the same aspect of his character, is amply documented. T'hami had invited to dine at the palace some French residents in Marrakesh, and with them a young Parisian woman who was visiting Marrakesh for the first time. The pièce de résistance of the meal was a whole roast sheep (*mechoui*), and in accordance with general Islamic custom, T'hami, as host, removed a succulent morsel with his fingers and held it out to her. Believing that he neither understood nor spoke French, she expressed herself freely to her companions, saying that this legendary figure was after all nothing but a pig. She added that she wouldn't mind having the enormous emerald ring that decorated his right hand.

At the end of the meal T'hami drew her aside and said softly and in excellent French, 'Madame, a stone like this emerald was obviously never made for a pig like me. Permit me to offer it to you.'

In 1930 T'hami found himself almost crippled by debts, and although he had raised large loans from El Byaz and others, they were not enough for his needs. At last he borrowed fifty-two million francs from a Belgian company, giving as security and under the moral guarantee of France all the lands to which he held title. Only after the Second World War was he able to repay this debt, owing to the enormous increase in value of the town properties he owned. In all his financial dealings he was advised by his three Jewish counsellors, Berrimoj, Attias and Mimram, who also served as intermediaries between himself and the merchants with whom he dealt. Berrimoj and Attias died before he did, leaving truly colossal fortunes. Mimram is alive at the time of writing, and is believed to be one of the richest living Moroccans.

It is against the setting of Marrakesh that T'hami El Glaoui is re-membered best, that incredible city that has changed so little in almost one thousand years of existence. The city was founded in 1062 by the first of the Almoravide dynasty of Sultans, and the very earliest of the mediaeval descriptions of it are but little different from T'hami's Marrakesh between the two world wars.

Marrakesh (always referred to by early European writers as Morocco City) stands on the great fertile plain of Haouz, some seventeen hundred feet above sea level, and forty miles from the foot of the High Atlas, whose mighty peaks tower another twelve thousand feet above it, remote, icy, snow-covered for the greater part of the year, a splendid backcloth for the splendour of the city itself. Some eight miles of now time-worn ramparts enclose the thronging hive of humans, ramparts pierced by ten great gates, each giving its name to a quarter of the city. Dynasty after dynasty of Sultans enriched Marrakesh with the finest architecture of their epoch; it became a royal city, the capital of the South, and many Sultans preferred their palaces there to those of Fez. By its geographical position the town became the great market place not only of the Haouz but of all the lands between the High Atlas and the Sahara, the clearing-house of the camel caravans from all the remote oases of the South with their loads of walnuts and oranges, grain and hides, spices, dates and precious metals. It was the largest slave market in all Morocco; by the time of T'hami's reign the recent disappearance, at least from the public eye, of that weekly auction, was the only external departure from the traditions of the city as they had developed over nearly ten centuries. Marrakesh was much as Europeans visualize the Baghdad of The Thousand and One Nights, but more beautiful than Baghdad ever was, for Baghdad lacked the savage glories of the Atlas as a background to the jewels of palace and garden, orchard and lake, and the glittering green-tiled minarets of the mosques. Over every traveller who visited it Marrakesh cast its strange heady spell – a spell that to many has survived the short French occupation and the partial westernization of the unique and essentially African city. Marrakesh is accessible, it has become perhaps the greatest tourist attraction of all North Africa, but the tourists, however great an impression Marrakesh makes upon them, make little impression upon Marrakesh. In 1904, Es El Ben Susnan wrote with a foresight worthy of Jules Verne, 'There are certain cities that cannot be approached for the first time by a sympathetic traveller without a sense of solemnity and reverence that is not far removed from awe. Athens, Rome, Constantinople, Damascus, and Jerusalem may be cited as examples; each in its turn has filled me with great wonder and deep joy. But all those are to be reached nowadays by the railway, that great modern purge of sensibility. In Morocco, on the other hand, the railway is still unknown . . . until the Gordian knot of Morocco's future has been untied or cut. Then, perhaps, as a result of French pacific penetration, flying railway trains loaded with tourists, guide-book in hand, and camera at the ready will pierce to the secret places of the land, and men will speak of "doing" Morocco, as they "do" other countries in their rush across the world, seeing all the stereotyped sights and appreciating none. For the present, by Allah's grace, matters are quite otherwise.'

Allah's grace did not last long in this respect, and the French penetration was not quite as pacific as Ben Susnan anticipated; nor could he well have known that T'hami El Glaoui would become a scratch golfer and cause a golf course to be laid out for his pleasure at Marrakesh itself. But Marrakesh is still to be approached with awe.

Marrakesh was not only the market place of all the southern riches; since early times it had become a pleasure town for the distant tribes-people who carried them there. The city had a perpetual floating population of some twelve thousand people: wild, pale-skinned Berbers from the mountain villages, black men from the edge of the desert, Arab tribes such as the Rehamna from the plains to the north and the west; they came, they sold their goods, and had money to spend, so that the city became a sort of perpetual fun-fair. Close to the tall Koutoubia mosque, one of the grandest in the country, a great irregularly shaped open space of beaten earth, the Place Dj'mma El F'naa has from very early times been given up entirely to the use of public entertainers, around each of whom would form a dense circle of spectators, its circumference touching that of the next ring, so that the effect in looking down upon the scene from some elevated building is that of a formally-patterned carpet made of some fifteen thousand human beings. The sound of human voices comes up like the muted rumble of some vast engine, an undertone to the perpetual staccato urgency of drums, the wailing of reed pipes, the clang of cymbals, the shrill tinkle of water-sellers' bells, the endless calling of the beggars – 'Allah! Allah! Allah!' The fluid circles form and dissolve and reform

Koutoubia mosque and the Atlas, Marrakesh

around the snake-charmers and sword-swallowers and fire-eaters, all of the Essaoui sect, their hair falling in blue-black cascades over their shoulders; gaudily dressed acrobats from Taroudant forming towers of multicoloured unidentifiable limbs; conjurers and mimers, and story-tellers who hold a circle of a hundred solemn-faced children in hypnotized silence; Berber dancers from the mountains, their white-robed lines swaying in rhythmic advance and withdrawal; whirling black Gennaoua dancers from the Sudan, whose little conical caps, tasselled and embroidered with cowrie shells are spun fifty feet into the air as each dancer reaches the climax of his performance; troops of Chleuch boy dancers with painted faces, waggling hips, and clicking castanets, their bare feet flicking through the intricate pattern of the dance while their eyes rove the circle for evening clients; performing monkeys, fortune tellers, clowns – all these and their exotic audiences have been part of the Dj'mma El F'naa for hundreds of years.

Towards evening the din becomes crescendo; the sun sinks and lights the towering snow peaks of the Atlas to orange and pink; the shadows of the thronged spectators in the Dj'mma El F'naa become long black spikes that join group to group like the bars of an iron grille; over their heads drift homing flights of the numberless white egrets that roost nightly on the roofs above the wool market, their breasts lit with the same fiery colours that glow on the mountain snows.

If T'hami El Glaoui had ruled from a less fairy-tale city his myth, which was so great a part of his power, might never have come into being; it would have been less easy to dazzle in, say, the drab setting of Casablanca.

10

The Glaoui Empire Completed

It would be convenient to examine the character and conduct of Si
Hadj T'hami El Glaoui in the light of his greatest public detraction, a
polemic entitled *Son Excellence*, appearing in 1932, and extending to
275 pages of journalese vituperation.

This book intruded, violently, upon an image already contradictory
– that of a gracious host and delicate diplomat, a scratch golfer and a
fantastic warrior, an athlete of sexual orgy and refined sadism, an ogre,
and a sage like Solomon. He was, probably, a product of European
intervention rather than of his own infertile soil, a figure standing
perpetually at an unacknowledged cross-roads. He was, in the public
eye, larger than life; the redeemer, the executioner, the ultimate. He
was more probably, as the greater Abd El Amir had said of himself, 'a
man like any other man', implicitly embracing all the follies of a strange
and destructive environment.

Son Excellence is a curiosity of literature, the more piquant because
there are exceedingly few copies left in the world. In the mid 1920s a
certain *cadi* (religious judge) called Abd El Hakim had set himself up
against the Glaoui, and as a result was arraigned on a charge of treason.
The Glaoui condemned him to fifteen days' imprisonment for seditious
activities. In the considerable fracas that ensued, he appealed to French
law. During the protracted legal proceedings that followed, Abd El
Hakim was defended by a left-wing French lawyer who dabbled in
controversial journalism. Losing his action, as was only to be expected
in the circumstances, this French lawyer called Gustave Babin entered
into a compact with his defeated client to destroy the great Moroccan
personalities of the South, beginning with the Pasha of Marrakesh,
Si Hadj T'hami El Glaoui, and going on to the minor Lords of the Atlas.

His book on the Glaoui appeared in its first edition in 1932. A considerable proportion of it is factually inaccurate, but it is not so much the falsehoods as the misconceptions that demand attention. He displayed a complete absence of knowledge of the traditional customs of the country; it was as if a Muslim attacking a particular Christian made major issue of the fact that he ate pork, urinated standing up, slept in the same bed as his wife, and did not shave his body; as if an Englishman attacking a particular Frenchman were to scream that this monster of depravity (a favourite epithet of Gustave Babin's) ate frogs and snails and gave his infant children wine to drink. For this reason his book is childish even where it is interesting. He made, in sum, the particular from the general, and in result the picture presented is almost wholly misleading. Had he attacked the Glaoui as an anachronistic instrument of colonialism doomed to disappointment, the point might have been well made, for France and her Moroccan delegates were both certainly enriching themselves at the expense of the bulk of the Moroccan people. To both, the concept of an independent Moroccan state was necessarily an anathema; by it each had all to lose and nothing to gain. Babin was a Frenchman, and he never brought himself to say that the true blame lay with France.

Much of the stupidity of this book is plain to any reader acquainted with Moroccan custom. To give but a few examples, Babin whispers with horror that the Glaoui had a private cemetery in his palace, ignoring the fact that for religious reasons palaces were almost always built in the immediate vicinity of a saintly tomb, and the numerous servitors of the family interred there; he speaks of an all too normal summer drought as if it were comparable with the real famine of 1929; he praises the Goundafi's personal generosity in giving soup to the poor, as if unaware that the giving of alms is one of the five fundamentals of the Islamic faith; he accuses T'hami of having been, in his boyhood, the M'touggi's lover, as if unaware that this form of homosexuality was an established custom; he accuses T'hami of 'stealing' his dead brother's women, without reference to the long and quite respectable establishment of this practice; he cites the loans made by France to T'hami as evidence of profligacy, without noting that all the Great *Caids* had made it plain that in default of customary pomp they would lack authority.

Because, however, the book contains less obviously parryable thrusts, it appeared to the present writer to be of great importance to record the personal comments of the Glaoui's surviving courtiers; those scattered and largely exiled remnants of a fallen régime would now have nothing to lose by revealing the truth as they knew it.

The first difficulty of all was to obtain a copy of the book, for the Glaoui had responded with alacrity to its publication. He bought from the publishers the entire remainder of the edition, and burned every copy. Quite a number were already in the bookshops or in private hands. These he bought – in the latter case often for fabulous sums – and those he could not buy he stole. Sometimes the books were well hidden, and there were a number of unexplained fires in private houses. T'hami followed up this very direct approach to the matter by bringing a libel action against Babin, which, owing to French intervention, was settled out of court. By 1960 the book was *introuvable*, and it cost me a year and a very considerable sum of money to acquire one of the few remaining copies. Having done so, I succeeded over the following two years in getting this copy annotated by important ex-members of the Glaoui's personal staff. These notes are indispensable, not only because they illumine the whole climate of thought of the old régime; they are, however, so voluminous, so replete with detailed ramification, and add so many names to an already crowded stage, as to preclude publication in their entirety. I have therefore limited myself to those passages which have been independently commented upon by more than one of my informants and have chosen the most informative version. I give in Appendix IV a brief précis of Babin's allegations, followed by the informed comment upon them. I have omitted the question of the Glaoui's ancestry, which appears more conveniently treated in another chapter.

At the date of the Babin incident in 1932, it was fourteen years since T'hami El Glaoui had inherited from his brother Madani; and, while he was still debarred from absolute power by the continued existence of his nephew Hammou at Telouet, his authority was by now supreme over all southern Morocco on the Atlantic side of the Atlas ridge, and he had become commonly known to the occupying power as the

Viceroy of the South. He enjoyed also less formal titles, such as 'the Lion of the Atlas', 'the Eagle of the Atlas', and 'the Black Panther'.

He had greatly increased his lands and riches, adding to the tribes under his direct authority the Sektana, Ounein, Ghouzioun, Zemrani and Mesfiouia. There can be no question but that some of these lands and more particularly those of the Zemrani and Mesfiouia were acquired by very dubious means, involving the despoliation and expulsion of the tribespeople. There exists a great bulk of writing on the subject, much in accusation and little in defence; it can be fairly assumed that methods were 'traditional'.

While T'hami's estates thus formed a veritable kingdom, his nephew Hammou's might have been termed an empire. From the old white *kasbah* of Telouet he ruled over immense territories that included the lands of the Ghaptama, Fetwaka, Dougana, Glaoua, Imeghran, Imegroun, Todghra, Dadès, Skoura, Ouazarzat, Mesguita, and the giant confederation of the Aït Waouzzit.

Blocked by Hammou's intransigence from exploitation of the lands to the south of the Atlas, the French had perforce to sit by and wait for him to die. Meanwhile they heaped power and honour upon T'hami, whose interests had become indivisible from their own. Under a thin but opaque veneer of French civilization the wood of the old Morocco was alive with its traditional worms; behind a flimsy façade of French institutions the Pasha of Marrakesh had absolute control of all police functions and of all justice. The function of Chief Justice had at first been assumed by T'hami's *khalifa* who came after El Byaz; the integrity of this man, Si Ahmed Zemmouri, son of T'hami's half-brother Hassi, formed the single exception to a rule of absolute corruption. Every man who had recourse to the law courts, whether as plaintiff or defendant, witness or accused, made a 'present' to the Pasha's *khalifa*, the gift being either made personally from hand to hand, or left in a sealed envelope at the *khalifa*'s office. A further gift, either in cash or in kind, was required when the court had risen. This amounted to verdict by auction; it was not one law for the rich and another for the poor, it was law for the rich and none for the poor. The Pasha himself, surrounded by members of his own coterie who had come to intercede, financially, for some protégé or other, frequently found it necessary to revise his verdict several times over 'in the light of new information received'.

The verdict always went to the largest 'information'; this had always been the custom. The old information was not returned.

As T'hami's status and responsibility to the French grew, so did his need for money. Besides the revenue from the great tribal lands he had assimilated, he received ten per cent on the gross sum of the *tertib*, or agricultural tax (instituted by Moulay Abd El Aziz), which he levied upon all lands under his command; and this, together with the customary *hediya* or present in cash or kind from all his subjects on feast days, constituted the greater part of his unearned income. He had also gone into business in a very large way, an enterprise for which his absolute power over the people gave him unique qualifications. He had cornered the market in all the most important products of southern Morocco, by the simple means of forbidding their sale to any but his own agents, and at prices distinctly advantageous to himself. By these means he had acquired a monopoly in almonds, saffron, dates, mint and olive oil. From the State he rented for the nominal sum of 25,000 old French francs the vast olive garden of Agdal; some indication of the profit accruing from this single item may be given by the sale to France of one year's crop (1948) on the branch, for 30,000,000 francs. Crops from the great olive groves of Taliouine and of the Haouz yielded no less than 300,000,000 francs.

In the early years the cultivation of his great olive groves had been entrusted to his own Moroccan agents, and the results had left much to be desired. In the early 1920s he took on a French manager, who worked on the basis of a percentage of the profits. Systematic European methods of cultivation and harvesting had a spectacular effect, and within a few years the profits had more than doubled. T'hami warmly congratulated his manager, adding, 'From these figures one can see at a glance that someone is working for himself.' 'Excellency,' said the Frenchman, 'I don't quite understand.' 'I will explain by illustration,' T'hami replied. 'Some thirty-odd years ago my predecessor as Pasha of Marrakesh, a certain Ben Daoud, who came before Driss Mennou, tried a man and condemned him to immediate imprisonment. Although this man was small and very fat he somehow managed to escape from the room and fled through the crowd who were waiting outside the tribunal. Ten soldiers pursued him, but he ran so fast that they never caught him up, and eventually they lost trace of him. Some long time later this man made honourable amends, and re-entered the good graces of the Pasha, who asked him how in the world such a small fat man had managed to escape the pursuit of ten stalwart soldiers. "Excellency," he replied, "I was running for myself, while your soldiers were only running for you!" '

T'hami's strictly business enterprises may be examined as well here as elsewhere, though some of the following list belong to years a little later in his career. Identifying himself with the French colonial policy of exploitation, he became, without the necessity of buying a single share, honorary president of l'Omnium Industriel du Moghreb (sugar, soap, and tea), president of the Mining Society of Bou Azzer du Graara (cobalt mines), president of the Metallurgic and Chemical Society of North Africa (plastic materials), vice-president of the Hygienic Drinks Company of Casablanca (Coca-cola, an American company), administrator of the Olivettes Company (olive oil). This is to name but a few from a formidable list.

After the death of Hammou in 1934, which removed the last apparent obstacle to absolute power over all the South, he interested himself increasingly in the mining projects which Hammou had already initiated. No one could hope then to obtain mining concessions without the support or at least the approval of the Pasha of Marrakesh, and it was his custom to let any aspirant know that he would not be averse to having a hand in the direction of the new concern and perhaps a little block of shares to go with it. If neither was forthcoming, tribal difficulties were likely to arise in the area, which would necessitate the Glaoui's personal intervention, perhaps at very great cost. The principal mining company of southern Morocco was Omnium Nord-Africain, founded by one of the first French business-men to settle under the Protectorate, a Monsieur Jean Epinat. This company, under the controlling interest of the Bank of Paris and the Low Countries, operated the only known cobalt bed in the franc zone; and its subsidiary, the Tifnout-Tiranimine Company, operated the great manganese bed of Taliouine. All mining labour was supplied by the Glaoui, but their wages were paid by the operating company. Monsieur Epinat and T'hami El Glaoui remained in close liaison until T'hami's final downfall in 1955, by which time Omnium Nord-Africain had through T'hami, its president, acquired the greater part of all mining concessions in Morocco. In 1928 and 1929, notably, T'hami entered into mining contracts with the tribal chiefs, contracts that were not unprofitable to himself.

A controlling interest in the Moroccan press was both an obvious strategic necessity and a profitable business venture. During the 1930s he acquired control of four out of the five French-owned Moroccan dailies, *Le Petit Marocain, La Vigie Marocaine, Le Courier du Maroc,* and *L'Echo du Maroc.* These newspapers had belonged to M. Pierre Mas, one of the great businessmen of the Protectorate, who also happened to be managing director of Omnium Nord-Africain. This combination of power and absolute press control became of enormous significance twenty years later, when T'hami El Glaoui was engaged upon unseating his Sultan from the throne.

Meanwhile, during the fourteen years since Madani El Glaoui's death in 1918, there had been many changes in the country. Lyautey, the 'architect of Morocco', had gone, leaving, it is said, with tears streaming down his cheeks. His unsuccessful attempts to quell the massive rebellion of Abd El Krim in the Rif mountains had led to his asking Paris in the summer of 1925, when the rebel army was only fifty miles from Fez, for General Weygand as second-in-command; the request was ignored and instead he received a telegram informing him that Marshal Pétain would take over command of all troops and military operations in Morocco. Lyautey tendered his resignation a few weeks later, refusing even to await the arrival of his successor Monsieur Théodore Steeg, former Prime Minister of France and Governor-General of Algeria. Despite the use of something like half a million European troops, Abd El Krim was not defeated until May 1926, French losses being three thousand dead and ten thousand wounded. In farewell to Lyautey, T'hami said, 'No matter who succeeds you, it is always you who will remain my master.'

Lyautey's policy had genuinely been that of a Protectorate, with the maximum possible contact with the protected people; Steeg's was essentially colonial, and under his régime the Sultan Youssef became a puppet for the signature of French prepared documents. The number of French administrative officials quadrupled itself in two years.

In 1927 the Sultan Youssef died, and the French, frustrating his elder son Idriss's attempt to take the throne, secured through T'hami and Abd El Hay Kittani's good offices the election of the third son, who began his reign in 1927 aged sixteen, as Sultan Mohammed Ben Youssef later known as Mohammed V. There is much evidence that he was chosen for his extreme youth, which together with his shy and retiring disposition eminently qualified him for the post of a puppet Sultan ruling through a ventriloquist conqueror. One must look far to parallel such an error in colonial judgment.

What Gustave Babin had failed to say, that the European régime in Morocco progressed for the benefit of the French and their European representatives, without regard for the mass of Moroccan people, should have been the true reproach against T'hami El Glaoui, and it was this factor alone that eventually brought about his downfall. A movement for the independence of the country was inevitable, and independence would mean not only the end of the French in Morocco but also the end of the Glaoui kingdom they had sponsored. The situation called for statesmanship of which Madani might perhaps have been capable; T'hami was not, for to the very end in 1955 he thought only in terms of traditional remedies.

The independence movement started as early as 1926 when Moulay Youssef was still Sultan. Like most similar movements, it began as a number of scattered groups, who later became unified under the single name of *Istiqlal* – independence. The movement did not at first demand the total ejection of the French from Morocco, but merely that France should admit once and for all the distinctions between a Protectorate and the colony that Morocco had become.

France replied in 1930 with a transparent move to divide the country against itself – the Berber *dahir* (imperial decree), which was not only designed to underline the racial and cultural differences between occupied Berber and occupying Arab, but to exonerate the numerically superior Berbers from the Islamic law ·called *chraa* exercised by His

Chereefian Majesty, and to substitute the laws of Berber custom (the varying laws imposed by the councils of small Berber republics) and of French law to all criminal cases. The young Sultan signed this *dahir* in all good faith, brought up as he had been to regard Lyautey as infallible and personifying the French. The Berber *dahir* did more to foster the independence movement and the ultimate downfall of the French régime than any previous action of the Protectorate; it was a signal failure to divide and rule. In the opinion of the present writer its greatest weakness was a failure to recognise that the majority of the Berbers to whom it was intended to appeal were already labouring under the despotic rule of the Great *Caids* – notably T'hami El Glaoui, Hammou El Glaoui, and El Ayadi of the Rehamma. The *dahir*, therefore, insulted the Arabs and the spiritual powers vested in the Sultan, without providing practical attraction for the bulk of the Berber population, who were unaffected by it; moreover it gave the Istiqlal potent ammunition for propaganda.

In 1934 Hammou died, and T'hami entered into his glory, consolidating the whole vast Glaoui empire under his own hands. He married his own niece, Hammou's principal wife Halima, and by her had a daughter, Lalla Fatooma; he absorbed the greater part of Hammou's harem into his own household, including Hammou's favourite concubine Mina, daughter of a blacksmith. T'hami's eldest son Brahim married one of Hammou's daughters, Lalla Malika.

Brahim, recalled from Paris where he was living, became *Caid* of Telouet, Ait Ben Haddou, Ouazarzat and Skoura. Resident at Telouet, he abandoned Hammou's old white *kasbah* and began the vast project of making from Madani's nearby stronghold the greatest fortified palace in the world. Of T'hami's other sons, Mohammed became *Caid* of the Mesfiouia, with his headquarters at Ait Ourir; Ahmed became *khalifa* of the Haouz; Abdessadek became president of the Chereefian Tribunal at Marrakesh. Between *caidats* and *khalifats* his own trusted relations now numbered some eighty, dispersed over a vast territory. The Protectorate, while consenting to the displacement of a large number of Hammou's old régime whom T'hami did not trust, was alive to the possibility of losing control over the whole of southern

Morocco, and in turn insisted on attaching to his regional governors French civil controllers or military advisers.

In 1935 the pacification of southern Morocco was officially completed. Since 1907 the French had lost in Morocco 27,000 dead and 15,000 wounded. Moroccan losses have been estimated at more than fifteen times those figures.

Apart from those towns possessing tribunals which dispensed summary justic, and apart from French tribunals dealing solely with the European population, all legal administration was now in the hands of

A halt in the Southern desert

T'hami and members of his family. Apart from the Chereefian Tribunal of Marrakesh, under the presidency of his son Abdessadek, T'hami had, as Pasha of Marrakesh, his own *salon de justice* which, as we have mentioned, was a not inconsiderable source of personal revenue. His verdicts and decrees were oral, and no records of the proceedings were kept; in this matter, also, he was emancipated from all French control. In the very rare cases of French intervention, T'hami almost invariably emerged triumphant, presenting his political role as indispensable to the occupying power. The following are representative of the curious courses of justice at the period.

A Jewish notable of Marrakesh wished to break his engagement to his fiancée. She, knowing of T'hami's susceptibility to female charm, put herself under his protection. His Chamberlain, Hadj Idder, received her and her equally attractive sister, at night and in the private quarter of the palace reserved for Europeans. T'hami gave them audience, and promised his protection, retaining a lawyer to whom he paid a large sum from his private funds. The Jewish notable, terrified of becoming the victim of T'hami's personal justice, approached the French tribunal through the Jewish Committee, and the tribunal in turn placed the matter before the French governor of the town. Learning of this move on the part of his opponent, T'hami changed ground with his customary agility, and requested the defending lawyer whom he had retained to put the whole matter through the official channels of the Chereefian Tribunal of Marrakesh, then presided over by his nephew Si Ahmed Zemmouri. Zemmouri had the highest reputation for integrity both among Moroccans and French, but T'hami invited him to deliver verdict in favour of the girl. The French judicial authority, represented by a certain Commandant Vitalis, got wind of this invitation, and forestalled possible bias by intimating that he would take the matter into his own hands if judgment were given according to T'hami's whim rather than in the spirit of true justice. As a result of this intervention the case was prolonged, and ended in a verdict unfavourable to the girl. Put greatly out of countenance by this turn of event, T'hami made her extravagant gifts of jewellery, and nursed his rancour against his nephew Ahmed Zemmouri.

We are reminded at this point of the anonymous comment upon a portion of Gustave Babin's book – 'The Glaoui never pardoned, never forgave.' So it was in this case. He used to the full his great influence with the Residency-General, and succeeded in obtaining from the Protectorate the destitution of Ahmed Zemmouri. Though, much later, the French had him restored to the minor position of *cadi* or religious judge, his career was broken.

More usually, however, the Glaoui had his way, either by intrigue or by recourse to violence, as in the following instance. One day his protection was sought by a rich private citizen who was the principal accused in a criminal case appearing before the Chereefian Tribunal of Marrakesh. T'hami, without concerning himself with the rights and wrongs of the matter, gave instructions to the new president, Omar ou Torza, at the same time making representations to the French judiciary authority Maître Giraud. Outraged by this interference, Giraud thought to cut the ground from under T'hami's feet by bringing the case before the tribunal at once, putting the date forward without announcement. It must have appeared to him that he had faced T'hami with a *fait accompli*. T'hami only learned of this manœuvre late in the evening before the hearing. Very early the next morning he left the palace and reached the courts before any functionary had as yet arrived. He sent his soldiers to the house of the clerk of the court, with orders to bring him and the documents in the case at once. If the clerk refused he was to be placed under instant arrest. The clerk and the dossier arrived under escort; T'hami took the dossier from him and tore it to shreds, handing the pieces back to him with the remark, 'Now tell your bosses to judge the matter.' He left the court at 8 a.m., courteously saluted by the entering Maître Giraud, who as yet had no idea of what had taken place. T'hami's protégé was acquitted and no more was heard of the incident.

The successful administration of the enormous area over which T'hami El Glaoui now ruled called not only for a suspicious nature but a highly efficient intelligence system, and he possessed both. He distrusted his servants and all of his functionaries but a handful of intimates, fearing (and often quite rightly) that they were in the pay of the French, or, later, in the pay of the independence movement. His spy network was enormous and costly, for there was no single administrative body of any importance which did not contain some secretary or small functionary corrupted by his generosity. Thus he was informed in advance of any complaints made about him to the Resident-General or to the Sultan, whether these were made by individuals or by tribes. He preferred his agents to be young and not too highly placed, and they would give their information either directly to him or to members of his immediate circle, either by telephone or by letter. His circle of intimates, in turn, would pass on to him all information of interest over tea-drinking sessions in the private quarters of the Palace, sessions at which the more important of his outside agents were often present as well. Concerning the affairs of Marrakesh itself, he was personally informed every morning between 10.30 and 11 a.m. of all that had taken place between 9 p.m. the evening before and 10 a.m. that morning; and again in the evening of the events of the day. Suspicion was enough – he never waited for proof nor gave any man the benefit of a doubt.

Much doubt has been cast upon the Glaoui's linguistic powers, so it may be worth recording here the facts as given to me by members of his personal entourage. Up till 1927 he spoke and understood little or no French. He began to learn in that year, and by 1931 he both spoke and understood adequately. By 1937 he was fluent, and also understood,

though did not speak, a little English. Despite his gradual mastery of French he never dispensed with an interpreter, though this may have been as much a means of gaining time for thought as by reason of strict necessity. The sequence of those employed as interpreters was: Ben Rummoukh, a Jew, from 1932–36 (when he died), M. Stora, a Frenchman from 1936–47 (when he died), Pérès, a Jew, until 1950, Mimram, a Jew (who had long been one of his financial advisers) until 1953, coeval with Berdugo, also a Jew. Mimram and Berdugo are both still alive, the one living in Paris and the other in Nice. From 1953 until T'hami's death in 1956 his son Abdessadek took over the work of interpreter.

This may have been an ill choice, for Abdessadek by no means shared his father's political views, and from early times had strong sympathies with the independence movement, the Istiqlal, which brought about the final downfall of the Glaoui régime. Of all his sons, only the eldest, Brahim, followed his father's politics absolutely and for better or for worse, leading him eventually to a sentence of fifteen years' exile from Morocco. The others were either uninterested in such matters or held views in definite opposition to the feudal régime. Ahmed, *khalifa* of the Haouz, had no politics, nor had Mohammed, *Caid* of the Mesfiouia, and he avoided trouble either with his father or with the Istiqlal or with the tribespeople over whom he ruled. Hassan was a boy, interested only in art, and later became a well-known painter in Paris, introduced to the public by Mrs Edward G. Robinson, wife of the American film actor. Madani, who had studied in Paris and Bordeaux, and later both in Algeria and Rabat, held views absolutely contrary to his father's; he saw far into the future, and considered the Glaoui empire to be a folly leading inevitably to disaster. He was a member of the Istiqlal, and

Old Berber earrings

later suffered imprisonment at his father's hands. Mehdi was an officer in the French army, and expressed no political views at all; nor did Abdallah.

They were not, in any case, a united family, for as is common in polygamous cultures the jealousies between their several mothers led to discord among the sons. Lalla Kamar, a Turkish lady, was the mother of Brahim, Ahmed, Abdallah and Madani; Lalla Fatma, a Berber from Telouet, was the mother of Mehdi; Lalla Zineb, daughter of the Grand Vizier El Mokri, was the mother of Hassan and Abdessadek; Lalla Halima, also from Turkey and ex-wife of Hammou, was the mother of Mohammed. T'hami feared his sons, and watched them for the least sign of political defection.

I I

The Image

T'HAMI's life during the 1930s was not yet overtly shadowed by the Istiqlal party, one which he never doubted would be controlled by traditional methods, and it was during these externally untroubled years that his myth reached its height. This myth he fostered by every means in his power, but chief among his stage properties remained an unequalled display of pomp and might. Each new French Resident-General was subjected to this treatment. In the case of M. Théodore Steeg, who succeeded Lyautey, the display required the co-operation of Hammou, but this T'hami was able to secure by persuading him that a demonstration of tribal might was in no way contrary to Hammou's spirit of intransigence.

The prelude to the exhibition was a banquet in the palace at Marrakesh, after which, in taking leave of his guest of honour, T'hami said, 'Excellency, tomorrow you are going to see the men and women of my country. They know little of France, but they know that they want peace. They know too that France is powerful. You have no need of soldiers of France to escort you – here peace reigns.'

The message that he had sent out to his tribespeople ran something as follows: 'El Hadj T'hami El Glaoui, Pasha of Marrakesh, requires you all, with your horses, your rifles and your women to line the route from Marrakesh to the pass of Tiz-n-Tishka. Every man will be armed and will see that his powder is dry. Every musician will come with flutes and tambourines. The women will wear their finest clothes; they will line the roadside and will sing with their finest voices as the procession of cars passes through their village. Every armed warrior will precede the procession to the pass of Tiz-n-Tishka, and will be there by dawn. On the arrival of the procession in the pass each man will fire his rifle twenty times.'

The procession was headed by the Glaoui's personal car, a giant 44 h.p. Renault of 1924, that jumped forward ten yards like some giant frog as each cylinder fired. At the wheel was his young Basque chauffeur Querlier, employed at the request of the French in 1927; Madame Querlier, then no more than twenty years of age or so, T'hami had placed in charge of his harem. (These two had replaced the previous French chauffeur and his wife, Monsieur and Madame Auguste. The Querliers acted as a general information service for the Glaoui and the French during periods of his absence from Marrakesh.)

The roads from Marrakesh to the Atlas passes were still under construction then; they were motorable, but only just so. Where they ran along the side of a river they were frequently awash, and to line a processional route was therefore a matter of hazard. On this occasion the snows were thawing, and the rivers were running high; many of the men and women were standing waist deep as the procession went by, and no doubt finding it difficult to sing in their finest voices. The men had been warned to be ready to push the cars if it proved necessary. It did. Steeg protested mildly about the display of nudity necessary for this purpose, since there were three French women among the guests; youths of the villages not unnaturally tucked their *djellabahs* up round their bare waists, but T'hami only replied with a smile, 'Is French anatomy so different from ours?'

Nevertheless the whole State party somehow reached Tiz-n-Tishka, and every village it had passed through had accorded the mass ovation demanded by the Glaoui's message. At the pass of Tiz-n-Tishka M. Steeg was confronted by a spectacle impressive even to his haughty, colonist's eyes, for no less than ten thousand mounted Berber warriors awaited them in the gorge, and each fired his rifle twenty times in salute. The noise was deafening; the fumes from the powder formed a huge drifting grey cloud against the mountain walls; and some French officials made rapid mental calculations on the expenditure involved in a salute of two hundred thousand rounds. The banquet took place in a vast tent of white wool, richly carpeted; several thousand women danced and drummed and sang, while several hundred black slaves were engaged in roasting sheep in traditional pit ovens and carrying the food on great silver dishes. At the end of the banquet the ten thousand mounted warriors formed a circle round the tent and saluted again the three figures of majesty, *Caid* Hammou, T'hami El Glaoui and the Resident-General.

Winston Churchill, who made T'hami's acquaintance in the early 1930s, also found such ceremonies impressive, and over the years there grew up between them a definite friendship, the mutual sympathy and respect that, as a post-Glaoui Moroccan put it to me, one great brigand feels for another.

T'hami seems, in fact, to have had an especial liking for the British, and said to a young English woman who was often his guest in the years between 1937 and 1939, 'If only it were the English and not the French who run my country!'

This young lady stayed often at the palace in Marrakesh and also at Telouet. When in Marrakesh she lived in the guest house attached to the palace, an annexe sumptuous but weirdly anachronistic. The vast bedrooms, walled and floored with magnificent Moroccan tiles, and carpeted with superb Berber rugs, contained hideous great brass bedsteads surmounted by brass crowns. Each of the numerous bathrooms contained two baths, and when she asked T'hami the reason for this, not without giggles, he replied in bewilderment, 'Don't Europeans like to talk together when they are having their baths?' This reply only increased her unseemly merriment, and the Glaoui appeared much distressed. He did not appear on the next morning, and his Vizier confided to the young lady that he had slept extremely badly because of the question of the bathrooms. He was, the Vizier explained, exceedingly sensitive to European opinion, and was afraid that she would mock his misunderstanding of western custom to other Europeans.

Over a period of eight months she saw him constantly; she rode his horses, played golf with him, dined with him as his personal guest every week, and as a result it was widely rumoured that she was to become one of his wives, though she had never for a moment entertained the thought. She was impressed by his exquisite manners and his thoughtfulness; he made no sexual approaches to her, and appeared actively to enjoy her company, but she felt that behind the façade he was both ruthless and treacherous, 'like every other oriental potentate'. She had the impression that both he and his eldest son *Caid* Brahim of Telouet had a literally insatiable desire for all that modern invention had to offer, but that at the same time they felt insecure without the traditional forms of pomp that made their status plain to the people.

Any departure from tradition in others was offensive to him; thus when in 1952 the son of the *cadi* (religious judge) of Marrakesh asked authorization to celebrate his marriage in European style, with bride unveiled and a procession of cars, T'hami refused point blank, saying that the ancient customs of the city must be respected. The young man, Bachir Ben Abbas Taarji (now Ambassador to the U.S.S.R.), defied this edict, and the cars were hired, but T'hami sent a detachment of his guards to countermand the order. Taarji riposted by celebrating the marriage in Casablanca, outside T'hami's jurisdiction, and in the manner he had planned. T'hami took sharp reprisals against the family, and, because the bridegroom was a member of the Istiqlal, the affair assumed a major political significance.

In sharp contrast to this insistence upon traditionalism in others, he took delight in displaying to European guests at Telouet his own small children of both sexes dressed in the briefest of shorts, after the manner of the French bourgeoisie on holiday.

During the English girl's stays at Telouet work on the decoration of the interior as a palace was in full swing, and everything was in chaos; there seemed to her to be thousands rather than hundreds of men engaged upon extension and beautification. *Caid* Brahim, then about twenty-two years of age, was full of enthusiasm for his plans, and constantly visited every part of the castle where work was in progress. At Telouet she went out riding daily with him or T'hami or both; behind them came carpet-bearers, carrying rolled on their heads great rugs which were spread on the ground at every stopping place so that the riders might admire the view in greater comfort. The head carpet-bearer was a man of great dignity and presence, tall, half-Negro, and very handsome; the English girl remarked on this to T'hami, and asked who he was. T'hami appeared a little embarrassed by the question; then he replied, 'As a matter of fact he is my uncle. He is not very clever, and this seemed to me to be the best way of employing him.'

She enjoyed life at Telouet, the luxury, the gracious living; she was not, of course, shown the dungeons and the just-living horrors they contained.

Her friendship with the Glaoui ended abruptly, when she dined one evening at the Italian Consulate; he hated all Italians with a bitter and ineradicable venom, probably because his mother, Lalla Zora, was of Ethiopian origin, and the brutal rape of Ethiopia by Mussolini was a thing of the very recent past.

T'hami at this time played golf to a handicap of plus four. (It is illogical, but strange, that the image of an amateur golf champion should be so hard to reconcile with that of an owner of active dungeons.) To Europeans who expressed surprise at his remarkable prowess, he would reply, 'Golf is not a new game to me. When I was a boy in the mountains I used to play a game called "*takoura*", which was very much the same. We used to play it on *jol* [pebble desert] with a stick whittled from an oak branch and a wooden ball.'

The construction of his private golf course, begun in the mid-1920s as a nine-hole course, and later enlarged to eighteen holes, had caused something of a scandal. The harm done by diversion of water supplies from cultivated lands was no doubt exaggerated by his enemies; in a land of habitual summer drought and periodic famine it was not a democratic piece of development, but the Glaoui was not democratic.

In 1924, following upon severe drought, there was an alarming fall in all agricultural produce, and Moroccan landed proprietors suffered severely curtailed revenues. T'hami, however, refused to share in a general retrenchment or resign himself to a lesser expenditure. He was confident in the future, and saw no reason either to alter his way of life or to expect less revenue from his lands. When the French general commanding the region of Marrakesh learnt at this time of a contract placed with a firm of specialists for the construction of a private golf course, he exceeded his duties and sent the Glaoui a letter, reproaching him with criminal waste. This letter was brought by a young officer of the general's command, and when the Glaoui had heard it read he merely remarked, 'Will you be so good as to tell the general that if I have a golf course made it must be with his full agreement, because

when it is finished I shall be in a position not only to hole out but to put a stop in *all* leakages.'

The course was constructed as planned, on the hitherto barren little stretch of desert, and at a cost of several million francs, and one of the best known professionals in France, M. Gustave Golias, engaged as instructor. He was later replaced by M. Massey; both are now dead, but the present (1965) manager of the golf course was the Glaoui's caddy.

Golf was more than a mild hobby; it became a passion and a ceaseless subject of conversation, rivalled only by talk of horses and of building, for he was as great a builder as had been Moulay Ismael.

On this golf course he organized championships every year, inviting players from all over the world, and throughout the period that the play lasted he gave orders to his *khalifas*, his sons and his entourage to give huge open air banquets. Many well-known personalities, including Winston Churchill, took part in friendly matches with the Glaoui, and it was on the golf course, too, that he initiated liaisons with the wives of various foreign diplomats whom he had invited. Before the Second World War he was never without European mistresses – some of them so highly placed that it can only have been with the full connivance of their husbands.

After 1939 T'hami became virtually impotent, and only one more child was born to him, a girl named Saadia, daughter of Lalla Zoubida, a girl from Tamdacht. Saadia was born in 1944, and he said of her with a smile that miracles could happen as well as accidents. Madame Querlier later became Saadia's governess.

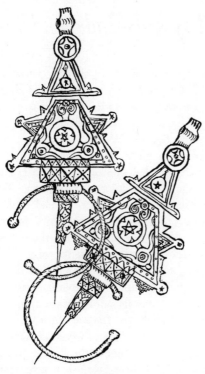

Haik *pins*

12

Towards Independence

THOUGH the great, convulsive crisis of Morocco was still years ahead, the embryo of the independence movement was already stirring. The French were blind not so much to the threat as to the futility of trying to deal with it by the traditional methods of colonialism. Even in these last years before the Second World War, every action they took towards its suppression gave the movement greater volume and impetus. In 1937 they exiled one of its young intellectual initiators, Allal El Fassi, to the French colony of Gaboon. (While in exile he learned to speak French – before then he had spoken only Arabic.) Others followed him to other French colonies, becoming martyrs in the eyes of their ex-colleagues, and fanning the hatred of France that was beginning to spread among the student group.

The other, coeval, move only contributed to the same end. From 1937, the French began to employ the Jewish youth of Morocco in all minor positions of Protectorate administration, as a blockade to the infiltration of newly-qualified Islamic Moroccan students whose political views might be anti-French. Over all Morocco some ten or fifteen per cent of minor posts under the Protectorate were nominally held by Moroccans, but of these more than seventy-five were in fact Jews. The small handful of Islamic Moroccans whom France proudly claimed to have educated were unable to find work in their own country; these formed the hard core of malcontents around whom the independence movement grew towards a virile maturity ten years later.

France was on the eve of war with Germany for the second time during her twenty-seven years occupancy of Morocco. Your enemy's enemy is your friend, and France was very definitely the enemy of the independence movement. Writing in *Son Excellence*, Gustave Babin made the incredible mistake of accusing the Glaoui of attempted collaboration with the Germans; this would have been unthinkable, for the Glaoui's very existence depended upon the continuation of the French occupation, while the downfall of the French at the hands of the Germans would have represented an enormous step forward to the independence movement. (Later writers who should have known better, such as Robert Barrat, prefaced by Mauriac, made the same mistake – this is perhaps best excused by a reminder that by that time feelings were running high enough to obscure fact.) The two Moroccans who would suffer most of all by independence were T'hami El Glaoui and *Caid* El Ayadi of the Rehamna, who were not on speaking terms with one another.

The collapse of France in 1940 found a strongly anti-Ally Resident-General in charge of Morocco – General Noguès. The rapid succession of Resident-Generals had reflected Morocco's unhealthy political atmosphere; after Steeg had come Colonel Lucien Saint, whose main claim to fame is the disastrous Berber *dahir*, aimed at frustrating nationalism by dividing Arabs and Berbers; and 1936 had seen Henri Ponsot, Marcel Peyrouton and General Noguès. Of him Eisenhower wrote that he was 'untrustworthy and worse', and Harry Hopkins recorded that he 'would not trust him as far as I could spit'. Noguès had, nevertheless, succeeded in reaching a genuine and affectionate understanding with the young Sultan Mohammed V.

With Germany in occupation of France, General Noguès willingly accepted his orders from the Vichy government, and the greater number of the larger French settlers in Morocco were unquestionably of the same persuasion. All these voices expressed a common viewpoint to the German Intelligence Service, that the independence movement was of no real significance in the country; and, effectively misled by this derogation, the German commission did not make any serious attempt to liaise with its leaders, who had in any case identified themselves with the Sultan's proclamation on the outbreak of war: 'From today and until such time as the efforts of France and her allies are crowned with victory, we must render her every help without reserve.'

The German Commission arrived in Marrakesh in 1939, and was officially welcomed by General d'Hauteville, commanding the Marrakesh region, Colonel Ribaud, and other southern representatives of the Protectorate. They remained in Marrakesh, living in the Mamounia Hotel, until the American landings in 1943. General Noguès and his subordinates remained, by order of the Vichy government, in close liaison with the Commission, but it was clear to the Germans that the pro-Vichy Protectorate officials represented an extreme minority, and they turned their attention to the two 'ruling' Moroccans, the Sultan and the Glaoui.

The Sultan Mohammed Ben Youssef – despite the fact that by now his personal sympathies lay wholly on the side of the independence movement – refused to receive the German Commission. This was from no sense of misplaced loyalty towards the occupying French, whom he detested, but because he had no wish to exchange them for a new master whose racial policies were an affront to the whole Moroccan nation. (About one-sixteenth of the country's entire population were of the Jewish faith, while more than double that fraction were of Jewish race but converted to Islam during the eighteenth century.)

Failing with the Sultan, the Commission tried to obtain audience from the Glaoui in 1942. What proposition they intended to put forward to this extremely improbable ally, whose fortunes were wholly linked to the French *ancien régime*, will never be known with certainty, for he, too, refused to see them. Four of their officers left the Mamounia Hotel one morning by car, and drove to the Glaoui's palace, where they presented an official card to the porter on duty. T'hami replied through his secretary, saying that he had no dealings with the German Commission, and if they had anything of importance to communicate they had only to address themselves to General d'Hauteville commanding the Marrakesh region, or to the Resident-General, Noguès, at Rabat. The four officers retired visibly ruffled by this message.

On the question of attitude towards the German Commission, the Glaoui and the Resident-General showed a common front, even though Noguès later resisted the American landings and caused much unnecessary bloodshed. Tangier, where T'hami had a summer residence, was at that time an international city, and it was there that T'hami's *khalifa* Moulay Larbi El Aloui made the acquaintance in 1942 of some of the members of the German Commission, on the golf course. These he invited to T'hami's Tangier residence, together with the Sultan's representative in Tangier, Mohammed Tazi. This caused Noguès to telephone to T'hami in Marrakesh, asking him if he was aware of his *khalifa*'s action. He said that he was not, and demanded explanation from Moulay Larbi, who replied that his acquaintance with members of the German Commission was fortuitous, and his invitation a matter of common courtesy. Neither the Glaoui nor the French were satisfied with this explanation, and he was relegated to the post of Vizier of Justice at Rabat. (Much later, the French restored him to grace, and he was made Pasha of Settat, in which post he died.)

The net of espionage, counter-espionage and intrigue that existed at the time is well illustrated by the incident of Omar the guide, which took place in the same year. Omar had obtained his plaque on the customary condition that he reported to the police everything of possible interest concerning his foreign clients. The Marrakesh police inspector, Bel Mokhtar, was charged with the surveillance of the German Commission, and he in his turn handed over the detailed work to Omar the guide, whose duty was to report without attracting any attention to himself all their comings and goings and the descriptions of their visitors. This was supposed to be a day and night job, hanging about outside the Mamounia Hotel as guides often do; but one evening, suffering bitterly from the cold, and believing the inspector to be away, he went home to warm himself and to sleep. He returned to his post very early in the morning, but during the night the inspector had made a surprise round of his spies and found Omar absent.

Bel Mokhtar submitted a report to the Glaoui, signed by the commissioner of police, in which Omar was accused of clandestine liaison with the German commission. Omar was charged, arrested and held at the Glaoui's disposition. The Glaoui instructed his Chamberlain, Hadj Idder, to bring Omar before him. Omar prostrated himself before the Pasha, kissing his shoes and crying, and told the whole truth, adding that this was a trumped-up charge to punish him for his disobedience.

Hadj Idder spoke for the guide, saying that he knew him to be an honest man who had no liaison with the Germans, and the Glaoui then asked Omar how much he earned from the police for his espionage. Nothing, Omar replied; only the plaque that allowed him to be an official guide. Then how much did he earn as a guide? That depended:

there were good days and bad days, generous tourists and mean tourists
– a maximum of five thousand francs a week. The Glaoui pondered a
moment, then he said, 'Here are five thousand francs, and from now on
you will work for me and not for the police. Give all the information
you acquire to my *khalifa*, Si Bel Abbas.' Omar became a faithful and
assiduous member of the Glaoui's information service, and as such
enjoyed immunity from any further police action.

In November 1942 Allied troops landed in North Africa. General
Noguès gave orders to resist American occupation, but on instructions
from General Darlan (Algeria) surrendered three days later.

In January 1943 the Allies convened the Casablanca Conference to
confer on the liberation of Europe from Nazi Germany. The conference
took place at the Hotel d'Anfa, outside Casablanca, and included
President Roosevelt, Elliot Roosevelt, Harry Hopkins, Winston Churchill, General Noguès, General de Gaulle, General Ribaud, the Sultan
of Morocco and his eldest son Moulay Hassan. The only two guests who
did not enjoy the party were General Noguès, who rightly feared his
early dismissal, and Winston Churchill, who suffered acutely from the
absence of alcohol on which President Roosevelt had insisted in
deference to the Sultan's religion. (His programme for the day, noted
to Harry Hopkins for information read: 'Dinner. At the White House
(dry, alas!) with the Sultan. After dinner recovery from the above.')

Roosevelt and the Sultan made a markedly favourable impression
upon each other, and the Sultan saw in America the possible instrument
that would liberate him from France. Roosevelt certainly did nothing
to discourage this belief, and six months later the Sultan sought a second
interview, this time in private and without the presence of any officer
of the French Protectorate. This meeting also took place at the Hotel
d'Anfa, and again Winston Churchill was present. For the description
of what took place at this meeting I have relied on the account given
to my informant by *Caid* El Ayadi of the Rehamna, who was at that
time a close personal friend of the Sultan.

Roosevelt spontaneously asked the Sultan for his opinion on the
French Protectorate, and the Sultan replied at length, saying that it was
no Protectorate but an oppressive colonialism, and that his aim was to

liberate his country. He described the growth of the independence movement, stating that it had his absolute support in so far as was consistent with his pledged word to the French to support them until they were victorious in the war against Germany. Roosevelt told him in reply that he could have confidence in the independent future of his country, and that meanwhile he should rigorously guard the mineral rights of his country from exploitation by the occupying power. This conversation appeared far from pleasing to Churchill, who did everything in his power to interrupt it by violent and loud fits of coughing which he punctuated only by reiterated excuses that this was due to a new brand of cigar that he was smoking. However, El Ayadi noted, he continued to smoke his cigar and to cough.

This meeting gave more impetus to the independence movement than any other single happening to date, for it convinced the Sultan that President Roosevelt stood solidly behind the concept of an independent Morocco. That same year the various fractions of the independence movement united under the name of the Istiqlal Party, founded by Ahmed Balafrej and Mohammed Lyazidi. Roosevelt, however, died two years later, and it became plain at once that Truman had no such clear-cut ideas.

General Noguès, receiving at least as much news of the Sultan's meeting with Roosevelt as to disquiet him considerably, decided to try to detach El Ayadi from the Sultan and ally him to the Glaoui, who could be counted upon to resist the Istiqlal to the limit of his powers. The Glaoui and El Ayadi were the two greatest feudal overlords, and their concerted opposition could do much to obstruct the Sovereign's policies, but unfortunately they were not on speaking terms. This obstacle the French finally overcame by arranging a marriage between the two families, and then turned their attention to using against the Sultan the massive weapon they had thus forged.

This weapon was not the responsibility of General Noguès, for in the same year as the Sultan's meeting with Roosevelt he was replaced as Resident-General by M. Gabriel Puaux. Noguès had formed a real and close friendship with the Sultan, too close for the war that was to follow, and when they said goodbye both were weeping.

Sultan Mohammed V, 1927–53 and 1955–61

In January 1944 Puaux was received by the Sultan for the purpose of discussing the general state of the country. The Sultan spoke at length, and, in the belief that Puaux intended to arrest leading members of the Istiqlal on a charge of collaboration with the Germans, said that he could only guarantee the good conduct of his subjects on the absolute condition that there must be no political arrests. The interview ended at 5 p.m.; at eleven o'clock on the same evening Balafrej, Lyazidi and sixteen other Istiqlal leaders were arrested. The following day there were riots at Rabat and at Fez, and French troops fired on the crowds, killing a number of men and some children.

Istiqlal published its manifesto, thoughtful and well-reasoned, opening with the sentence, 'The essential condition for the revival of Morocco is its independence, because a country unable to enjoy the various attributes of sovereignty is inevitably destined to remain the slave of that which holds it down.'

The Sultan, fearing bloodshed which he believed could be avoided, associated himself less actively with Istiqlal, though his belief in the necessity for independence never wavered. The general state of Morocco's unrest ran steadily from bad to worse, and the hopes of the Protectorate were more and more centred upon T'hami El Glaoui.

In March 1946 Erick Labonne succeeded Puaux as Resident-General. Labonne's first action was to liberate the exiled leaders of Istiqlal, including Allal El Fassi, who had been in Gaboon since 1937. More, he received these nationalist leaders weekly at the Residency. 'We are dealing,' he wrote to the Council of Government on 22 July 1946, 'with the necessity of giving all sections of the Moroccan people, and to its youth both male and female, a feeling of certainty that life in all its aspects is wide open to their own efforts, the use of their own intelligence, and the exercise of their own faculties.'

In April 1947 he conceived the idea of a State visit of the Sultan to Tangier, as a reminder to all Morocco and the outside world of his spiritual sovereignty over the whole country, including the international and Spanish zones. The speech he would make at Tangier was carefully prepared, and contained a paragraph announcing solidarity with France, and recalling the friendship that united the two countries.

Three days before his departure for Tangier there was violent rioting in Casablanca. The cause remains obscure, but appears to have started in a brothel quarter as a quarrel between French Senegalese soldiers and Moroccans. The Senegalese returned to their barracks and fetched their rifles and ammunition. Fighting lasted two hours, and there were more than two hundred killed and wounded, including women and children. When the Sultan read his speech at Tangier, he omitted the paragraph concerning France, for at the moment it could have seemed no more than a mockery; but the Press had already been circulated with the original text, and the worst conclusions were drawn as a result of its omission. It was regarded as a declaration of war.

Monsieur Labonne did not long survive this incident. He was felt by the massive colonial interests to be far too progressive, and on 14 May 1947 he was replaced by General Juin. Labonne had, in any case, come too late; Morocco had, over the past thirty-five years, come to expect nothing from France but lies and deceit.

Juin was clever, able, a politician by instinct, and a man of great personal charm, but with the notable failing that he could tolerate no one with similar qualities on his staff. Under his régime the great French industrialists became the people of importance in Morocco, their interests considered necessarily identical with those of metropolitan France.

Juin had something of T'hami El Glaoui's love of pomp and splendour and protocol; he liked glittering uniforms, beautiful women and lavish parties, and he enjoyed the magnificence of the Residency-General. Years later an old Negro slave, showing me the cracking painted plasterwork of the great reception rooms at Telouet, said in halting French, 'It was beautiful. Very beautiful – more beautiful than General Juin.'

Juin arrived with the intention of removing from the Sultan even the vestigial powers that he had enjoyed under previous Resident-Generals. He began this campaign by an oblique move; he added to the seven ministers allowed to the Sultan five Moroccan delegates of the Grand Vizier, each of them attached to the French administrative departments of finance, commerce, health, public works and agriculture. By this step the *mahkzen* lost what little autonomy had remained to it, for all meetings now required French representation. The Sultan signed this

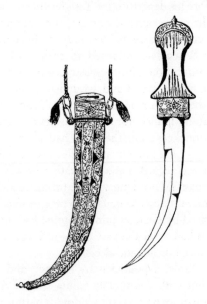

dahir, but refused to sign many more whose objects were transparently to put the French Resident-General upon the Chereefian Throne of Morocco.

Force failing at least temporarily, the President of the French Republic, M. Auriol, tried blandishment. In 1950 he invited the Sultan with all his family and his court to visit Paris in October. After some hesitation the Sultan accepted, with a proviso that this should be made the occasion for a discussion of Morocco's problems. On 11 October the Sultan arrived in Paris with his whole vast retinue, numbering four figures, and with him he brought T'hami El Glaoui, for the two were not yet sworn enemies. The Sultan received the most extravagant welcome that one Head of State can accord to another, and at first the negotiations appeared promising. But as the Sultan grew more precise in his demands a creeping paralysis set in, until, having received no reply to his last note to the President, the Sultan cut his visit short and returned to Morocco. T'hami El Glaoui remained in Paris at the request of M. Auriol. It was as though an echo of Madani's voice came down the long years, 'You do not know my brother T'hami – he is a dagger with which one may strike, but which one must afterwards discard.' For the French did both.

13

The First March of the Berber Warriors

JUIN had come to Morocco with instructions from the French Government that if the Sultan showed himself too obstructive there should be 'either a voluntary abdication or a deposition provoked by the French authorities themselves'.

The basis of his policy to that end was to create open enmity between the Sultan and the Glaoui, and thus to confront the Sultan with the whole of T'hami's might in open opposition to him.

The plan was carefully thought out, and executed with precision. At the Imperial Palace the instrument of French propaganda was a cousin of the Sultan's, Moulay Larbi El Aloui; while in the case of T'hami the Protectorate made use of every available source, French and Moroccan. Under the orchestration of General Juin, the Glaoui received insistent reports from many apparently different sources that the Istiqlal was primarily directed not at the French but at the Glaoui empire, and that this was the personal responsibility of the Sultan. At the same time Moulay Larbi El Aloui encouraged the Sultan to believe that Juin was not fundamentally opposed to the Istiqlal, and pointed as evidence of this fact to his institution of a bi-partite Government Council, whose elected members included prominent Moroccan nationalists. (In writing his own account of his proconsulate, General Juin wrote, 'I found it quite legitimate that [the Sultan] should show himself to be a patriot and anxious for the emancipation of his people. I even declared this publicly.') The true threat to the Sultan's policy was therefore the Glaoui, who had refused at any time to meet a member of the Istiqlal, and by doing so had defied his Sultan.

The desired climate of mutual suspicion and animosity between Sultan and Glaoui had been created by the time of the winter assembly of the Government Council in November 1950. The first few days of session were stormy, the nationalist members making forthright speeches, and General Juin allowing himself a considerable display of public anger. Matters culminated on 12 December in a speech by Mohammed Laghzaoui, which accused the French of exploiting Morocco for her own ends, without regard to the welfare of the people. General Juin interrupted him, shouting, and formally expelled him from the chamber. Laghzaoui rose to leave, and as he did so he was followed by nine others, the only Moroccan members who had been elected by their countrymen as opposed to having been nominated by Juin.

This, the curtain-raiser to the whole drama, took place on the eve of the feast of Mouloud, one of the great religious occasions when all Pashas and *Caids* came to Rabat to prostrate themselves before their Sultan in private audience, with the words '*Allah ibarek fi amer Sidna!*' (May Allah bless our Lord) and to present him with the customary gift, or *hediya*. The Glaoui had always been the first to be received, and the magnificence of his gifts was legendary. Now he was requested by the French to use this audience for the purpose of remonstration with the Sultan about his political policies.

On this occasion it was not he but the ten Istiqlal members of the Council of Government who were the first to have audience with the Sultan. Moulay Larbi El Aloui was charged with lighting the fuse by saying to the Sultan, 'I want to tell Your Majesty that that nigger Hadj T'hami El Glaoui is going to reproach you with having received Laghzaoui in private audience after he had been expelled from the Council chamber by General Juin.'

The Glaoui, knowing nothing of these preparations, left the Hotel Balima by car at 9 a.m. on 21 December 1950 with his son *Caid* Brahim and his Chamberlain Hadj Idder. In the second car were his courtiers and secretaries. The Glaoui and his son arrived in the *mechouar* or inner court, and waited for seven minutes – an unprecedented delay that was tantamount to a stinging insult. At length the Sultan's Chamberlain appeared and said, 'Excellency, His Majesty is ready to receive you.' The Glaoui followed him, and after having made his obeisance began immediately upon an attack on the Istiqlal and the Sultan's support of it, saying that these hooligans would bring the name of the throne into world disrepute. The Sultan cut him short, saying, 'Listen, Your Excellency. From now on you will have to change your outlook, because we are going to work for the independence of Morocco.' The Glaoui expostulated that the country was not ready for independence, that it was not unified, that the family of Glaoui had sworn perpetual loyalty to the French. The conversation went on so long that those who were waiting outside began open speculation as to what could be going on between the Sultan and the Glaoui.

The moment that the French had planned came at last. The Glaoui lost his temper, and, rising to his feet, shouted, 'You are nothing but the shadow of a Sultan! You are not the Sultan of Morocco – you are the Sultan of the Istiqlal!' With that he left, and passed through the astonished courtyard with his face twisted by anger. He entered his car without giving any explanation to anyone, and returned to the Hotel Balima.

Immediately after he had left, Moulay Larbi El Aloui entered to the Sultan and asked, 'What did you do with that nigger? Why didn't you have him arrested or expelled from the country?'

T'hami, his anger but little cooled, was in session with his courtiers at the Hotel Balima, discussing the effects of what had happened, when the Sultan's Grand Vizier, El Mokri, telephoned requesting the Glaoui's presence at the Palace immediately. The interview was brief. 'Excellency,' said the Grand Vizier, 'His Majesty desires me to tell you that he refuses to receive you ever again, or to have any further dealings with you of any description. You are to return to the South immediately, and you are never again to set foot in any of His Majesty's palaces.'

The French had achieved the first step in their elaborate plan for suppression of the Istiqlal.

The next step, lasting only a few weeks, was a tour by the Glaoui of all his southern domains, to assure himself of the full support of all his *Caids*.

On 26 January 1951 General Juin demanded of the Sultan that he should denounce the Istiqlal. The Sultan replied that he could not denounce any party – as Sultan he was above all political parties. Juin dropped all pretence, and replied, 'Your reply is unacceptable. Either

you disown the Istiqlal party or you abdicate from the throne. Otherwise I shall depose you myself. I am now leaving for Washington. On
my return we shall see what we have to do.'

On his return on 12 February 1951 the General was even more
exacting and even tougher. The Sultan demurred; then finally signed
a proclamation drawn up by his Viziers, a proclamation so vague and
equivocal that its exaction under duress could have been doubted by no
one. General Juin wrote later, 'Understanding that I was being trifled
with, I severed all relations with the Palace.'

Mounted Berber warriors

The Sultan telegraphed to the President of the French Republic,
M. Auriol, asking for intervention, but the reply, received on 25
February, was not encouraging.

Juin gave the word to T'hami El Glaoui to move in accordance with
their prearranged plan. What followed was a piece of trickery so
gigantic that it must be difficult to find its parallel in the history of any
nation. Just as the Sultan Moulay Hafid had acquired himself an army
by inviting all the members of the Gennaoua sect to a banquet at his
palace and then keeping them there, so T'hami launched the whole
might of his southern mounted warriors against Fez and Rabat without

giving them an inkling of the true reason. They marched on the northern cities in their thousands, some believing that they were to undergo compulsory vaccination, some that the Sultan was giving a free distribution of sugar-cones, others that there was to be a great feast of which they had no detailed knowledge. The author has spoken to one who believed that the warriors of his tribe were to parade in honour of the Sultan. They did not, in short, know that they represented a spontaneous revolt of the Berber tribes against the Sultan of Morocco, demanding his deposition.

It was as such that General Juin presented them. The *mise en scène* was complete; French armoured troops surrounded the Sultan's palace to protect him from the peaceable and bewildered multitude encamped around the city. On 25 February 1951 General Juin presented his ultimatum, through the Sultan's Minister of Protocol, Si Mammeri; if he did not sign he would be deposed in two hours. After many comings and goings between the French Residency-General and the Palace, Juin obtained the documents he required, which included an official condemnation of 'a certain party' by the Grand Vizier, and an additional paragraph from the Sultan recognizing France's generosity towards Morocco.

General Juin wrote that he himself felt a great personal relief, and once the documents were signed he was able to turn to the great chiefs encamped outside the wall and convince them that all they had to do now was to take their tribesmen home peacefully. (They didn't even get their sugar, or a vaccination.)

It was a compromise, and an unsatisfactory one from all points of view. It satisfied Juin's vanity, but it had altered nothing. Nor had it satisfied the Glaoui's determination to see the Sultan dethroned; an event which he had felt certain of accomplishment forthwith when he gave orders for the tribespeople to march.

In April 1951 the Istiqlal united with two other opposition parties, giving to the nationalist movement a unity and solidarity that it had never possessed before.

At the end of August 1951 General Juin was recalled, and General Guillaume put in his place. Guillaume was not a novice to Morocco;

he had been a local commander during the pacification of the Middle Atlas, and had been director of political affairs under General Noguès from 1940 to 1943. He arrived charged with the mission of re-establishing friendly relations with the Sultan and creating a spirit of co-operation.

His first action was to reassure the southern chiefs and *Caids* that they had nothing to fear in the way of vengeance from the Sultan for their part in General Juin's *mise en scène* of massed tribesmen outside the walls of Rabat and Fez. T'hami El Glaoui, however, had already made up his mind absolutely that there was no means of implementing such promises other than by deposition of the Sultan, and by the time of General Guillaume's arrival he was wholly and absolutely dedicated to this end.

Meanwhile the Sultan, who despite the recent happenings maintained an inflexible determination to independence, benefited greatly by an able propaganda service, notably in Cairo, the United States and in French left-wing intellectual circles. The spearhead of this propaganda was the tenet that the Sultan alone, as spiritual leader of his people, had the right to speak in his country's name; as he himself said to a French journalist, 'Morocco thinks through the person of her Sovereign.' Rom

Landau, a European Jew long resident in Morocco and a prolific writer, gave his wholehearted support to the Sultan's policy, and published in this same year a biography, *The Sultan of Morocco*, that did much to put the Sultan's plight in its true perspective.

Guillaume tried to create an impression of frankness and bonhomie in presenting the Moroccan picture to the world; a 'nothing to hide – come and look for yourselves' atmosphere that was the very opposite of the measures he was in fact taking – arrests and expulsions of pro-Istiqlal foreign journalists, restriction of visas, threats and sanctions. His true policy was in no essential different from that of his predecessor General Juin, under whose remote thumb he was, indeed, freely rumoured to be.

On 4 October 1951 the Arab Group demanded that the Moroccan question should be put before the United Nations. On 18 November 1951, the Sultan said in his Speech from the Throne that he hoped for a new relationship with France, based upon full national sovereignty. T'hami El Glaoui's reaction to this speech was a series of urgent injunctions that the French should waste no more time in deposing the Sultan. He put forward precise suggestions as to the method of doing this, and urged traditional methods for total extirpation of the Istiqlal party. The French President M. Auriol was confronted by an increasingly formed world opinion, and though the Glaoui's proposals were noted and filed, the day of deposition was still indefinitely postponed.

On 20 March 1952 General Guillaume transmitted a letter from the Sultan to M. Auriol, requesting permission to form a representative government capable of negotiating with France in the name of the Palace. At the same time the Istiqlal issued a statement offering to guarantee French rights and interests in Morocco under a new convention; offering, in effect, coexistence within a Morocco governed by Moroccans. This cut the ground sharply from beneath the feet of the French colonial propagandists, who had persistently represented the nationalist aims as total expulsion of the French. Since it was not very easy to see what to do in face of these shockingly moderate requests, the French did nothing. The Sultan received no reply to his letter until 17 September – a lapse of almost six months. When this reply did come it was devious, evasive, largely irrelevant, and wholly unacceptable;

parts of it, indeed, were contrary to the terms of the Protectorate Treaty of 1912.

The Sultan answered on 3 October, politely as always, more in sorrow than in anger. It is at this stage that one is struck by the inflexible pertinacity of his attitude in the face of what must have seemed over-whelming odds.

On 7 and 8 December 1952 there were massive riots and mass murder in Casablanca. Owing to an official policy of distortion and suppression of fact, the exact number of fatal casualties has never been determined. The official announcement was thirty-eight Muslims and five Euro-peans. Eye-witnesses put the number of Moroccan dead at a minimum of five hundred on the second day alone, the majority of these deaths being caused by machine-gun fire into the heart of the crowds. European deaths have been established as four. 'In fact the machine-guns fired from the intersections of the main streets, and literally mowed down the dense crowds of rioters, causing at least five hundred deaths.'

The overt cause of the riots was the assassination in Tunis of an Arab nationalist named Ferhat Hashed and a resulting strike among Moroccan workers. A first press headline was contradicted the next day in such small type as to be hardly legible; by that time reprisal lynchings by Frenchmen had already taken place, counter-reprisals by Moroccans, and machine-gunning by French police of Moroccan crowds. At the same time there were incidents in Rabat and Beni Mellal. At Rabat five Istiqlal leaders were arrested, and a crowd gathered demanding their liberation. An unidentified passing car fired on this crowd, killing three Moroccans. At Beni Mellal seventeen were killed.

These incidents were followed by the mass arrests of all the prominent nationalists and Istiqlal leaders. In addition to several thousand house arrests and local deportations (exile to Glaoui tribal territory and to internment camps in the South) seventy-five Istiqlal leaders were actually incarcerated, and a hundred and sixty-seven other Moroccans were sentenced to one year's imprisonment for rebel activities against the French. General Guillaume is stated to have told a French government functionary that he would never accept an official commission of inquiry into the events at Casablanca – he would sooner resign. The investigation finally came in 1954, and it did at least establish that the Istiqlal was innocent of any involvement in the riots; none of the charges against the great number of prisoners could be upheld. The inquiry also revealed acknowledged torture of prisoners – an official remarking, 'Well, the Gestapo would have done worse.'

In the eyes of the world, and considerably aided by the commentaries of Mauriac and others, the Casablanca massacre did enormous harm to the French cause.

By this stage it must be emphasized that the motives of all conflicting parties, whether basically ideological, mercenary or world-political, were strongly overlaid by individual animus and venom. The events of the past few years, many contrived, some fortuitous, had combined to produce elements of strong personal hatred, strictly emotional even when they were capable of rationalization.

T'hami El Glaoui, now sworn to depose the Sultan and humiliate him as he himself had been humiliated, was engaged in rigorous personal measures against every citizen of the South who was even remotely suspected of nationalist sympathies. The dungeons of his many southern *kasbahs* were at this time fuller than at any date since the official pacification of the South in 1934.

Even his own household was suspect. One of his wives, Lalla Chems, a well-educated Turkish lady of great intelligence, exchanged continual correspondence with her parents in Turkey. Because she wrote in Persian script she found herself under her master's suspicious surveillance, and had to entrust the posting of her letters to Mme Querlier, his Basque chauffeur's wife whom he had placed in charge of his womenfolk. (Chems had had a strange history. In 1925 she had been given in marriage by her parents to Hadj Omar Tazi, who sold her to T'hami for a large cash sum, though the transaction was represented as an exchange of gifts. She wrote in urgent protest to her parents, who immediately sent her brother to Morocco to investigate. He was bewildered to find her living as a queen in T'hami's palaces and expressing herself thoroughly contented with her lot. He and T'hami then became friends, and exchanged frequent presents thereafter, the Turkish presents consisting of rare cigarettes carrying T'hami's insignia in gold letters. It was Chems, who herself remained childless, who initiated the idea of a French metropolitan education for T'hami's sons, and their marriage to French women. She remained his favourite wife until the end.)

Neither his confidants nor his own sons escaped the purge. One of his trusted entourage T'hami dismissed on a charge of spying for the Sultan, saying, 'Go, and take your parents with you. I will not have spies in my own house; consider yourself fortunate that my dungeons are already full.'

Links of an Hispano-Moorish silver necklace

One of T'hami's sons, Madani, had long foreseen the disaster that lay before the House of Glaoua, and saw clearly that the present measures could not in the end be regarded as more than delaying tactics. To his father, who chanced to be in Paris, he wrote a long and reasoned letter, in which he pointed out that the nationalist movement in North Africa – personified at that time by Tunisia – was bound to triumph, and that T'hami's policy could do nothing but detract from Morocco's wellbeing and the name of Glaoui. As a result of this letter, Madani was instantly arrested and imprisoned, first under the custody of his brother *Caid* Brahim at Telouet, and subsequently that of his brother Mohammed at Aït Ourir.

T'hami's son Abdessadek, *khalifa* and interpreter to his father,

City gate

maintained an external political neutrality, but was secretly of the same mind as Madani, and was in fact a clandestine member of Istiqlal, fearing France and fearing his father.

An incident in connection with T'hami's political arrests illustrates the absolute terror that his power could inspire. A group of innocent relations of some of the arrested men decided to petition for the release of those whom they could prove to be without Istiqlal connections, and to this end they presented themselves at the Dar El Glaoui at the hour when he was accustomed to give audience. Led in by the Chamberlain Hadj Idder, they went through the usual protocol of homage, and when they had composed themselves T'hami asked what they wanted. They fidgeted, looked furtively at one another, and said nothing. T'hami stared icily at their silent spokesman, and remarked, 'I have received you because I assumed that you had something to say. What is it?'

'Excellency,' stammered the leader, 'We are come to ask whether the deliveries of meat can be made earlier in the mornings. The hour of the present deliveries is really extraordinarily inconvenient both for the merchants and for the customers who buy from them – and we knew that if we presented the case directly to Your Excellency, Your Excellency would immediately understand the difficulties and give orders for them to be rectified. . . .'

'Very well,' said T'hami, 'the matter will be looked into. You may go.'

14

The Deposition of Mohammed V

THE New Year 1953 opened with a majority French slogan, used ironically by *Paris-Match* as headline to a distinctly anti-colonialist article, 'The Sultan must change or we must change him.'

No such alternative events presented themselves to the mind of T'hami El Glaoui; he was going to depose the Sultan whether the French decided it to be necessary or not, and he had already gone far in his preparations.

It is at this point that we should reintroduce Abd El Hay Kittani, to whom passing reference has been made on page 112 of this book. His brother had been beaten to death at the hands of Moulay Hafid in 1912, and he had sworn vengeance upon the whole of the Alaouite dynasty.

Kittani was a *Chereef*, or descendant of the Prophet, through the extinct Idrissite dynasty of Sultans, and he was the head of an important religious brotherhood or *zaouia*, the Kittaniyine. For a long time such brotherhoods had played an important part in Moroccan life, for religion and politics had always proved inseparable. The *zaouia* were off the orthodox path of pure Islam, akin to the veneration of *marabouts* or local saints, and had always been distrusted by Sultans, as undermining the central spiritual authority of the throne. (There were seven principal *zaouias*, the others being the Tijaniyine, to which the Glaoui belonged, the Derkaouiyine, the Nasiriyine, the Kadiriyine, Ouezzanayine and Aissaouiyine.)

The Kittaniyine had their headquarters at Fez, and counted, between Morocco and Algeria, some fifteen thousand members. Kittani himself (who owed his name to an ancestor's popularization of the cotton – *kitan* – tent versus the traditional skin article) had the white-bearded blue-eyed head of an old Norse patriarch. He was one of the greatest religious scholars in all Morocco, and also possessed a magnificent and largely pilfered library. He was a personal friend of T'hami El Glaoui, and an agile and assiduous political schemer. These two now united to depose the Sultan, and so vast were these forces that Juin and Guillaume had released that it is doubtful whether the French could by now have stopped them had they wished.

T'hami and Kittani formed a joint plan of action, each using his energies in the sphere where he was most likely to be successful. T'hami was to rally all the southern *Caids* and notables to sign a petition denouncing the Istiqlal and the Sultan as its leader; Kittani was to unite all the seven *zaouia* in the same protest, demanding the Sultan's deposition. These campaigns were to run simultaneously during the spring of 1953.

T'hami's grand tour of the South, conspicuously attended by glittering French uniforms, was not wholly successful. He collected some two hundred and seventy signatures, but amongst these there were only two Pashas and some fifty *Caids* – who significantly did not include El Ayadi of the Rehamna. The temporary alliance achieved by General Juin had given place to the older and more stable rivalry and mistrust. El Ayadi had now declared his loyalty to the Sultan. It was easy for Kittani's opponents, who now included a strong body of metropolitan French intellectuals, to show that the remainder were unimportant lackeys of the Glaoui-French régime, and already compromised by participation in the march on Fez and Rabat in 1951.

Kittani's paper success was more complete, but its intention – in demanding the Sultan's deposition for reasons of 'modernist heresy' – went beyond that envisaged by France, and on the last day of Kittani's congress a telephone call from Paris requested him to confine his text to denunciation of the Istiqlal.

France had, in fact, foreseen the danger that the spirit of vengeance animating T'hami and Kittani had minimized – the immediate and uncompromising intervention of the *Oulema*, the orthodox religious council of Morocco, without whom no Sultan could rightfully be either deposed or elected. The *Oulema* denounced both Kittani's congress and T'hami's petition – saying of the first that the *zaouia* lacked any authority to make protest against the central religious authority, and of the second that the signatories were puppets in the hands of a puppet. In this they over-stressed the overriding authority of the French, for the matter was now a struggle to the death between the last of the Lords of the Atlas and the reigning Sultan. In the final analysis it was the French who were now the tools of the Glaoui's vengeance rather than the reverse, even though it was they who had intentionally created the quarrel.

Not only did the Glaoui fail to obtain the more influential names as signatories to his petition, but he earned their public protest, for the Pashas of Rabat, Casablanca, Fez and Sefrou published a violent denunciation of the Glaoui, stating that even the signatures he had obtained had been 'extorted'.

In May T'hami took his petition to Paris in person, and was received in private audience by the President, M. Auriol. He went on to London to attend as a personal guest of Winston Churchill the Coronation of Queen Elizabeth II. The British Press seemed to be ill-informed of his status at the ceremony. The *Daily Telegraph* of 23 May announced that he would attend as an official guest; *The Times* was more accurate in this respect, but predicted that he would 'present the Queen with a gold crown, set with emeralds, and made by craftsmen of Marrakesh, and the Duke of Edinburgh with a gold dagger'.

The crown and the dagger were to be his price for the honour he coveted most – an English knighthood, the final seal of respectability. Moulay Abd El Aziz's Minister of War, Mehdi El Menhebbi, had got one by attending the Coronation of King Edward VII, and no other had ever been granted to a Moroccan. The precedent seemed, no doubt, auspicious, but T'hami had either overlooked the difference in status between an official and an unofficial guest, or he had thought that the crown and the dagger would adjust the balance. They did not; they were refused, and the reasons were clearly enough explained in a letter to the *Guardian* (then *Manchester Guardian*) from Mr Fenner Brockway, Labour M.P. for Eton and Slough, on 10 June 1953.

'Sir, All of us will recognize the right of the Prime Minister to invite his personal foreign guests to the Coronation, but it should be made clear that the visit of El Glaoui, the Pasha of Marrakesh, was entirely unofficial. This was indicated by the refusal of the Palace to accept Coronation gifts which El Glaoui brought to the Queen, on the ground that only presents from foreign sovereigns or heads of states are acceptable.

'One would have thought, however, that Great Britain, as a signatory to the Pact of Algeciras, which recognized the sovereignty of the Sultan of Morocco, would have invited to the Coronation if not the Sultan himself then Crown Prince Moulay Hassan. Such an invitation would have placed in a proper proportion the visit of El Glaoui, who has been endeavouring for the past few years to bring about the deposition of the Sultan. The most recent attempt took place only a few days ago in the form of a petition signed by two hundred and seventy Pashas and *Caids* against the Sultan. According to *Le Monde* of June 4th "the Glaoui does not seek to conceal he is at the origin of this document".

'The petition, which was handed to the French Residency in Rabat, goes so far as to attack the religious orthodoxy of the Sultan. This has provoked a sharp rejoinder from the Moroccan Palace, and an indignant reply from the religious authorities, the *Oulemas* of Fez. The Palace adds that a great deal of outside pressure was brought to bear upon the *Caids* to persuade them to sign the petition. There is no doubt that a new campaign is being launched to lower the prestige of the Sultan, whose loyalty to the rights of the Moroccan people has proved such an awkward obstacle in retrograde quarters.

'As for El Glaoui it is enough to quote again from *Le Monde*, "The Moslem orthodoxy of the Pasha of Marrakesh, the purity of his intentions and his democratic aspirations cannot be seriously invoked . . . it becomes more than ever urgent to define not only a Moroccan but a North African policy."

'There is a danger that El Glaoui's presence in London for the Coronation will be interpreted in Morocco and in North Africa as a reflection of official British attitude. This would be most regrettable, as there is no doubt that the great majority of the people of Morocco are supporters of the Sultan in his claims for the independence of their country.

'Signed, Fenner Brockway.'

T'hami's return journey through Paris produced an incident so bizarre that one feels that it could have happened nowhere else but in France.

General Juin, now promoted to Marshal, had also been elected to the French Academy, perhaps the highest non-military honour to which a Frenchman could aspire. It would have been bizarre enough if this institution could at the same moment contain the philistine figure of Marshal Juin and the taut intellect of François Mauriac, who led the main stream of support for the Sultan of Morocco and condemnation of French policy in North Africa. But this paradox was magnified and exploited by Marshal Juin's gamin impudence in inviting T'hami El Glaoui to be his guest on the occasion of his maiden speech at the Academy and using this speech for a major attack on the Istiqlal. It should be remembered that by nature of his new post of military command in Europe he had no official right to intervention of any kind in Moroccan affairs.

In the presence of T'hami El Glaoui and of François Mauriac, Juin made an inflammatory speech, praising the Glaoui and saying of the Istiqlal that its methods were 'ingenious but criminal. In its external policy it tries to multiply its allies by an active propaganda involving the grossest falsehoods. Thus, à propos of the repression of troubles which it had itself stirred up, it has tried – not without success – to mobilize to its side what we may conveniently call the "religion of the heart". Consciences which are ready to get excited about unsubstantiated reports and are excessively susceptible to moral and spiritual arguments have deliberately made common cause with the Istiqlal. Certainly, we cannot doubt the sincerity of this crusade in reverse.'

Mauriac replied at length and with spirit the next day, on the front page of *Le Figaro*, dealing the new boy Juin a sharp rap over the knuckles for his impertinence. 'By this public aggression against another member who has for twenty years occupied a seat in these precincts which Marshal Juin has just succeeded in penetrating, he is doubtless unconscious of having fulfilled the most ardent wish of those economic powers which, protected against taxation, hold Morocco under their power – and whose game we are not allowed to upset.'

T'hami did not return to Morocco until early August, and when he did so his plans were already complete. Guillaume was on sick leave at his Alpine home. T'hami began an immediate tour in company with

A Glaoua *kasbah* in the Dadès valley

(Courtesy Agence France-Presse)

T'hami El Glaoui and Marshal Juin

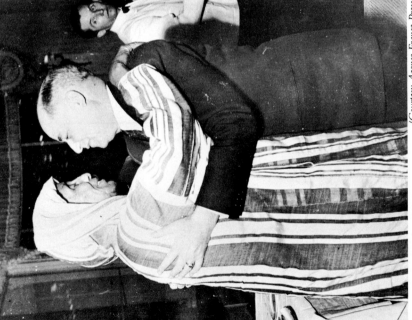

(Courtesy René Bertrand)

The brittle alliance: *Caïd* El Ayadi of the Rehamna (left) and T'hami El Glaoui (right)

The heart of the conspiracy: the Glaoui's palace at Marrakesh during the plot to dethrone the Sultan Mohammed V, 1953

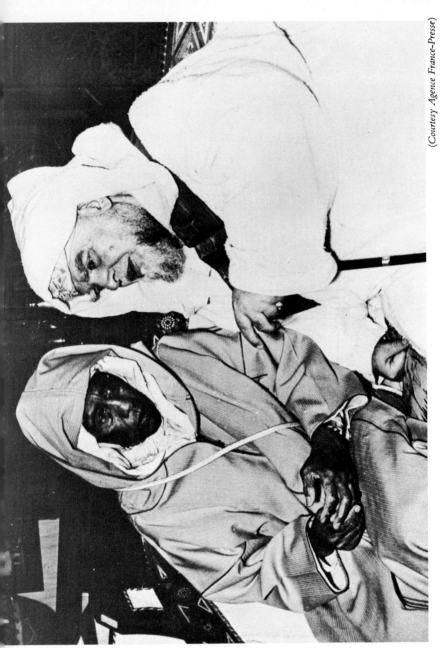

(Courtesy Agence France-Presse)

T'hami El Glaoui (left) and Abd El Hay Kittani plot to dethrone the Sultan Mohammed V, 1953.

Above: Rebels' banquet—*kous-kous* covers for a reception of notables at the Glaoui's palace in Marrakesh, 1953. Below: Minstrels in the Glaoui's palace in Marrakesh, to entertain the rebels' banquet, 1953

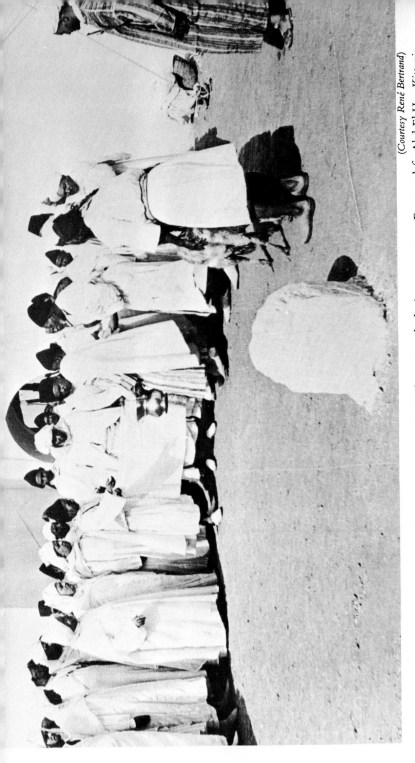

(Courtesy René Bertrand)

The puppet Sultan, Ben Arafa, about to sacrifice a sheep for the *Aïd El Kebir* at Marrakesh, August 21, 1953. Extreme left, Abd El Hay Kittani; third from left, T'hami El Glaoui; left, behind the Sultan, *Caïd* Brahim El Glaoui. Sacrificial stone in the foreground.

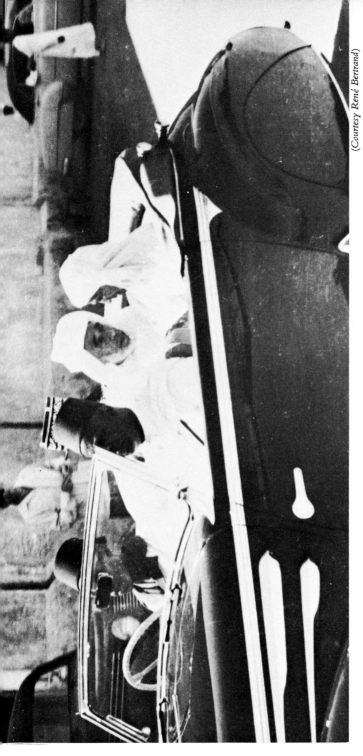

(Courtesy René Bertrand)

The Sultan Ben Arafa leaves with T'hami El Glaoui to entrain for Rabat. In the back of El Glaoui's Delahaye are General d'Hauteville (hidden), the Sultan Ben Arafa, and T'hami El Glaoui.

Children of Telouet

(Courtesy René Bertrand)

T'hami's Sultan, Ben Arafa, arrives at Rabat by train from Marrakesh. Left to right: General d'Hauteville, T'hami El Glaoui, the Sultan, Commandant Franqui, *Commissaire de la ville.*

The first attempt on the Sultan Ben Arafa's life, Rabat, September 11, 1953; an open car charges the Sultan's horse as he rides to the mosque. The imperial parasol has fallen at right of picture.

(Courtesy *United Press International (UK) Ltd.*)

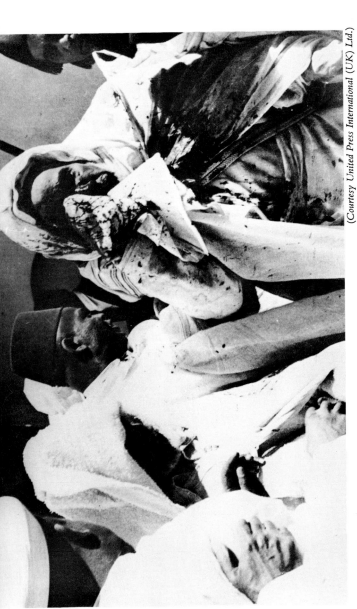

The second attempt on the Sultan Ben Arafa's life, Marrakesh, March 8, 1954; the Sultan (right center) bleeding from a grenade thrown at him in the Berrima mosque. Hadj Idder at center.

(*Courtesy United Press International (UK) Ltd.*)

The grenade thrower, Ahmed Ben Ali, immediately before he was shot by T'hami El Glaoui

(Courtesy United Press International (UK) Ltd.)

T'hami El Glaoui, spattered with the Sultan's blood, advances to shoot Ahmed Ben Ali.

Rabat, October 26, 1956. T'hami El Glaoui enters the throne room to submit to the Council of the Throne.

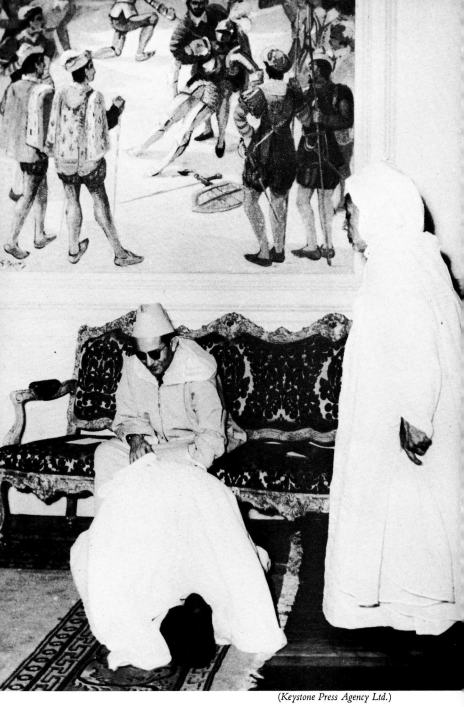

Paris, November 9, 1956. At the chateau of St. Germain-en-Laye T'hami El Glaoui kisses the feet of the Sultan Mohammed V whom he had deposed.

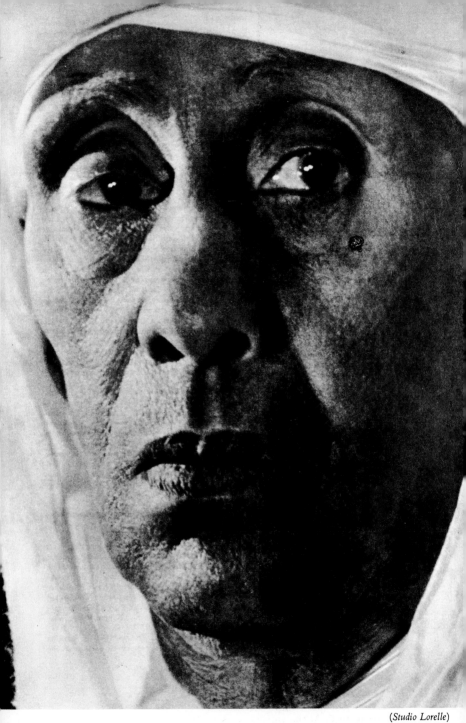

(Studio Lorelle)

T'hami el Glaoui shortly before his death in 1956

Kittani, and was reported by the Press to have received tremendous popular ovations at Oujda, Taza and Terouel. At the same time the Sultan's palace was surrounded by vast numbers of Moroccan citizens from the cities loyal to the throne, and who had come in their thousands to demonstrate their fidelity. Tribes who were unable to leave their lands sent a single representative.

On Monday 9 August the Crown Prince Hassan was informed that on Wednesday the 11th at the shrine of Moulay Idriss the Glaoui and Kittani would name a second Sultan and that thousands of Berber warriors were even then massing on Marrakesh for a march on the northern capitals. Their purpose this time would be to force the hand of the *Oulema* to the deposition of the Sultan and the official election of his replacement. Guillaume was recalled.

On 11 August no new Sultan was proclaimed, but at the shrine of Moulay Idriss the followers of Kittani and the Glaoui sacrificed two black bulls and took solemn oath never to rest until the Sultan, a heretic and an enemy of Islam, had been chased from the throne. This they swore before Allah and before Moulay Idriss. As a result, they were formally excommunicated the next day by the *Oulema* of Fez, on the instructions of the Sultan.

On 12 August General Guillaume was called to Paris by night. He returned the following day, and announced at Casablanca his immediate programme of action – maintenance of order and introduction of reforms. The same afternoon, having surrounded the Palace with his armed security forces, he obtained the Sultan's signature to certain 'reforms' on which he had hitherto maintained an intransigent attitude. These included delegation of all legislative power to the Grand Vizier El Mokri (then 103 years old)[1] and to a council composed half of French, half of Moroccans. This document would remove the last of the Sultan's temporal power. The Sultan asked Guillaume's representative what would happen if he refused to sign. The answer was ready and un-equivocal – 'One telephone call to Paris and you are deposed.'

While this unedifying scene was taking place inside the Palace, the Sultan's younger son Moulay Abdallah, who had been out when the security guards took up their positions, tried to re-enter. He was

[1] It has not been established whether El Mokri's age had been calculated by lunar or calendar months,

prevented, and protested that he was the Sultan's son and had a right to enter his home. A guard drew his pistol, cocked it, and replied, 'One more step and I fire.'

The Sultan signed at 6.15 p.m. and in doing so removed the last excuse for his deposition by the French. At 6.30 Si Mammeri, the Minister of Protocol, telephoned to General d'Hauteville, commanding the Marrakesh region, telling him of the Sultan's submission, as he had been informed that this knowledge was necessary to halt the Glaoui's movement for deposition.

On 14 August M. Bidault, the French Foreign Minister, cabled to Guillaume ordering him to call off the Glaoui and to oppose any rising of his tribesmen.

The *Oulemas* of Egypt published a statement condemning T'hami El Glaoui and his followers as instruments of imperialism. The Afro-Asian Group in Paris requested United Nations to prevent the deposition of the Sultan. At Marrakesh the Glaoui sent for an elderly uncle of the Sultan, Moulay Mohammed Ben Arafa (always afterwards known as Moulay Arafa), a son of Moulay Hassan, who had been living in retirement in Fez. The new Sultan had been chosen.

Much has been written in derogation and defamation of Moulay Arafa, but there is little evidence that any of it is true. He was a peaceful old gentleman who led a quiet life and, like most old gentlemen, enjoyed certain luxuries that were traditional to his way of life and his country. There is, on the other hand, much evidence that he accepted his new role with reluctance and hesitation, but he was no match for the massive pressures put upon him.

On 15 August General Guillaume went to Marrakesh to confer with the Glaoui, taking with him a member of the French Foreign Office, M. Vimont, whom Paris had despatched in a belated attempt at independent observation. All the Glaoui's following were at his palace, together with the 'ultras' of French-Moroccan colonialism, Boniface, d'Hauteville and Vallat, head of the Rabat department of Home Affairs. The incendiaries, as the French writer Barrat remarked, had been sent to put out the fire.

Vallat addressed the crowd, asking them for twenty-four hours' moratorium. The Glaoui agreed. But on the same day Moulay Arafa was proclaimed in Marrakesh as spiritual leader of the people of

Morocco, though only the *Oulema* of Fez could elect a new Sultan. The true Sultan said, 'They have taken away my temporal power by making me sign that protocol. They encroach upon my spiritual power by allowing this false *Imam* to be named. What is there left.'

During the following three days there were riots in Casablanca, Rabat, Oujda and Marrakesh itself. At Oujda alone the dead numbered six French, two Spaniards, two French-Algerians, two pro-French Moroccans, three Algerian-French Jews, one Moroccan Jew and more than thirty of the rioters. More than eighty of both factions were seriously wounded. At Marrakesh an *Imam* cried out in the mosque, 'In whose name shall I pray – Mohammed or Arafa?' – and was instantly stabbed to death.

The rightful Sultan, Mohammed V, issued a communiqué declaring himself to be the sole Sultan, spiritual and temporal, and calling upon the Muslim peoples of the world to recognize him as such.

Once more there were two Sultans in Morocco.

On 17 August the Glaoui published a statement. 'Tomorrow my enemies may come upon me. If the spiritual side has been our incentive, the temporal must look to the Protectorate.' Guillaume and Vimont flew to Paris for conference. Throughout all the Arab world there were demonstrations against the colonial powers and demands for United Nations intervention. Late at night Guillaume and Vimont returned, and made it known for the first time that the Sultan had in fact signed the reforms on 12 August. They sent for the Glaoui, who arrived at Rabat at 5 a.m. having published a communiqué from (with very few exceptions) all Pashas, *Caids* and religious leaders, demanding the total and final abdication of Mohammed V. He had also, for the second time in two years, set his Berber warriors marching on the capital in their thousands. Once again they were ignorant of the purpose of their march, and acted only upon the orders of their *Caids*.

On 18 August the Glaoui published what appeared to be an ultimatum to the French and to the Sultan alike; it was his culminating assertion of power.

'Yesterday, alas, French blood flowed. Moroccan blood, too. Tomorrow orders may be issued from the Imperial Palace, headquarters

of the Istiqlal, that will cause new seas of blood to be spilled, to be announced in further communiqués. We who represent tradition, loyalty, the future of the country, warn the French Government. It bears a terrible responsibility, which we do not envy. Our own is enough. If, against our expectations, it does not reply immediately with the firmness that the Moroccan people desire, France will have no more place in Morocco. What we say is serious, very serious. We are aware of the meaning and the gravity of our words. Those who are our friends today could become the enemies of France. They still have confidence. May God grant that they are not deceived, if the worst is not to follow. There is not one moment more to lose. For us this moment is decisive. Who is not for us is against us, for the time for prevarication is over.

'For forty years I have been the friend of France because I have been at the service of Morocco. Today I wish to save Morocco from anarchy and annihilation. I would like to believe that France understands that there are limits to my loyalty.

'Being a man of this country, I cannot prevent France from acting as she pleases. But this country, Morocco, I shall save cost what it may and without other considerations, even though that mean the renunciation of a friendship close to my heart and to which I have sacrificed my goods, my life, and a son.' (His son Mehdi had been killed at Monte

Cassino while serving with a regiment of Spahis. It had become a custom among the feudal overlords to send one son – never a favourite – into the French army.) 'God grant that my words are understood before it is too late.'

That same afternoon the French President received a delegation of the pro-Sultan organization, France Magreb, headed by its leader François Mauriac, and including two members of the French National Assembly, Reitzer and Clostermann. Three members of the French Cabinet threatened to resign if the Sultan were deposed; resignations that would have resulted in the dissolution of Parliament. The Sultan, who was in constant telephone communication with Paris, and surrounded by his French supporters in Morocco, received the information that Guillaume was instructed to calm down the Glaoui while trying to avoid using force against his tribesmen. The Glaoui issued a statement that his ultimatum, which had been telephoned to Casablanca, had been misunderstood and mistranslated. The Sultan believed that there was still hope.

Acting on instructions from Paris, Guillaume urged T'hami to halt his warriors' march summarily and to ensure that they approached no nearer to Rabat or to Fez. But T'hami replied, 'Even if I wanted to I could no longer stop the movement of the tribes!'

Each, from the highest downward, had his scapegoat – it could be said that the Resident-General had exceeded the policy of the French Government; that the Glaoui had exceeded the policy of the Resident-General; and now, the Glaoui claimed, his tribesmen were exceeding his own. Guillaume telephoned this reply to M. Bidault, asking, 'Must we fire upon our own friends? Those who wear our own military decorations?' He was asked to wait for a reply.

But the Glaoui's tribesmen were now encamped outside the city walls. Reitzer and Clostermann, returning exhausted from Paris, met some of them on the road, gay and friendly. Asked what they were doing there, the Berbers replied, 'We don't know.' 'But who sent you?' 'The *contrôleur* [French local governor].' These were the infuriated tribesmen whom the Glaoui could not stop even had he wanted to.

The last gaps were closed. A rioter, arrested after the Oujda incidents on 16 August, stated under 'interrogation' that the orders for the massacre of Europeans had come from the Imperial Palace, and more particularly from Crown Prince Moulay Hassan. Proof was in the hands of the police. . . .

Rabat was surrounded by French armoured troops, ostensibly to protect the Sultan's person from the tribal uprising.

At midday on 20 August Guillaume received Paris's answer to his question. 'We give you *carte blanche*.'

At about 1.45 p.m. Guillaume telephoned to the Palace demanding to see the Sultan immediately. A few minutes later a column of shock troops entered the Palace courtyard and disarmed the ceremonial Black

Tour Hassan, Rabat

Guard. These had only parade weapons, without ammunition, but when they had been relieved of their toys they were made to stand facing the wall with their hands above their heads, and they were kept covered by sub-machine-guns. Then two Residency cars arrived, containing General Guillaume, the chief of security police M. Dutheil with two inspectors, and the Chereefian councillor, M. de la Tour du Pin. Guillaume and the councillor entered the throne room, while the police waited outside it.

It was the hour of siesta, and the Sultan had been about to eat. He had just time to put on a *djellabah* over his pyjamas. Guillaume demanded his immediate abdication in favour of his younger son Moulay Abdallah, then sixteen years old. The Sultan refused. Guillaume called to Dutheil, and turned to the Sultan with the words, 'You are deposed!' The two inspectors went to find the two young princes, who were also in their pyjamas, but were allowed to slip on a *djellabah* over them. The three were marched at pistol point to the waiting police cars, the Sultan pale but dignified, the two princes hardly concealing their tears. They were conducted to the airport in separate cars.

The cars drove to the military airport of Souissi, some mile and a half distant from the city. There the Sultan and his sons were placed in separate rooms, under constant guard, and refused permission to speak to each other. Moulay Hassan protested that his father, in his present state of exhaustion, was in no condition to undertake an air journey. In response, the Sultan's doctor was summoned to the Residency and asked whether the Sultan was fit to fly. He was refused permission to make any examination, and would not commit himself.

The royal party were bundled into an unheated Dakota. The aircraft, an ex-paratroop unit, had no seats, and was not pressurized. There was straw on the floor. They were denied both food and water (the aircraft could supply only beer, which, being alcoholic, was against the Sultan's religion, and the 'service' did not provide for food). The plane took off for Ajaccio, Corsica, at 3.15 p.m. At ten in the evening they arrived in Corsica as apparently unannounced and unexpected guests of the local governor, who treated them with the courtesy and protocol due to a reigning monarch. The Sultan and his sons were still in their pyjamas, and had no luggage whatsoever.

They were followed into exile three days later by the Sultan's three legal wives, his six legal children, some black slaves, and twenty-one white concubines.

The next day many Moroccans detected the features of the ex-Sultan in the moon; those who proclaimed and hailed this phenomenon were promptly put in prison.

T'hami El Glaoui returned to Marrakesh to celebrate with the southern *Caids* the feast of Aid El Kebir and the deposition of their Sultan. In panache it had outshone his brother Madani's deposition of Moulay Abd El Aziz.

15

T'hami's Hour

FROM the moment of the deposition of Mohammed V, whom the French instantly but somewhat precipitately christened Mohammed the Weak, Morocco took on the aspect of an occupied country under Nazi Germany; there were curfews, multiple arrests, interrogations under torture, terrorism and counter-terrorism, dungeons and death. Morocco became overnight a total *bled es siba*.

During the night following the Sultan's deposition, French police beat at the doors of the members of the *Oulema* or religious council of Fez, ordering them to be at the Palace in the morning to sign the proclamation of the new Sultan Arafa. One, Si Mohammed Ben Larbi El Aloui, refused, saying that if Arafa were proclaimed he would afterwards have to be executed, quoting the *hadith* (apocryphal Koranic saying) that 'if there are two *Imams* the second must be killed'. In the morning his house was surrounded and he was refused exit. A very short time elapsed before his arrest and removal from the scene. One other refused, a Koranic professor of the Ben Youssef University of Marrakesh, and he was beaten to within an inch of his life.

So, under menaces, threats and open brutality, the same *Oulema* who had only eight days earlier signed the sentence of excommunication on T'hami and his followers signed on 21 August the *beya* proclaiming Moulay Arafa the new supreme *Imam*.

On the same day all mosques were closed for fear of demonstrations. At Rabat, despite police precautions, a procession of women formed, screaming and waving portraits of the deposed Sultan; they were dispersed with tear gas bombs, and two were killed. At Meknès there were a hundred and twenty arrests, including every known supporter of the Istiqlal.

Sultan Ben Arafa

On 23 August many of the people tried to gather in the mosques to recite before Allah their allegiance to Mohammed V. At two mosques, those of Karaouyne and Moulay Idriss, they were allowed to enter, shut inside, and made to exit one by one. They were then arrested as they left, and sentenced by tribunal to imprisonment varying between one and two years.

On 27 August Moulay Arafa arrived in Fez, preceded by a throng of southern tribesmen whose *Caids* had received orders that they were to line the route and give the new Sultan great acclamation 'or they knew what would happen to them'. Arafa arrived flanked by T'hami El Glaoui and Abd El Hay Kittani, and received a satisfactory salutation from some twenty thousand mounted Berber warriors firing their rifles. There were no civilian enthusiasts, for police had sealed off all exits from the *Medina*.

On 1 September the ex-Sultan's mother died at Fez, seemingly of a broken heart. The crowds who would have followed her cortège to the cemetery were forcibly dispersed, and a cordon of police sealed off the route of the brief procession, which was followed by none but soldiers and officials.

The French had, in fact, momentarily lost control to the Glaoui. In Marrakesh he had brought thousands of his Glaoua tribal warriors into the town to maintain order, wild men from the mountains over whom M. Jean Mougin, the French Police Inspector, had no authority. Four of these men were stationed at the entrance to every street in the *Medina*, and they were told to use their own discretion where any suspect was concerned. Mougin had urged that they be ordered to show respect to any foreigner inhabiting the *Medina*, but in the event he was powerless. An Algerian, well known in the town, returned from a journey, carrying with him a small valise which contained his personal effects. The tribesmen halted him roughly, and ordered him to open it. He did so, but at the same time had the unwisdom to ask, 'What would have happened if I had refused?' Without another word he was marched, with sub-machine-guns pressed into his back, to the Dar El Glaoui. T'hami was away, and his *khalifa* put the Algerian in prison without more ado. A relation of the prisoner, a notable of Marrakesh, went immediately to Inspector Mougin to obtain his release. Mougin replied, 'We deeply regret, monsieur, that we can do nothing on his behalf. Our authority is overridden by the Pasha's warriors – they have been given *carte blanche*, and they have as much power as the Resident-General himself. They have even imprisoned our own police officers because they were armed. It is too late now to try to check all this. The only authority now is the Glaoui.' At that the prisoner's relations went direct to T'hami. He had only just returned, but received them at once. He ordered the release of the prisoner; and, having discovered that his *khalifa* had held him captive out of personal spite, sent the *khalifa* to prison instead. (It was the ex-prisoner himself who, in response to the pleadings of the *khalifa*'s family, finally secured his restoration.)

On Friday 28 August Arafa led prayer for the first time, in the small mosque of Boujeloude, chosen for its insignificance in order to lessen the likelihood of demonstration, and none but trusted members of the reactionary movement were admitted. Elsewhere the mosques were empty, for prayers were offered – on pain of death – in the name of Arafa and not of Mohammed V. By the twentieth day of Arafa's reign nearly *thirteen thousand* people had been arrested on charges of treason, and Morocco's dungeons were as full as at any time in the country's history. Unmentioned by the now wholly censored Press, there were daily riots, murders and atrocities throughout all the land.

On Friday 11 September Arafa paid his first ceremonial visit to the

mosque at Rabat, only some three hundred yards from the Palace. He rode, as it was customary for the Sultan to ride, in state, beneath his crimson parasol and surrounded by his courtiers. Before the imperial party had covered half the distance to the mosque an open white car, driven by a young man carrying a dagger in his right hand, charged straight at the Sultan's horse, unseating him and hurling the crimson parasol to the ground. Before the assassin could get his knife to the fallen Sultan – indeed before he could get clear of his own car – he himself was killed by an unidentifiable mixture of blows and bullets.

On the following Friday, 18 September, the most elaborate precautions were taken to safeguard the aged Sultan. He travelled in the State coach, and on each side of him rode dense ranks of the Black Guard with their swords drawn, and their non-commissioned officers carried cocked sub-machine-guns. The foot guards closed ranks, and all along the route mobile guards faced outwards towards the crowd, alert for the smallest suspicious movement. Immediately behind the Sultan's coach rode T'hami El Glaoui, mounted on a bay horse and carrying, resting on his left arm, a repeating carbine. Instead of dismounting, as was customary, and entering the mosque on foot, the imperial coach was driven in and out of sight of the crowds.

By that date Moulay Arafa had already signed over all his legislative powers to a council consisting of Frenchmen and Moroccans handpicked by General Guillaume in close conjunction with T'hami El Glaoui. The fact that this council violated absolutely the original Protectorate Treaty seems of little importance in contrast with the monstrous rapacity and brutality that had preceded its formation.

The attention of the whole civilized world was focused upon Morocco during the twenty-five bloodstained months of Arafa's reign, and the chorus of protest grew from the isolated voices of the French intellectuals to a rumble of thunder from even the right wing Press of other countries. Few in France or Morocco, other than T'hami El Glaoui himself, can have believed in the possibility of maintaining this extraordinary sham State, and even he was far from satisfied with the culmination of his life's work, for he had expected certain rewards that were not forthcoming.

The choice of Moulay Arafa as successor to Mohammed V had been neither sudden nor obvious; it had been reached by a process of elimination. When the necessity for deposition had become a foregone conclusion, the French, in consultation with Abd El Hay Kittani, had favoured one of T'hami's own sons for the post of puppet Sultan – Si Ahmed El Glaoui, *Caid* of the Guich, a semi-invalid from kidney trouble, who was married to a French wife and had displayed no interest in politics. T'hami, however, had firmly resisted this project, both because he would have refused to make obeisance to his own son, and because he recognized that direct control of northern Morocco in the name of a Glaoui would provoke revolution difficult to contain. He had, however, characteristically expected to benefit from this refusal; he did not doubt that his family would be rewarded by *Pashaliks* and other important functions outside his southern kingdom. In his eyes it was to be, for the House of Glaoua, the greatest period of expansion beyond southern Morocco.

He had reckoned, however, without the effect of his published letter of 18 August, in which he had seen fit to challenge the French, a mistake that the elder statesman Madani would surely never have made. Their eye upon him was now wary; all the southern *Caids* were forbidden to leave their own commands, and he himself was not consulted about nominations outside his own territory.

A Glaoui dynasty of Sultans would not, in fact, have been so preposterous a proposition from a genealogical point of view as might have been supposed, for there is little doubt that his family could have claimed the requisite Chereefian descent from the Prophet. It was customary for his enemies to say that while the Goundafi and M'touggi were of ancient lineage the House of Glaoui could not be traced further back than the past century, but in fact this was not true, and there are not a few mentions of the family in the seventeenth century, and one as early as the eleventh century. During the 1920s he issued a statement to the Press on his lineage:

'My family comes from a village not far from Mecca. Our patriarch was Omar Ben Abd El Aziz, a contemporary of Haroun El Rachid. This family later came to Morocco and collaborated with the Sultans until the Alaouite dynasty. It was followed by Moulay Rachid of Tafilelt, who later became Sultan. Moulay Ismael is my ancestor; Abdessadek El Mezouari was my grandfather [this appears to be a slip for great-grandfather]; my signature is El Hadj T'hami El Mezouari El Glaoui.'

There is no reason to doubt that this was in essence true, and that like most other great Arab families the Glaoua tribe reached the High Atlas cols by way of the south-eastern oases, but there is equally little doubt that the family was of no real importance before the eighteenth century, and of no national importance before the visit of Moulay Hassan and their acquisition of a cannon. The Chereefian Arab ancestry was, in any case, a two-edged sword; his role as the natural leader of the Berber people, 'the pure Berber type' as the French termed him with a somewhat naïve disregard for the colour of his skin, would have been heavily compromised by descent from the Prophet in the male line and an Ethiopian mother.

Whether at any time he had considered setting himself up as a *rogui* –

and it seems improbable that the thought never crossed his mind – he had in any case finally abandoned the idea in favour of his family controlling all Morocco under a puppet Alaouite Sultan; and, finding this ambition thwarted too, he was far from content. It was the very beginning of a deep mistrust between himself and France, like the first crack in the wall of one of his mighty *kasbahs* that were almost all soluble in water.

The French themselves were at work now to break the vast structure they had formed to depose the Sultan, and one of their first actions was to undermine the newly-formed alliance between T'hami and *Caid* El Ayadi of the Rehamna, an alliance that had now served its purpose and might prove menacing in the future. With the full connivance of the French, El Ayadi declared himself to T'hami to have been in error in supporting the deposition of Mohammed V, and no doubt felt safe enough in making this assertion – but his advice had come from France, not from the Residency in Morocco, and as a result T'hami succeeded in having him destituted and his passport withdrawn.

Besides nearing his downfall, T'hami was, though he did not yet know it, a dying man. For some time he had been subject to fainting fits, lasting from six to twenty minutes, during which he foamed at the mouth and appeared in great pain, but retained no memory of the incident after recovering consciousness. Sometimes he was aware of a lapse of time, and asked what had happened, but his entourage were afraid to tell him the truth, and would say either that they had noticed nothing or that he had fallen asleep for a moment. At this time he was attended by a Swiss doctor resident in Marrakesh, a Doctor Jacquoud, a man of considerable brilliance, who may or may not have known the true nature of the disease, but spoke only of heart trouble, and warned T'hami that he must live under a strict régime which he never followed. He was already an old man, though like all great figures of myth and legend he had seemed to become ageless in the eyes of his people, and he had already made the necessary arrangements – which included great expenditure – to be buried by the tomb of Sidi Ben Slimane in Marrakesh, where other members of his family were already interred – his brother Madani, and Allal and Hammou and Hammou's brother

Mohammed, and the perfumes and the winding-sheet were already prepared by those who hoped that the blessings of T'hami's departed spirit would descend upon them.

Meanwhile, though the condition of Morocco declined into an epilepsy of violence and brutality, his spirit showed little overt sign of departure. In December there were riots and explosions in Casablanca, and a little later it was discovered that a restaurant much patronized by students was serving savoury stews composed of nothing but human flesh. It was an obvious and profitable way of disposing of a continuous burden of embarrassing corpses, and in fact it was only the extreme carelessness of the cooks that led to discovery. A medical student who had asked for a second helping found himself holding on the end of his fork the distal end of a human penis, and promptly fainted. His companions rallied round him, and together they took the evidence to the police. But the officers on duty, seeing a group of medical students who had obvious access to such anatomical souvenirs, treated the whole thing as a hoax, and it was not for several hours that they decided to investigate the restaurant. No steps had been taken to hide anything; all the stew-pots were still full of appetizing human remains. No doubt the staff were executed, but it was also quite possible, as an Arab wit put it, that they were eaten too.

The second attempt on Arafa's life was made on 8 March 1954. During his first official visit to the southern capital of Marrakesh, he led Friday prayers in the Berrima mosque. He had hardly begun when a hand grenade was thrown at him, wounding him in the face and covering his white robes with blood; wounding, too, the Chief of Protocol Hadj Abderrhaman Hajjoui, and killing several minor personages. T'hami and his sons were unharmed. In the ensuing chaos everyone turned out to be armed to the teeth, the blood-spattered Sultan waving a pistol just like everyone else. The bomb-thrower, a young man named Ahmed Ben Ali, was detained in the mosque; its doors were barred and each man searched separately as he left, but no further evidence was discovered. T'hami escorted the wounded Sultan back to the Palace in the big white Delahaye; then he returned to the Berrima and shot Ahmed Ben Ali himself.

After this incident Arafa is reported to have said, 'All this is really a bit too much for me – I simply can't go on with it.' In fact he did not; the poor harassed old gentleman rarely appeared in public again. When he moved he insisted upon an impenetrable guard, and as far as possible he kept to the confines of his palaces, aching only for the seclusion from which he had been so rudely extracted.

French troops were poured into Morocco to deal with what no one could now deny was a colonial rebellion. It was more; it was a civil war in Morocco and a war by the greater part of Morocco against her French colonists who had promised a Protectorate and had tried to

Kettle and charcoal brazier

produce a colony in which the Moors were slaves. In 1954 there were more French soldiers in Morocco (200,000) than at any time since the beginning of the French 'penetration'.

It is some measure of the Glaoui's personality that in the midst of all this he continued, with apparent outward calm and graciousness, to receive casual foreign visitors in his customary grand manner; a British film unit, for example, engaged in making a film against the background of Morocco, and of whom he said, 'Let them record what remains of my country before it is too late.' He listened, during this same period, with apparently courteous interest, to Mr Peter Scott explaining how he caught wild geese in nets and ringed them so that their migration could be fully understood by the world of science. Apprised of the fact that Peter Scott was the son of Scott of the Antarctic he remarked, 'His father wanted power over the earth, to place the British flag at the South Pole – this son wants power over the birds of the air whom no one will ever own.'

16

The Submission of T'hami

THE situation could do nothing but worsen. Morocco, despite the enormous metropolitan reserves poured into her to stabilize the situation, remained a political pawn, her febrile agonies a question of numerical vote in the motherland. Hence there was no true or lasting rapport between the Residents-General in Morocco and the French central authorities at the Quai d'Orsay, and the despairing Viceroys succeeded each other quicker than ever. In 1954 Guillaume was replaced by M. Francis Lacoste, who liberated most of the imprisoned nationalists, a move so unpopular with the intransigent colonists that he was quickly removed in 1955 and in turn replaced by Gilbert Grandval. The astonishing thing is that by that date any Frenchman could be found to fulfil the office, certain of betrayal both by his own and the occupied country. Yet the post of Resident-General was hotly competed for, most notably by General Koenig, then Minister of Defence, who did not conceal his bitterness at losing it, and told Grandval that he would certainly be assassinated. No Resident-General could feel himself even representative of his own country or sure of its support – policy in Morocco was no longer a matter either of national or imperial expediency. It was, for the metropolitan French ministers, a question of prediction and assessment of majority French feeling and therefore of votes. It is not too much to say that there was no united French policy, no policy at all other than that of opportunism in the light of the stop press news. A large number of French politicians had decided over the cognac that without looking very much further there was no immediate solution for peace in Morocco other than the restoration of the ex-Sultan Mohammed V.

T'hami El Glaoui was, to say the least of it, anxious on this point, and again and again he was reassured that whatever the outcome might be there could never be any question of restoring the old Sultan – who had now, for greater security, been transferred to exile in Madagascar.

Grandval replaced Lacoste on 22 June 1955, by which date de Gaulle had expressed the opinion that there was only one solution to the Moroccan problem – the restoration to the throne of the rightful Sultan Mohammed V. Grandval's opinion on arrival was that this could cause the enmity of the numerous tribes reputedly loyal to T'hami El Glaoui.

On the same day that he accepted the appointment, Grandval had a meeting with the Grand Vizier El Mokri at Vichy. El Mokri was then almost 106 years old,[1] and had been eighty-five years active in politics, but he was astonishingly alert and on the spot. He said at once that as a personal cause of difficulty Moulay Arafa could be discounted; that he was an old man who only wanted to lead a peaceful life free from intrigue and danger. This was a tactful way of answering an unspoken question; Grandval was highly sceptical of the trust placed in the Glaoui-Arafa faction, and recognized that any solution could only come about through a new occupant of the throne.

His personal contact with Arafa opened inauspiciously. On his way to the palace he was greeted by cries of '*Vive Grandval! Vive Mohammed Ben Youssef!*' Learning of this, Arafa displayed an absolute grasp of the fundamentals, saying that the Moroccan people couldn't care less who was Sultan; all they wanted was the independence of their country and the departure for ever of the French. Nothing but massive use of force, he said, could abate the present wave of terrorism. He showed himself at fault, however, when he added, 'If Mohammed Ben Youssef comes back they'll eat him.' (He did not, presumably, mean this in the literal sense of the Casablanca restaurant.)

Grandval then made his formal speech to the Sultan, which was followed by a deathly silence, because the Arabic translation had unfortunately been mislaid between the various departments of the Residency. Grandval's subordinate Colonel Guermouche stepped into the breach with a brilliant and lengthy extemporization in Arabic, but the *gaffe* caused Arafa a friendly giggle. Grandval was busily summing

[1] See note on p. 223.

him up, and at that first meeting formed the impression that had he not been surrounded by his courtiers he would immediately have confided his desire to surrender a highly uncomfortable throne.

On 14 July Grandval invited the Glaoui to lunch at the Residency. They had not met for ten years, when T'hami had accompanied Mohammed V on a visit to Nancy, where Grandval was commanding the 20th Military Region. Nevertheless, T'hami greeted him as an old friend, and began immediately to complain of his almost total exclusion from the Residency since the deposition of the Sultan Mohammed V. Guillaume, he said, he had only seen once, on 20 August 1953, and he hadn't even listened to the advice he had asked of T'hami. Grandval began to assure him that things would now be completely different, but T'hami interrupted him to remark maliciously that the past two Resident-Generals had given the same promises.

He then summed up the situation as he saw it, which was, for the purposes of the moment, extremely simple. Arafa was Sultan; the instigators of the deposition of Mohammed V had taken vows of loyalty to him, and surely France wouldn't want her friends to betray their solemn word. There were only two sides – the minority trouble-makers and the majority loyal to the French. Lacoste had made a great mistake in setting so many of the trouble-makers free, and the only solution now was force on a scale never used before. It was a mistake to confine Arafa to his palace, denying even the tribal leaders access to him; he should, on the other hand, be encouraged to show himself as often as possible to the Moroccan people and in the greatest conceivable pomp. Grandval remarked that these did not appear to be the Sultan's tastes, but T'hami replied that one should be able to make him appreciate the responsibilities of his position more fully. He did, however, admit that in the possible event of Arafa actually choosing to abdicate, there would be the problem of a vacant throne to consider. One would have to choose a new Sultan who belonged to neither of the present factions.

Grandval proposed a round table conference, but T'hami would not consider the idea of including the nationalist leaders. He did, however, concede the presence of one of his worst enemies, Si Bekkai. Si Bekkai, who had been an officer in the French army and lost a leg in the Second World War, had resigned his office of Pasha of Sefrou in protest against the deposition of Mohammed V. The interview ended cordially, with an absolute pledge from Grandval that the ex-Sultan would never be brought back, and assurances from the Glaoui that the French could count upon him come what might. Neither believed the other.

On the same day a bomb exploded at Casablanca, killing and wounding many. Grandval returned from the funeral of the six European dead on the 16th, to meet Kittani at the Residency. He found the old *Chereef* repulsive beyond words, and little emerged from the conversation beyond Kittani's protestations of loyalty to France and his numerous and virulent hatreds.

On 17 July there were further riots in Casablanca. A young Spaniard was stoned to death by the mob; a unit of the French Foreign Legion took brutal reprisals. In the past three days the official casualty list – which was certainly conservative where Moroccan dead were concerned – amounted to fifty-five Moroccan and eleven European deaths, and 218 Moroccans and eighty-eight Europeans seriously wounded. Thirty of these Europeans were victims of individual assault. A further 150 Moroccans were arrested and tortured. Not one Frenchman was arrested, though many were guilty of indiscriminate murder.

On 20 July Grandval expelled from Morocco the president of a 'reprisal' organization known as Présence Française, a certain Dr Causse, who had on the 18th approached T'hami El Glaoui with a view to producing a joint uprising against this monstrously pro-Moroccan Resident-General.

On 21 July Grandval flew to Marrakesh to take possession of his southern Residency, the old Bahya Palace, and was welcomed with the same cries of '*Vive Grandval! Vive Mohammed Ben Youssef!*' – but not in the *Medina*, where T'hami's soldiers were in force. He was greeted by T'hami and his three sons, *Caïd* Brahim, *Caïd* Ahmed of the Guich (or Haouz) and Si Abdessadek – the latter now acting as his father's interpreter, as his liberal sympathies were known and T'hami preferred to have him under his eye. (In June he had been in correspondence with M. Jacques Lemaigre-Dubreuil, owner and publisher of *Maroc-Presse*, the only newspaper to expose the true French policy. Dubreuil was murdered by French 'anti-terrorists' – a body organized under the name of O.D.A.-T., *Organisation de Défense Anti-Terroriste*, who did not hesitate to kill their own countrymen or to stone to death completely innocent Moroccans – only twenty-four hours after he had been conferring with the new French Premier, M. Edgar Faure.)

As these four were returning to Dar El Glaoui from Grandval's Residency of the Bahya Palace their car, the big black Bentley which had for some time been T'hami's preferred vehicle, collided – seemingly accidentally – with a group of demonstrators. A scuffle followed, in the course of which T'hami's guards opened fire, killing five Moroccans. T'hami himself got out of the car brandishing a sub-machine-gun. The French Colonel and his aide, who were riding with him, also dismounted; but the aide, seeing that his Colonel had no weapon, bounded back to the car to procure one. T'hami turned exactly as the aide had grabbed a pistol from the back seat, and, taking him to be an enemy, T'hami aimed his sub-machine-gun at him and pulled the trigger. By a miracle, it did not fire. As soon as the party had gained the forecourt of the Dar El Glaoui, T'hami, furious at the failure of his weapon, tried it out again, and fired a volley into the air; which, it is rumoured, killed a stork that happened to be passing by.

At their talk that afternoon Grandval assured T'hami once more that Mohammed V would never be recalled. Leaving the Dar El Glaoui at the end of the conversation, Grandval learned that besides the five killed in the morning incident there were many wounded, and that feeling was running high in the *Medina*, which he was due to visit that afternoon. Fearing more cries of '*Vive Mohammed V!*' and T'hami's probable retribution, he cancelled his visit.

That evening he was for the first time guest at one of T'hami's fabled *difas*, or banquets, and was duly impressed by all he saw – the vast host of Glaoua tribesmen armed with cudgels; the splendour of the palace; the hypnotic rhythm of the dancing Berber women; T'hami's fantastic collection of arms and more especially spears, of which Grandval wondered how many lives their steel had extinguished.

Next day he was received by the *Caid* of the Ouzguita, Moulay Hassan, and here again, deep among the Berber tribes, he heard the cry, '*Vive Mohammed Ben Youssef!*'

On 23 July Grandval met T'hami again, in a very much worse humour. He had decided, he said, to send his son *Caid* Brahim to Paris to make contact with certain of his friends. He himself, he said, would not see the Sultan until Grandval had done so.

Berber dancers

Only two days later, however, he discovered in Rabat that T'hami had paid an unexpected visit to Arafa and asked him whether it was his intention to remain upon the throne, and that together they had drafted a letter to the President of the French Republic. In face of this pressure put by T'hami upon the Sultan and the President, Grandval felt his mission of conciliation to be plainly ridiculous. He himself went to see Arafa, who made no mention of any letter to the President, but in reply to Grandval's previous suggestion of forming a representative government he presented a list of eighty-five names from which to select ministers. These were largely people without influence in the country, and none hostile to Arafa; however, consultation with a dozen of the best known revealed that they would not anyway accept any post that was not bestowed by Mohammed V.

Caid Brahim's visit to Paris was not a success. He returned to give his father the unwelcome news that the French Government policy was already fixed: vacation of the throne; constitution of a Moroccan government approved by Mohammed V and comprising all viewpoints; and the moving of Mohammed V from Madagascar to Paris. Such a policy, *Caid* Brahim's Parisian friends said, would gain two years, and, though it could not prevent action in favour of Mohammed V developing if the throne remained vacant, the delay and the French extreme right wing would together give T'hami a chance for counter-offensive. By now it was clear to Grandval that the voluntary abdication of Arafa would lead the Istiqlal to demand the immediate restitution of Mohammed V and the total eviction of the French from Morocco.

On 25 July Grandval visited Fez. Mobile police fired upon a crowd who had no hostile intent; the only visible results of his visit were seventeen Moroccan dead, fifty wounded, ten French casualties among the security forces, and murderous feelings stirred up the *Medina*.

On 31 July Grandval again entertained T'hami to lunch, and found him utterly intransigent. He would not consider the dethronement of Arafa unless he was immediately replaced by yet a third Sultan and would hear nothing of Grandval's argument that such a man would find himself in exactly the same untenable situation as Arafa. When Grandval drew his attention to the terrible state of Morocco, he replied violently, 'You have only to do as the British do with the Mau Mau!' The only practical assurance received from T'hami was that if France acted against his advice he would not rise against her, but would take no further part in public affairs of any kind.

As a result of this meeting Grandval formed his own policy – the abdication of Arafa, the formation of a Council of Regency comprised of the moderate elements of all parties, and a simultaneous message from Mohammed V to his people that this was their legitimate government. All this he felt should take place before 18 August, for the 20th was the anniversary of the Sultan's deposition, when fresh horrors might be confidently expected.

Time was extremely short. He calculated that it would take twelve days to form the Regency Council and send a delegation to Madagascar to obtain Mohammed's support. Five more to get T'hami out of the way by formal invitation to Paris from the French President, convince Arafa of the need to go, and secure the co-operation of Pashas and *Caids*.

The French Government undertook to approve or disapprove the policy in principle by 6 August, if he would now set forth the details by telegram. This would leave him the twelve days he required.

On the evening of 2 August he received a telephone message from Premier Faure requesting him to postpone sending the telegram, as its divulgence would cause parliamentary upheaval. Instead, the Premier would immediately despatch by air a member of the Cabinet, M. Edouard Morgaut. Grandval decided to put a blind eye to the telescope. He greeted Morgaut with the news that his telegram had already been despatched when the aircraft left. In consternation, Morgaut telephoned to Paris for advice, and was told to remain with Grandval, who now felt himself to be under surveillance.

On 3 August Grandval received the reply to his telegram, and it contained nothing but trivial questions and delaying tactics. He realized then that it was going to be made impossible for him to obtain Government decision before the beginning of the recess on 5 August.

At this point T'hami, who in keeping abreast of events had been even more active than Grandval, threw his bomb. On 2 August, unknown to Grandval he had again sent *Caid* Brahim to Paris, this time carrying a letter addressed by the Glaoui to the Prime Minister. This letter ascribed to Grandval policies and projects far removed from reality, and at the same time stated that under no circumstances would Arafa resign his throne except under inexcusable duress.

It was a master-stroke, for the whole of Grandval's plan had been based upon Arafa's voluntary resignation, and also upon the assumption that T'hami would not overtly oppose himself to it. The Glaoui's letter brought all plans to a standstill, for the Resident-General could hardly do violence to the peace-loving old Sultan or quarrel openly with T'hami, the Friend of France.

The dilemma was not even allowed to remain secret, for a copy of the letter intended, it is said, for General Koenig, somehow got delivered instead to *Paris-Presse*, who gave it their whole front page – or rather what little was left of it below the monstrous headlines.

While Grandval did not underestimate the astuteness or power of his opponent, he was also an able detective, and it did not take him long to discover that the master stroke had not been so simply delivered as appeared at first sight. It was clear to him that Arafa and the Glaoui had not acted upon their own initiative. The Glaoui's letter was dated 1 August, the day after Grandval had intimated to him intentions quite other than the letter attributed to him, intentions which were in principle perfectly acceptable to the Glaoui. Grandval did not, in short, believe that T'hami was the true author of the letter. As additional evidence to this effect, the Chief of Protocol, Si Abderrhaman Hajjoui, forwarded on 4 August a letter dated 28 July, announcing that Arafa wished to become President of a Moroccan Republic through the mediation of Grandval himself. The contents of this letter were known to the Press before it was sent. To Grandval the conclusion was inescapable – the letter purporting to have been written by the Glaoui in conjunction with Arafa had been drawn up not in Morocco but in Paris, and its pretended authors had done no more than append their signatures to a document already prepared.

This conclusion gave Grandval much food for thought. He knew for certain that T'hami was in constant liaison with the ex-Resident-General Marshal Juin, and that Juin passed on to the Prime Minister all information that might hinder Grandval's cause. The solution was not obvious; T'hami certainly had the right to confide in a past Resident-General, and the past Resident-General had the right – even, possibly, the duty – to inform the Prime Minister of what he knew.

At this stage it became finally plain to Grandval that both the Sultan and T'hami were pawns in the hands of French politicians who were playing a game quite contrary to that which he himself, Grandval, had been instructed to play. The battle was going to be won or lost in Paris, not in Morocco. Grandval told the French Premier, M. Faure, exactly what he thought, and as a result the Premier was able to 'damp the powder of the bomb so that it wrought less havoc than its engineers had hoped'. But Grandval wrote those words months before the bomb exploded – backwards, into the face of its engineers.

Grandval now feared a massive civil war in Morocco, and on 3 August appealed to the French Minister of Defence, General Koenig, to send a further division of the French army to Morocco. Koenig demurred, but eventually sent a detachment of lesser strength from Algeria. Grandval invited for discussion two Pashas considered loyal to T'hami El Glaoui (Mokhtar Ben Hammou, Pasha of Meknès, and Mohammed Ben Bouamor, Pasha of Marchand), and found that both believed the Glaoui's letter to have originated in Paris. Both were willing to intervene with T'hami, but were equally certain of his intransigent determination to keep Arafa on the throne. Any other course he would regard as a step towards the restoration of Mohammed V and, automatically, his own downfall.

Grandval now decided upon further direct talks with Arafa, and to that end went to the palace on 5 August. He harangued Arafa about the massive responsibilities resting upon his shoulders, but the Sultan interrupted him to say that all his powers had been taken away by General Guillaume and that he now possessed neither authority nor responsibility for events. This provoked Grandval to go straight to the heart of the matter; he told Arafa that there was no possible solution other than his renunciation of the throne. The Sultan seemed in no way put out by this, and asked for confirmation in writing. Grandval now understood that the only personal influence preventing the Sultan's return to peaceful retirement was that of his Chief of Protocol, Hajjoui.

After this meeting Grandval called together all his French regional commanders and outlined to them the plan he had put forward to Paris. He encountered complete hostility, closed minds, and refusal to consider the logical implications of the situation.

On 6 August Grandval received a telegram from Paris informing him that his proposals would now go before the Cabinet, but that they would require extremely close study. Time was running out; there remained only fourteen days before the anniversary of Mohammed's deposition, when Grandval foresaw mass riots that would finally commit France to a policy of open force. The following day he telephoned to Paris, but in the course of a very long conversation he could obtain no definite assurances whatsoever. On 10 August he flew to Paris and visited de Gaulle, who could give him no comfort. 'Your plan,' he said, 'will neither be accepted nor rejected. The Premier of the so-called Government will try only to gain time. If things go wrong he won't hesitate to abandon you and put all the blame upon you.'

Grandval then went to see the Premier, and placed on record his opinion that if effective action were not taken before the 20th there would be disaster. The Premier replied that the Government had a plan, a method and a calendar. The calendar, Grandval pointed out, ignored the fatal day of 20 August, for the plan was to call upon Arafa for immediate constitution of a representative Moroccan government composed of members agreed by a committee of five French Ministers. The members of this Moroccan government were to be invited to Paris on 18 August, which would do nothing to avert riots in Morocco on the 20th.

Grandval went on to interview other ministers, each holding individual views different from those of their colleagues, and only now did he learn that his own instructions received on 6 July, to work towards the installation of Mohammed V and his family in France, had never been made known to the Cabinet, for the Premier had believed that this would bring about the downfall of the Government.

He was now also shown, for the first time, the official French reply to the Glaoui's letter. 'The President has received the Pasha's letter and has forwarded it to the Resident-General, asking the latter to make known to the Pasha of Marrakesh the Government's point of view.'

Grandval, like other men, had his breaking point. It came when he was shown by Premier Faure the list of forty-three names from which Arafa was asked to form a government. He looked at the list and exclaimed, 'But this policy of yours can only lead to the direct return to the throne of Mohammed V!' Faure replied coolly, 'Have you ever doubted that that was my policy?' Both men lost their tempers; Grandval shouted that he would no longer play this comedy of blind man's buff, and demanded that his resignation be accepted forthwith. Faure accepted it with heat, and doors slammed. However, Grandval had hardly got outside the building when a panting messenger asked him to return to see M. Faure. Faure begged him to withdraw his resignation, and Grandval, swayed only by the possibility of thus averting mass slaughter on 20 August, at length agreed. He returned to Rabat on 14 August. Six days to go.

The list of members of the prospective Moroccan government had included the Istiqlal leaders Lyazidi and Ben Barka, and representatives of the P.D.I. (Partie Démocratique de l'Indépendance). Now (15 August) all these refused to take any part in the proceedings, and simultaneously Arafa refused to form a government largely composed of his enemies. Five days to go.

On 16 August the Pasha of Rabat, Si Abbes Tazi, sought urgent audience with Grandval. He arrived at ten in the evening, and his message was not equivocal. Arafa wanted to abdicate at once, and was already occupied with arrangements about the palace which the French had bought for him in Tangier. He sent his terms by Tazi in writing: the safeguard of his honour and that of his sons; personal safety; liberty of movement; maintenance of material interests. He refused to go by air, and Tazi had prepared the details of a secret departure. Tazi would invite the Sultan to dinner, from where he would leave clandestinely for Casablanca and take ship to Tangier. During the hours following his departure his family would rendez-vous at the house of one of his sons, near to Rabat airport, and fly to Tangier.

At dawn on 17 August Grandval telegraphed the proposals to Paris, asking that they should be made known to none but M. Faure, but this request was not followed, and in a short time the whole secret plan was common knowledge both in Paris and Morocco. Arafa, fearing for his life, refused to go through with it, though his one desire remained to vacate the throne as quickly as possible. Three days to go.

The Paris replies to Grandval's telegrams were now so irrelevant that he had the sensation of conducting a dialogue with a deaf man. On the 18th he was summoned to Paris for discussions, but with his private certainty of an imminent blood-bath he disregarded his instructions and remained in Rabat.

At midday on the 18th he received news by telephone from M. Faure of a Cabinet meeting in Paris at which, amid scenes of wild disorder, he had obtained the Cabinet's consent to the formation of a fully representative Moroccan government. He ordered Grandval to fly to Paris immediately, and overrode all objections. Grandval arrived in Paris at 10 a.m. on the morning of the 19th. One day to go.

In Paris each member of the Cabinet produced his own new list of proposed Moroccan representatives, but they were chosen only from well-tutored pupils. The second item on the agenda was the departure of the delegation to Madagascar to invite Mohammed V to France. Everyone agreed that this must take place on the 26th, but the actual decision was postponed to a conference at Aix-les-Bains on the 22nd. There was also discussion on who should head this delegation, but M. Faure remarked blandly, 'We shall have plenty of time to talk about it at Aix on the 22nd.'

Grandval was in despair; it was now late on the very eve of the dreaded day, and conditions could not have been more inflammatory if they had been contrived to that end.

He landed at Rabat at 2 a.m. on the 20th, and at 7 a.m. the Director of the Interior, General Leblanc, telephoned to him with the opening words, 'It is war.' Massive rioting had broken out at Khenifra, and the General asked authorization to use aircraft. The *Medina* was surrounded by troops, but mounted tribesmen were visible on all the ridges that could be seen from the town. Grandval gave his authorization, but on the condition that use of aircraft should be limited to low flying dispersal of tribal cavalry, and that no shot be fired or bomb dropped. This was only the beginning; during the next few hours the situation was repeated at Boujad, Safi, Ouezzane, Petitjean, Casablanca and Rabat. Already the number of dead and wounded had surpassed Grandval's worst predictions, and he could not have been blamed had he wished the whole French Cabinet and the preceding Resident-Generals to have been included among their number.

But news of the final horror was still to come. At 8.30 a.m. the French Civil Controller was warned by the *Caid* Bel Hadj Ben Bouazza, that numerous mounted tribesmen of the Smah'la tribe were marching on the town of Oued Zem, where the presence of nearby phosphate mines had established round a military post a colony of several hundred Europeans. The defences were negligible, for in the small hours of the morning the majority had been dispatched to protect the inhabitants of Boujad after rioting had broken out. The Civil Controller left with the *Caid's khalifa* and a strong police escort to try to calm the advancing tribal cavalry and persuade them to return to their homes. The whole party, to a man, was slaughtered on its first encounter with the outriders of the Berber warriors, and no news reached the town to prepare its people for the onslaught. The Smah'la, their appetite merely whetted by this first taste of blood, descended on Oued Zem.

Reinforced by dissident elements in the *Medina*, they first took the north-west part of the town, and began to pillage, to murder, and to burn. Such Europeans as could be found were massacred with fanatic savagery. All European patients in the hospital were slaughtered in their beds, including women, children, and a baby of only two months. The chief doctor was decapitated and hacked to pieces. By 10 a.m., when half the town was a smouldering rubble, the situation was accidentally discovered by a naval aircraft. The now distraught Grandval, who had so long, so urgently, and so vainly warned Paris of what would happen on 20 August, now gave General Leblanc virtual *carte blanche*, but still with the proviso that no Moroccan life must be taken unnecessarily. By midday parachute troops and units of the French Foreign Legion had restored some sort of order to what was left of Oued Zem, but

Grandval's injunctions had been ignored in a flame of vengeance and racial hatred.

Twenty miles away, the French engineers at the mines of Aït Amar were savagely attacked by their Berber workers, reinforced by local tribesmen. They barricaded themselves in their office building until they were eventually relieved by the Foreign Legion, but by that time fourteen of them had been killed – unpleasantly.

M. Faure's calendar had indeed ignored 20 August.

Dadès valley kasbah

As General de Gaulle had predicted, Grandval got the blame. The majority Paris reaction was that the military commanders had worked miracles with their small and complex tactical resources, but if Grandval had done his job all this could easily have been avoided. In protest, General Leblanc handed in his resignation, saying with masterly under-statement that the true intentions of the French Government had been concealed from him.

Morocco was undergoing a crisis unparalleled in all her long history of destruction and bloodshed. Despite the traditional tendency for all demonstration and rioting to end in pure plunder and pillage, it was no longer possible to ignore the fact that the demonstrators were activated by an absolute demand for the restoration of Mohammed V. The actual date of 20 August, chosen for concerted action, was evidence enough that this was a particular rather than a general rage against the occupying colonial power. The Sultan Mohammed V, deposed in 1953 by the 'beautiful' General Juin, now held the French Government of M. Faure entirely at his mercy. The pejorative phrase 'Mohammed the Weak' seemed now a little off-key.

Grandval now finally made up his mind to resign office. He had remained only because he had thought – wrongly, as it turned out – that he might be able to save Moroccan and French lives, that he might somehow be able to avert the catastrophes pre-ordained by French policy. He had failed, and the knowledge of failure must have been bitter indeed. On 25 August he had received news of the death in an air crash of his only remaining trusted military commander, General Duval. He was thus left without political or military support, at a time when he had the greatest possible need of both.

Among the French viceroys in Morocco Grandval towers head and shoulders above them all – greater even than Lyautey, for he was that great rarity, a truly civilized human being who was against violence and repression.

He left Morocco, secretly, on the afternoon of 26 August 1955, letting it be known that he was paying a brief visit to France, and would return in forty-eight hours. The Moroccan people did not mourn his departure – he was just another Frenchman gone, and good riddance. In Morocco now there should be some monument to this honest man who was so grossly exploited and deceived by his own country.

T'hami El Glaoui was ignorant of none of the current intrigues and events, but he was himself reaching the point of despair. Although there were still politicians in Paris who said, 'The Glaoui will never yield', he knew with finality that he had been betrayed by France, and he had neither hope nor faith in the future. He sensed, too, that no matter how great privileges had accrued to him through this alliance it was now over and finished – that he was indeed the dagger discarded. It was at this stage that he said, 'I will never trust a Frenchman again, nor speak to one if I can avoid it.' It was at this stage, too, that metropolitan France coined an adjective '*glaouisé*', which meant neither more nor less than 'betrayed'.

T'hami, old and sick, knowing now through the intervention of French and Swiss doctors that he had cancer and had but a short time to live, was desperately in need of some kind of support. It did not exist – in any real sense – either in France or Morocco; as a result he turned back to his religion. It would be easy to say that since the return to power of his deadliest enemy, Mohammed V, could no longer be avoided, he chose the obvious course of opportunism, but this would be to ignore his real needs. For many, many years he had become accustomed to all that went with great power; overnight, almost, he had lost these things, and his search was now atavistic, for security. For a time he continued to give the old answers, almost ritualistically; on the massacre of Oued Zem he said, 'There is only one way to deal with rebels. Kill them, or put them in prison.' 'But, Excellency, there are not prisons enough in all Morocco to contain the enemies of this present state. It is time to think upon new lines.' 'It has nothing to do with me, it is the responsibility of the French security forces under the French army.'

Grandval was replaced by General Boyer de Latour, Resident-General in Tunisia, and M. Faure assured the world at large that the Moroccan question would be solved by 12 September. The conference at Aix-les-Bains was held according to arrangement, and was attended by a number of invited Moroccan nationalist leaders. By 12 September no solution had been reached, and Arafa was still Sultan in Rabat. Every kind of pressure was put upon him by the extreme right wing to remain there at all costs, including personal and unauthorized visits and telephone calls from members of the French Government. Conducting this whole mad orchestra of an old world spirit of colonialism was the ex-Resident-General, Marshal Juin.

Faure now had a definite policy, but the work of the colonial lobbyists was enough to thwart it at every turn. This policy was, briefly, the abdication of Arafa and his temporary replacement by a truly representative Council of the Throne, pending the return of Mohammed V. Arafa left Rabat for his Tangier palace (the same palace to which the deposed Sultan Moulay Abd El Aziz, his uncle, had retired in 1907), but there was no Council of the Throne, and a cousin of Arafa's, a son of Moulay Hafid, named Abdallah Hafidi, was left as a sort of khalifa of the throne for which there was no precedent. Further demonstrations and bloodshed followed throughout the first fortnight of October.

On 15 October General Latour announced the formation of a

Council of the Throne, but the Istiqlal refused to accept its members as representative of the country. The Council, nevertheless, existed. By now the Berber tribes of the Middle Atlas and the Rif mountains were in a state of open rebellion, and there was civil war in Morocco. A body under the name of the Army of Liberation had been formed, claiming immediate independence and the territorial gains of the Rio d'Oro right down to the Senegal river. The brains of the organization were represented by a Tangier lawyer named Yusfi, a Doctor Khatib, and a M. Basri – all later imprisoned by their own people in independent Morocco's first attempts to restore order to the country.

By 20 October arrangements had been completed for Mohammed V to be flown from Madagascar to Nice on the 31st. By the 26th T'hami El Glaoui, old, sick, and finally betrayed beyond redemption, accepted the inevitable. Early in the morning, accompanied by his son Abdessadek, his Chamberlain Hadj Idder and his Secretary Mohammed Khizzioui, he left Marrakesh in his black Bentley and took the route for Rabat via his palace in Casablanca.

He broke his journey to eat there. A short time after his arrival three leading members of the Istiqlal party requested audience. T'hami had always resolutely refused to speak to any member of the Istiqlal, and the fact that he received these three, Ahmed Bennani, Abbas El Kebaj, and Ahmed Guessous, and allowed their introduction by his son Abdessadek, was evidence of some volte-face. After a somewhat surprised exchange of courtesies, for their visit was a result of rumour only, and they were far from certain of their reception, they asked whether it was true that he was about to make some declaration, and if so whether this declaration was truly in favour of the restoration of Mohammed V. T'hami replied, 'I am about to make a declaration of the profoundest importance to me, to my children, and to the people of Morocco. I am now on my way to speak to the Council of the Throne.' They asked then whether they might see the text, but this he refused. Guessous then asked T'hami's pardon for the hatred he had harboured against him. T'hami seemed moved, and gave it freely.

It is at least probable that the instigator of this unprecedented meeting was Guessous. His parents had been killed at the French capture of Taza when he was a small child. He was adopted by a French officer, who was killed only a year later, and he was then adopted by another French officer, who gave him a French education. As a member of the Istiqlal, and at the same time an employee of the French agricultural administration for the Marrakesh region, he had been charged by his party to try to make contact with T'hami and to reason with him. But though he made a friend of Abdessadek and the two spent many evenings together, T'hami had refused absolutely to receive him or to be influenced in any way by Abdessadek's recommendations. Not long before the time of which I am writing Guessous had met a prominent French member of Moral Rearmament, M. Chavannes, who had persuaded him to visit their headquarters at Caux sur Montreux. Here, to the great embarrassment of Chavannes, the first speech was a glowing picture of the Glaoui's life and ménage, and that of his son Mohammed at Aït Ourir. Chavannes protested at the tactlessness of this speech, and arranged that Guessous should have lunch with the speaker the following day. At this lunch Guessous was told that a man was as far from God as he was from his worst enemy, and he had replied, 'If I am as far from God as I am from T'hami El Glaoui I shall certainly never see heaven!' But the thought may well have pricked him, for he was a man of great sincerity and profound religious convictions.

At 3.15 in the afternoon the black Bentley took the road for Rabat. The Council of the Throne awaited T'hami. Hafidi, son of the Sultan Moulay Hafid; Hadj Fatmi Ben Slimane, ex-Pasha of Fez; Si Bekkai, ex-Pasha of Sefrou; Si Taib Spihi, Pasha of Salé; and Si Tahar Ou Assou. Ben Slimane, as President of the Council, received T'hami and asked him whether he had come to acknowledge allegiance to the Council of the Throne, and whether he wished to make any declaration. T'hami entered the throne room, and before the Council he made the speech that set his whole life's work at nought: 'I identify myself with the will of the Moroccan people for the restoration of the rightful Sultan Mohammed Ben Youssef and for his immediate return from Madagascar.' The brief session of Council closed with scenes of incredulous jubilation.

T'hami and his retinue left the Palace to find a vast throng awaiting them outside, among which were clamorous journalists of all nations. They pressed round him as he entered his car, saying, 'Excellency, show us your declaration!', but the old man was now showing signs of acute fatigue and replied, 'Address yourselves to my son Si Abdessadek.' Abdessadek silenced the crowd, and read aloud the text of the declaration which, he said, had already been published at Agadir by its Pasha Hadj Ahmed Ben Ayyoun, so that the tribespeople of the Sous should know the truth. Then the black Bentley turned and took the road for the South.

As soon as T'hami had regained his palace at Marrakesh, he telephoned to *Caïd* Brahim at Telouet, and told him to release Madani. Madani reached Marrakesh the same day, and his father said to him, 'You know what I have done. You are now free and in Marrakesh – do nothing rash.'

Berber dancers

17

The Hand of Allah

MOHAMMED V and his household arrived in Nice on 31 October 1955, and proceeded on 2 November to a very temporary headquarters in Paris, the Hôtel Henri IV. All pretence was at an end, and in France he was received with the full honours due to a reigning monarch. Every single Moroccan who had proclaimed himself against Mohammed V recanted with hysterical speed and emphasis, and poured into Paris to do homage to him. Arafa abdicated, Kittani followed T'hami's lead, the Council of the Throne resigned on 6 November.

On 8 November T'hami El Glaoui left Marrakesh for Paris to render homage to the Sultan whom he had deposed. In the evening he arrived at the Hôtel Claridge. From there he telephoned to the Crown Prince Moulay Hassan at the Sultan's headquarters in the Château of Saint Germain-en-Laye to ask whether he might obtain audience, and received answer that the Sultan would see him at ten o'clock the following morning. Before leaving for this appointment he telephoned to Quai d'Orsay to inform the French Government of the request and the reply; an action which may appear as a very belated attempt to keep a foot in each camp, since there could not now be said to be more than one camp in any case. Then he set out for Saint Germain-en-Laye, in company with his son Abdessadek, his Chamberlain Hadj Idder and his Secretary Si Mohammed El Khizzioui. There he found every Pasha, *Caid*, and other notable of Morocco waiting to be received by the Sultan. Only three had been refused audience, Abd El Hay Kittani, the F'kih Bourgba, Minister of *Habous* (religious property), and the Pasha of Mogador.

T'hami waited in the anteroom, and for the first time in his life he was kept waiting for a whole hour. Four photographers had been authorized to enter; many who had not pressed against the windows, feasting upon his humiliation. At length the *Caid* Briech, in charge of the introduction of the Sultan's subjects, announced that His Majesty awaited the Pasha of Marrakesh.

T'hami went in alone, discarding his shoes, to the room where the Sultan sat upon an ornate Louis XVI sofa. He knelt, advanced the last few paces upon his knees, and touched his forehead to the ground before the Sultan's feet, while the Sultan's minister performed the ritualistic action of pressing down upon the old man's shoulders – a ritual indeed, for T'hami could prostrate himself no lower. Almost in a whisper he begged the Sultan's mercy upon one who had lost the road and gone astray, but Mohammed V replied, 'Let us forget the past. We have need of you both for our person and for our people. It is not what you have done that matters, but what you do in the future.' T'hami was helped to his feet and backed unsteadily out of the Sultan's presence. In the waiting-room he made a statement to the Press of the words that had passed between himself and the Sultan.

When he got back to the Claridge he found a deputation representing the political parties whom he had opposed, Pashas, *Caids* and *cadis*, who thanked him in the name of their peoples for his act of contrition. He replied, 'It was the proper thing to do.'

It was as though the cancer of which he was dying chose this moment of his spiritual defeat to begin the final assault upon his body. He regained his room in a state of near-collapse, and was immediately seized by rending agonies in the stomach. After a few moments he lost consciousness, and did not regain it that day.

In the evening the Crown Prince Moulay Hassan telephoned to T'hami's eldest son, *Caid* Brahim of Telouet, to invite him and Abdessadek to dine. This extraordinarily improbable repast, which did not end until midnight, was attended only by T'hami's two sons and the Sultan's two sons, Moulay Hassan and Moulay Abdallah, and during the course of it they discussed in a lively and entirely friendly manner the events of the past two years. It appeared then as if there was to be a true reconciliation between the throne and all the members of the House of Glaoua.

Two days later, on 11 November, T'hami's tremendous will had reasserted itself over his tortured body enough to make immediate plans. *Caid* Brahim telephoned to Saint Germain-en-Laye to request for him a second audience with the Sultan. This was granted, and T'hami asked permission not to accompany the Sultan to Rabat, but to remain in Paris until he was well enough to travel. The Sultan granted his permission, and T'hami sent *Caid* Brahim to Marrakesh to prepare the tribespeople for the triumphal return of Mohammed V to Rabat. The Berber warriors of the South were to march upon the northern capital once again, but this time with the full knowledge of their purpose.

T'hami's long life, with its splendours, its follies and its dramas, was almost over. The dagger had been used and discarded.

He remained for five days in Paris, while the Sultan received his tumultuous welcome to Morocco, and during those days the cancer that was consuming his entrails began to take absolute command. But he was determined to die in the city he had ruled for forty-three years, and on the sixth day he was flown to Marrakesh by a special plane. There he remained at his palace of Dar El Glaoui for a further five days, under constant medical surveillance, before being moved to the Marrakesh hospital. On 7 December he was operated upon by four French surgeons, but both they and he knew that there was no chance of significantly prolonging his life. At the end of December he returned to the Dar El Glaoui, with the knowledge that there were only days to go.

On the last morning, 30 January 1956, with his family united around him, he rallied himself and spoke with great lucidity. To *Caid* Brahim he said, 'Listen, my son, take care of your brothers, and our friends, and the people of our houses and our lands. Look after their interests to the very end. When you have an enemy, watch him – I've had plenty, and I know.' A quarter of an hour later he made his last effort and pronounced the *chahada*, the profession of faith, *La illa Lah Mohammed rassoul Allah* – 'There is no God but Allah and Mohammed is his Prophet.' Then the heavy eyelids closed, and he did not regain consciousness. The Lion of the Atlas, the Eagle of Telouet, the Black Panther, the Mountain Gazelle, the last of the Lords of the Atlas, died at 11.30 a.m. aged seventy-eight.

A little before midday the following day he was buried where he had chosen to be, at the shrine of Sidi Ben Slimane. His body was carried down from his room in a modern lift. Wrapped in black, uncoffined, it was placed upon a crude wooden stretcher and carried upon the heads of four Glaoua warriors, out into the garden past the squatting figures of the religious brotherhoods of Marrakesh who chanted verses from the Koran, past the windows of the women's quarters from which T'hami's widowed wives and concubines watched with cries of hysterical grief the departure of their master; out into the vast press of people who accompanied T'hami upon his last journey. Half-way between the palace and the cemetery the cortège halted in the Place Bab Riad El Arouss, while the French accorded military honours to the dead body of the ally whom they had betrayed. M. Dubois, the last of the Resident-Generals, made a speech recalling the splendours and heroics of T'hami's life, and ended with the words, 'He was a legendary figure, one such as our modern age will never know again.' Then the cortège passed on into the precincts of the shrine of Sidi Ben Slimane, and T'hami was buried there as he had ordained. Now, the people of Marrakesh say that every Friday night a great black cobra comes up out of the tomb and remains, hood erect and poised as if to strike, until the first light of dawn.

The day after T'hami's funeral his six principal sons left in company with the Minister of the Interior, who had represented the Sultan at the funeral, to render homage to His Majesty. The Sultan said that T'hami's death was a loss not only to them but to him. He asked T'hami's sons to look after their father's women, servants and property, and added that the doors of the Imperial Palace were always open to them. He gave them two letters to the *cadi* of Marrakesh, authorizing them to divide their father's heritage among them. They left for Marrakesh overjoyed at his magnanimity.

But there were forces at work in the country stronger than any one man's pledge. A year after T'hami's death *Caid* Brahim was condemned to fifteen years' exile from his country. Six months later the Army of Liberation arrested four of Brahim's brothers, Abdessadek, Mohammed, Abdallah and Hassan, and held them prisoner for three days. On the fourth day they were transferred on government orders to the custody of the *Caid* at Ouled Said. On the sixth day a *dahir* was published ordering the confiscation of the goods of all those who had worked for the French régime. The most notable of all these families were those of the Glaoui and of the Grand Vizier El Mokri. The four brothers remained imprisoned at Ouled Said for eighteen months, and were then set free, but their heritage had passed into the hands of the State, the herds of their tribespeople had been confiscated, and all the contents of the many Glaoui palaces and *kasbahs* had been sold.

It was sixty-five years since the Sultan Moulay Hassan had presented the Krupp cannon to Madani El Glaoui at Telouet.

By 1960 there were very few people left at Telouet; the great fortified palace, which alone had held a thousand, was crumbling; the once teeming feudal village dependencies were inhabited for the most part only by the now listless Negroes who had once been the servitors of the Glaoui family. The few Berber Glaoua who remained seemed incompletely dressed, for they no longer carried the habitual Moroccan

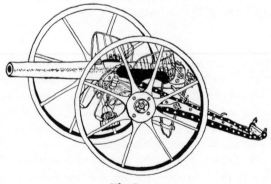

The Cannon

dagger slung upon a cord round the shoulders; the tribe were now forbidden to carry arms of any sort. The daggers had been discarded. The remaining people were administered by a *Caid* from a northern province, and their customs, legends and traditions were fast vanishing under the chill wind from the north.

On a day of March sunshine and great empty stillness I stood with one of the black servitors below the ruined *kasbah* of *Caid* Hammou. Behind was the stony desert plateau, encircled by the mighty painted peaks from which the snows were beginning to thaw, irrigating to a vivid emerald a wide basin of green sward below me, at the centre of which lay a shallow lake of flood-water. All around the margin of this lake, and on the short turf stretching away from it, lay the dead bodies of storks, the sacred bird of Morocco, and their carcases were visible, too, upon their bulky nests which capped the *kasbah* towers. They had died, though I did not know this, because they had eaten of locust-swarms poisoned by helicopter. I asked the Negro why they were all dead. He looked at them and he looked back at the great silent *kasbahs*, and said, 'I do not know – the hand of Allah lies heavy upon Telouet.'

APPENDIX I

The Aftermath — Marrakesh in 1956

I was only a child when these things happened, but I remember them well, though I don't like to remember them or to think that I laughed to see a man burnt alive. It was a short time after the Glaoui's death, and I was a child of about nine, living with my parents in Marrakesh as we always had. I had just eaten the midday meal, and I was playing in a street of our quarter with other children of about my age when someone came running and calling out, 'Come and see the fun! They've broken open the Glaoui's garage at the Dar El Glaoui and they're smashing his cars!' We ran with him and we found a great crowd round the garage and men smashing a big black car – I think it was a Delahaye. Then they set fire to it and everyone watched it burn, talking and shouting excitedly. Suddenly someone in the crowd yelled out, 'Let's have vengeance on the other traitors!' Others repeated it, and in a moment or two a wild yelling crowd had formed in the Riad El Arrouss beside the Dar El Glaoui, all shouting, 'Death to the traitors!' They began running towards the house of a man who had been one of the Glaoui's judges – his name was Kittani, but I don't think he was any close relation of Abd El Hay Kittani, a very cruel man who had punished the young people who were against the Glaoui by making them sit naked upon bottles that had been broken half-way up, and then confining them chained in dungeons with just enough food to live. I ran with the crowd, and when they reached his door and beat upon it he opened it himself. He held the Koran open in his left hand, and at his right were his small sons. He began to speak at once, asking for mercy and for pity, but immediately one of the foremost of the crowd shouted 'No pity for traitors!' and struck him a great blow on the head with a cudgel. He fell, unconscious, and they seized him and put him on a *kourrissa*, the hand-cart on which people push goods about, and rushed him outside the city walls at Bab Doukkala. All the young people were stoning him, and stripping him of his clothes. They put him upon a rubbish dump, poured petrol over him, and set him alight. I remember the smell and the way his skin blistered and burst. We were laughing, all of us, and that is something I am ashamed, bitterly, to remember.

The crowd went back into the town, this time led by a jeep manned by four quite young boys with masks over their faces. They made for the house of one of El Glaoui's intimates, a man called Bou Raghba [*pronounced* Bourgba] who was hated by all his neighbours. I ran behind them, laughing and excited as we all were. I suppose there's no point in saying I was just a child, because the adults were behaving in the same way. We were showing of what stuff human beings are really made, without the disguises and pretences behind which we hide.

When we reached Bou Raghba's house it was barred and shuttered and Bou Raghba himself began to fire upon us with a sub-machine-gun from an upper window. In the first burst of fire he killed two of the boys who had been driving the jeep, and wounded many of the crowd, including us children. Then the leader of the mob decided to attack the house by following the roof-tops from the next street. They did this, and threw down incendiary bombs; this stopped him shooting, and while he was suffocating in the fumes they broke down the door, and a man who was an old soldier of France, and who had been wounded by Bou Raghba's first shots, went in first and shot at Bou Raghba with a rifle. Then he was dragged out as Kittani had been. They stripped him quite naked and hauled him through the streets – I remember how his shaven head looked like a jelly, because the skull had been dashed to pieces. We all thought it was funny – why? Then they burned him too, on the same rubbish dump.

Another party of rioters seized the *Chef de Quartier* of Bou Doukkala, a man named Mghinia. I remember him particularly because my mother had ticked off one of his children for fighting me in the street, and as a result he had sent a deputation of his guard to intimidate us. My father had to pay them blackmail money and because of this we went hungry for a long time. My mother said that Allah would curse this man for what he had done, and when he was burnt alive that day she said that Allah had answered her prayers. When the rioters reached the burning place he held out his *shaccara* (the leather bag all Berbers carry) and took from it a huge sum of money. He said, 'I know I am about to die, but in Allah's name give this money to my children.' The crowd yelled 'No mercy!' and pushed him on to the fire, throwing petrol over him at the same time. I remember how, as he burnt, the hand holding the purse of money raised itself, clenched, above the flames, and remained visible long after the man must have been dead.

I think nothing worse ever took place in Marrakesh, even in the terrible old days. Nothing could be worse. My father, who could remember the dynastic wars and horrors of the days of Moulay Hafid, said, 'No man has the right to burn another and thus deprive him of resurrection – it is the privilege of none but Allah himself.' It is said that when the Sultan Mohammed V heard of these happenings he did not eat for seven days.

Although no police intervened in the course of these horrors, the new Pasha of Marrakesh, El Skalli, placed his guards round the corpses that smouldered all night, so that the women of the city could not take pieces of them for use in black magic, for the relics of these burned enemies were thought to be potent. Indeed El Skalli did more, for he took to himself the orphaned children of Bou Raghba, and I remember that as he put his arms around them he said, 'This terrible happening, this shame, can never be wiped out in any of our lifetimes.'

You have made me remember these things – remember the real story behind what is still called 'The Place of Burning', and have made me ashamed for remembering. We Moroccans are a violent and a cruel people – but is not all humanity the same before they begin to think? Please do not disclose my name. I was a child, following a mob.

Walter Harris's Description of his Dealings with Moulay Hafid after his Deposition

'Almost immediately after his arrival at Tangier began the discussion of the terms of his abdication, for only its more general lines had been settled at Rabat, and in a very short time the ex-Sultan's relations with the French were seriously embroiled. Moulay Hafid did not apparently regret having abdicated. He knew that his continued presence on the throne in the actual circumstances was out of the question. What he did regret was that he had not made better terms for himself, and he still hoped to be able to extort more money and more properties. Thus the negotiations were being carried on by him in a spirit of grasping meanness, that rendered any solution impossible. At the beginning of his reign, only four years before, he had shown signs of an elevated and patriotic spirit, and really intended to do his best to maintain the independence of the country. But he had quickly realized how impossible his self-set task was. He became unscrupulous, neurasthenic, and cruel. He made enemies on every side – amongst his own people by his barbarities and his extortions, and amongst the Europeans by his cynicism and intransigence.

'So it came about that in a very short time after his arrival in Tangier his relations with the French authorities were strained to breaking-point. It was at this moment, when everything seemed almost hopeless, that the writer was asked, independently by both sides, to intervene in the interests of peace.

'This invitation to intervene came about as follows. There had been a terrible scene between the ex-Sultan and the French authority charged with the negotiations, and Moulay Hafid had used language so unparliamentary that any further meeting was out of the question.

'Early one morning the writer received the visit of a French official, who implored him to become the medium of the conversations and proposals, paying him the compliment of saying that he seemed to be the only person who had any influence over the ex-Sultan, whose conduct was bitterly resented in high quarters.

'Scarcely had this person disappeared when the ex-Sultan himself arrived. His nerves appeared to have completely given way, and he was in a state of the deepest depression. Throwing himself upon a sofa, and in tears, he poured out all his woes, real and pretended, attacking the French with a vehemence that was as violent as it was unjust. "You," he said to the writer, "seem to be the only person who has any influence upon these villains. Will you continue the negotiations?" Under the circumstances there was nothing to do but to accept.

'An hour later the conversations had recommenced. The ex-Sultan spent the whole day at the writer's villa, and could scarcely be persuaded to eat or drink. During the writer's absence at the French Legation, Moulay Hafid took his departure – and that was not all he took, for he carried away with him the choicest specimens of the writer's Arabic manuscripts. Being of a literary disposition, the temptation of the illuminated books was too great. The writer never saw them again, but it is only fair to state that His Majesty sent a present in exchange the same evening – a gold and enamelled dagger.

'During the following weeks the principal points of the negotiations were successfully solved – the question of the pension, funds for the construction of a palace in Tangier, the retention of certain large properties in the interior, and the future of the ex-Sultan's wives and children.

'Then came the question of the debts, about which there ensued a long and acrimonious discussion. It had been accepted on principle that all debts that had been incurred directly, and in certain cases indirectly, in the interests of the State, should be considered as Governmental debts, and be paid by the French Protectorate Government, while all private debts should be settled out of the ex-Sultan's private fortune.

'Now this distinction of debts was rendered extremely difficult by the systems under which Morocco had been governed. The Sultan of Morocco was always an absolute monarch, and, as such, the revenues of the country were his. There had never been any distinction between public funds and private funds – all belonged to the Sultan. As a rule, the expenses of the State, as well as the palace upkeep, were paid by bills drawn upon the custom-houses of the 'coast. It was therefore no easy task to arrive at an agreement as to what were State and what private debts, so inextricably mixed had they been in the past.

'There was, for instance, a bill for a fine marble staircase, ordered in Italy for the palace at Fez. The French authorities argued that this very expensive staircase was merely a piece of wild extravagance on the part of Moulay Hafid, and that accordingly he ought to pay for it. The ex-Sultan, on the contrary, insisted that the palace was the property of the State – he had argued just the other way when he had been called upon to explain why he had brought away with him certain valuable fixtures – and that any additions and improvements he had made to it were all to the advantage and interests of the State. It was, he said, his successor and not he himself who would benefit by the marble staircase. The Protectorate Government allowed the justice of this argument and paid the bill.

'The sequel to this incident is worth the telling. A few months later, when the ex-Sultan was signing a contract for the construction of his new palace at Tangier, he eliminated one of the several marble staircases marked in the plan. He had, he said, a very superior marble stair which would do admirably in its place. The writer ventured to ask if it was the same one about which there had been so much discussion. "It is," replied Moulay Hafid. "You see, it had not yet left Italy, so I telegraphed and had it delivered here instead of being sent to Fez.'

'A still more complicated claim was for some hundreds of yards of very expensive and very fine crimson cloth. Naturally the Protectorate authorities scheduled this amongst the private debts. The Sultan protested. The cloth, he said, had been purchased for Governmental purposes – in fact, for the trousers of the Imperial kitchen-maids – for there are several hundred slave-women employed in preparing the palace food. The Protectorate Government refused to be responsible for this debt. The ex-Sultan drew up an historical treatise to prove that Imperial kitchen-maids were part and parcel of the State, and passed, like the palace itself, from Sultan to Sultan. The principle was accepted, but the debt was disallowed, on the ground that these good ladies did not require such expensive stuff for their nether garments. A cotton material, they argued, would have equally well served the purpose. The Sultan's reply was unanswerable and crushing. "In Europe," he said, "it may be the custom for the Imperial kitchen-maids to wear cotton trousers, but in Morocco we have more appreciation of the dignity of their position."

'There was nothing more to be said. The debt was paid by the Protectorate Government.

'The long discussions which the writer, practically unaided, had to maintain with the Sultan were not always facilitated by the surroundings in which they took place. There were no regular business hours for these conversations or for the examination of the voluminous documents which they often necessitated, and which were always in the wildest disorder, but which none the less required a careful perusal. Whenever and wherever His Majesty felt inclined he would burst out with his grievances, and as at all costs he had to be kept apart from the French authorities, the whole storm used often to fall on the writer's head. At times the ex-Sultan, struck by a brilliant idea how to escape the payment of some small sum, would arrive at my villa at dawn – at others I was hastily summoned to the palace at midnight. The debts were discussed and argued over in every possible situation, and any one present, native or European, high authority or slave, was dragged into the discussion. There were two aged ladies whose opinion was constantly asked. One was an old black slave nurse, the other a Berber woman, quite white, who was the Sultan's soothsayer and fortune-teller. Her advice was always good and to the point, and she never hesitated to tell the ex-Sultan that he was acting foolishly when occasion required, and she rendered distinct services toward the unravelling of these complicated questions.

'Sometimes it was when seated on mattresses and rugs in a garden, surrounded by his slaves, that Moulay Hafid would argue that all debts were State debts, and that private property never had legally existed, and that individual responsibility – especially for debts – was contrary to the highest principles of divine nature. He discoursed with great facility and great literary ability. He had a classical Arabic quotation at hand – often most skilfully misquoted – to prove his every argument. He could persuade others quickly, and himself at once. Leaning slightly forward, swathed in his soft white robes, he would speak slowly and with great distinctness and charm, with an accompanying slow movement of his right hand – and then in the middle of it all his attention would be attracted by his elephants or his llamas or a group of cranes that would come wandering out of the shrubberies, and turn his thoughts and his conversation into new channels.

'While the two elephants were being brought from Fez to Tangier at the time of the abdication, one of them escaped on the road, and being an unknown beast to the villagers of the countryside, it met with many adventures. Wherever it appeared arose panic and consternation, and the whole male population turned out with such weapons as they could lay their hand on to drive away this terrible and unknown beast. The country population, however, possessed little but very primitive firearms, whose range was short, and whose bullets dropped harmlessly off the sides and back of the huge pachyderm, thereby increasing the panic. The elephant, luxuriating in the spring crops, grazed undisturbed, while from as near as they dared to approach the outraged proprietors poured volleys against its unheeding bulk. But one day it found itself on the road again, and came rolling along into Tangier none the worse, but remarkably spotted all over with the marks of the spent bullets.

'It was during one of these long discussions of claims that news was brought to the Sultan that one of these elephants was lying down in its stable and was unable to rise. This information, of course, put an end to all business, and we set out at once to see what had happened. Sure enough, the female elephant was lying on her side, every now and then struggling but vainly to get up.

'After everybody present had given an opinion, and every effort had been made to put the poor creature on her legs – from twisting her tail to lighting a lucifer match under her hind-legs, which failed, of course, even to singe the skin – Moulay Hafid arrived at the conclusion that only by the aid of a crane could the elephant be raised.

'A heavy beam was found, and made fast to ropes hung from the roof. Two other ropes were passed under the elephant's recumbent body, one just behind her front-legs, the other just in front of her hind ones, a manoeuvre that entailed considerable labour.

'When everything was ready the slaves began to haul. With cries and shouts of mutual encouragement they managed to raise the elephant till she was swinging suspended in the air, and then set to work to lower her gently on her feet. In this they would no doubt have been successful had not the forward one of the two ropes slipped back, with the result that the unfortunate pachyderm, suspended now only from aft, stood on her head, and remained hung up in this posture until she was lowered to earth once more, this time with her face to the wall in a more impossible position than ever. But in spite of all the difficulties, after much shouting, swearing, and a good deal of real hard work, she was restored to a standing posture.

'There were many occasions when our conversations were in less pleasant places than the gardens. There was a room, for instance, in a hideous villa that Moulay Hafid had bought as it stood, and greatly admired, that seemed haunted by the microbe of irritability. Not only was its decoration appalling, but it was full of a host of objects which the ex-Sultan had brought from Fez, amongst them innumerable musical-boxes, clocks of every shape and form – he evidently particularly fancied a kind made in the shape of a locomotive engine in coloured metals, the wheels of which all turned round at the hours, half-hours, and quarters, and mechanical toys. Everything, or nearly everything, was broken, and an Italian watchmaker was employed in trying to sort out the wheels, bells, and other internal arrangements of this damaged collection of rubbish. It was in this room that he had set up his workshop, and nothing pleased Moulay Hafid more than to sit and watch him.

'Now it was not unseldom the writer's duty to break to the ex-Sultan the news that the French authorities refused to pay such and such a debt. With all oriental autocrats it is best to break bad news gently, for they are usually wanting in self-restraint, and are not accustomed to blunt facts. Often it required considerable time and a neatly-expressed argument, couched in Arabic at once diplomatic and literary, to carry out the task successfully and escape an access of temper. I would begin with a little discourse on the origin of revenues, the ex-Sultan would listen attentively, and then just as the moment arrived to bring generalities into line with actual facts, the Italian watchmaker would meet with an unexpected success. Clocks would begin to strike and chime, or a musical-box, old and wheezy, to play, or an almost featherless stuffed canary in a cage would utter piercing notes in a voice that moth and rust had terribly corrupted – or from near the Italian's chair some groaning mechanical toy would crawl its unnatural course over the carpet, eventually to turn over on its back and apparently expire in a whizz of unoiled wheels. The ex-Sultan's attention would stray. There was an end of business, and it generally led to the ordering of a meal to be served to every one – at any hour and on any excuse – at which the watchmaker, who might have only just finished a repast, was the guest of honour, and was forced to eat incredible quantities of very rich, but very excellent, food. And what was left of the royal repast was handed out of the windows and served to the slaves and gardeners.

'Perhaps the most difficult claim to settle was that of the Sultan's Spanish dentist, for not only was it extremely complicated, but it also became almost international. It might naturally be supposed that the dentist's bill was for professional services; but no – it was for a live lion. In the early days of his reign the Sultan had engaged the dentist at a regular stipend, and he had become a permanent member of His Majesty's household. For a time he was kept busy patching up the mouths of the Court, but the task was at length accomplished, and the ladies' teeth glistened with gold. The dentist remained unemployed.

'Now there is no possible reason in the world why dentists shouldn't be employed to buy lions. It is not, of course, usual, and so sounds incongruous. In Morocco, views as to the limitations of professions are much less restricted than with us. In Moulay Abd El Aziz's time, a very few years ago, one of the duties of the Scotch Court-piper was to feed the kangaroos, the professional photographer made scones, a high military authority supplied the Sultan's ladies with under-linen, and the gardener from Kew was entrusted with the very difficult task of teaching macaw parrots to swear. And so it was not surprising that the dentist became a buyer of lions.

'In the first flush of his success at the beginning of his reign, Moulay Hafid was setting himself up as an orthodox Sovereign by Divine Right, and this necessitated a menagerie. It is one of the attributes of royalty which has almost disappeared, except in the East, though at one time universal. It is perhaps fortunate. The hurried entrance of an excited rhinoceros amongst the guests at a garden party at Windsor Castle would prove embarrassing, and so, to a lesser degree, would be the presence of a hyena at the evening service at St George's Chapel; but in Morocco similar incidents would have attracted little or no attention. The father of Moulay Hafid, Moulay Hassan, allowed his tame leopards to roam about his reception-rooms; but his son, more timid by nature, confined the leopards in cages, and replaced them in his drawing-room by guinea-pigs. The effect lost in majesty, but the afternoon callers were less nervous.

'So the dentist was sent to Hamburg to buy wild beasts from Hagenbeck. But he erred. He should have returned with the menagerie and shared its glory. He delayed, and when he arrived in Fez a few months later the novelty and glamour of the wild beasts was passed, and the reception that he and the belated unpaid-for lion – the last of a series of lions – met with was by no means enthusiastic. Moulay Hafid had discovered that the upkeep of so many sheep-eating beasts was expensive, as the tribes, on the eve of revolt, refused to supply the sheep, and insultingly demanded payment.

'So far the claim presented no insurmountable difficulties, but there were complications; for the Sultan, immensely attracted by the mechanism of the dentist's operating-chair, had some time previously ordered from the dentist, and paid for, a throne to be constructed on the same mechanical principles. This throne had never been supplied, so there was a counter-claim. The Sultan stated that he had paid for the lion; or if he hadn't, then it was a State debt, for which he was not responsible, and demanded the delivery of his mechanical throne. The question was still under discussion when the term of the dentist's contract expired, and the ex-Sultan notified him that it would not be renewed. But the dentist held a trump card, for the ex-Sultan had lodged him, rent free, in a little villa situated on one of His Majesty's Tangier properties. The dentist refused to quit, and the Spanish authorities upheld him, for by the capitulations each Power protects the interests of its respective subjects. A body of slaves were sent to eject him. They found the villa barricaded, and were met with pistol-shots. The complications were becoming serious, and international in character. The Sultan, the French authorities, the Spanish dentist, the black slaves, the writer, a British subject, and the German lion threatened to cause annoyance to the Governments of Europe if recourse was made to firearms. I made an impassioned appeal for conciliation on everyone's part. After much delay and no little difficulty, an interview was arranged between the ex-Sultan and the dentist, at which as mediator I was to be present. Each was studiously coached in the part he was to play: the dentist's plaintive appeals to the generosity of the ex-Sovereign were carefully rehearsed, as were also the Sovereign's "gracious reply", while the writer's little speech on the blessing of brotherly love was a gem of the first quality.

'Moulay Hafid was seated on a divan studiously reading a book when the dentist entered and made his obeisance, but this obeisance – polite but intentionally curtailed – did not meet with His Majesty's approval. Instead of, as arranged, smilingly acknowledging the dentist's salutation, the ex-Sultan continued reading half aloud in a sing-song drawl.

'A long period ensued, broken by one of the suite, who said, "My lord the King, the dentist is here."

'Without raising his eyes from his book the ex-Sultan asked in the softest of voices:

' " Has he brought my mechanical throne?"

'Now that wasn't on the programme at all! There was to have been no mention of such distressing objects as dentist-chair-thrones or lions. There was to have been purely and simply a reconciliation: a sum of money promised to the dentist if he would quit the villa, and a general abandonment of claim and counter-claim. But alas! before any one could intervene the dentist shouted out:

' "Pay me for my lion!"

'And then the fat was in the fire. For some moments the atmosphere boiled with vituperative allusions to lions and dentist-thrones, until, while the writer restrained the infuriated potentate, the dentist was, struggling and shouting, removed from the presence-chamber.

'By dint of great persuasion the writer eventually brought about a settlement. The Sultan did not get his throne, nor did he pay for the lion, which the Protectorate Government took over, not having been informed that it had meanwhile died. The dentist received a sum of money in payment of all his claims. The writer, whose solution it was, got the thanks of none of them, all three parties concerned expressing themselves as distinctly dissatisfied with the settlement arrived at.

'In 1912–13 the modern palace which the latest of the abdicated Sultans, Moulay Hafid, has built himself at Tangier, and which covers several acres of ground with its immense blocks of buildings and its courtyards, was still rising from the level of the soil, and His Majesty was temporarily housed, with all his retinue, in the old *Kasbah* at the top of the town. It is a spacious, uncomfortable, out-of-date, and out-of-repair old castle, and it formed by no means a satisfactory place of residence, for it was not easy to install 168 people within its crumbling walls with any comfort or pleasure. When, too, it is taken into account that many of these 168 people were royal ladies with royal prerogatives as to their apartments – to say nothing of their pretensions to the "most favoured ladies' " treatment – it can be realized that the solution was not easy. Even in the most luxurious of quarters the ladies of the palace are said to give considerable trouble, for jealousy is rife; and if one of them receives more attentions – personal or in presents – than the rest, there are often disturbing scenes – and rumour says that the "Arifas" – the elderly housekeepers charged with keeping order – not unseldom make use of the equivalent of the "birch rod" – a knotted cord.

'The royal ladies completely filled all the available accommodation in the *Kasbah*, and the Sultan was able to reserve for his private use only a couple of very shabby rooms over the entrance. Here he would, apologetically, receive his guests until the purchase of the large garden in which he constructed his new palace furnished him with more convenient apartments; for there was a villa in the garden which had been erected by its former owner, a wealthy and respected Israelite, who had for years filled the post of Belgian Vice-Consul. This villa, which still exists, is an astounding example of extraordinary taste – a pseudo-moresque copy of a toy-house, over which plaster and paint of every colour had been poured in amazing profusion. Plaster lions guard its entrance, more like great diseased pug-dogs than the king of beasts, and to add to their attractions they were then painted all over with red spots. A scalloped archway crowned the front door, and the former owner had once pointed out to the writer that each of the thirty-two scallops was painted a different colour, which was quite evident. Inside, decoration had run riot in the wildest way. The ceilings dripped with plaster protuberances in reds and gold. Mouldings pursued their strange courses all over the parti-coloured walls, enclosing odd-shaped panels painted with views of lakes and mountains and impossible fishing-boats – designed and executed by some local genius. Chandeliers of coloured glass hung suspended from the ceilings, and the windows were fitted with panes of green and purple. The Sultan was in ecstasies, and furnished these astounding apartments with chairs and sofas covered in red plush trimmed with blue and yellow fringes, and studded with blue and yellow buttons. On the walls he hung promiscuously a score of clocks of all sizes and shapes; he littered tables with mechanical toys; he piled up musical-boxes in every corner; he hung cages of canaries in every window, and adorned the chimneypiece with baskets of paper-flowers – and then he sat down, happy, to enjoy civilization.

'Amongst many mechanical toys which Moulay Hafid possessed was one which in its absurdity surpassed any toy I have ever seen. It was – or had been – a parrot, life-sized, seated on a high brass stand which contained music. Moth and rust had corrupted, and there was little left of the gorgeous bird except a wash-leather body the shape of an inflated sausage, with the two black bead eyes still more or less in place, and a crooked and paralysed-looking beak. The legs had given way, and the cushion of a body had sunk depressedly on to the brass perch. One long red tail-feather shot out at an angle, and round its neck and sparsely distributed over its body were the remains of other plumes, of which little but the quills remained. On either side were the foundations of what had once been its wings, consisting of mechanical appliances in wood and wire. Anything more pitiful than this relic of parrotry could not be imagined.

'Every now and then, apparently for no reason, this strange toy came to life. The sausage-like body wriggled, the broken beak opened, the tail-feather shot out at a new angle, and the framework of the wings extended itself and closed again with a click; and then after a mighty effort, which gave one the

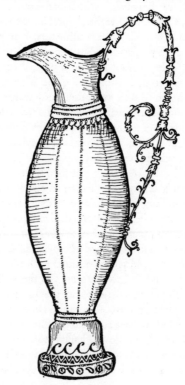

impression that the ghost of a bird was going to be sea-sick, the whistling pipes concealed in the brass stand began to play. The music was at a par with the bird – notes were missing, and the whole scale had sunk or risen into tones and demi-tones of unimaginable composition. To recognize the tune was an impossibility, but the thrill of the performance was undeniable. It seemed as though there was a race between the bird and the pipes to reach the climax first. Both grew more and more excited, until suddenly there was a long wheeze and longer chromatic scale from high to low, and, with an appealing shake of its palsied head, the parrot collapsed once more into its state of petrified despair.

'Moulay Hafid was completely content. He realized that at last, after the sombre pomp of the palace at Fez, he had settled down to modern life and refinement, and had attained "taste".'

APPENDIX III

Extract from *With Mulai Hafid at Fez* by Lawrence Harris (1909)

Letter from the Vizier for Foreign Affairs to Sultan Moulay Hafid to Mr Lawrence Harris (not to be confused with Mr Walter Harris) authorizing him to be the sole British correspondent in Morocco.

PRAISE BE TO GOD ALONE

(And there is no power and no strength except in God the high and great.)

To the most learned and able critics the leaders of the London papers.

With thanks to God, may He be ever exalted, and trusting you may have always good health and great prosperity for yourselves as well as your magnificent Government, which is always so steadfast in friendship. We have received your letter through the hands of the intelligent representative Mr Lawrence Harris, containing your kind expressions of sincere friendship which were addressed to His Majesty Our Lord the Sultan, may God strengthen him. And after he had apprehended, may his grandeur last, and rejoiced over its kind words and sweet expressions, he commanded me, may God exalt him, to answer you categorically.

As to the above mentioned representative he has joyfully arrived, and was received by His Majesty with favour and consideration, and he communicated to His Majesty, on your behalf, the messages with which he was commissioned of greetings and congratulations upon what God has bestowed upon him in confirming him on the Throne of the Greatest Caliphate. May those greetings return to you full of all the blessings you wish, and may you enjoy all happiness and dignity and greatness, and this is what we pray to God to bestow upon His servant.

As to your recommending the said representative, and your wish that he might be favoured by His Majesty and meet with distinguished treatment, Our Lord the Sultan has granted him an interview which has pleased him, and he, may God preserve him, received all his news and information, and he was received as an intelligent and wise representative. As to recommending him, this has been done, and as a proof of his being thoroughly looked after His Majesty, may he be glorified, has appointed him as correspondent here to the intelligent Director of the journal *The Graphic*, one of the three great papers; may he be preserved. Therefore all communications and correspondence and letters between both concerning the High *Mahkzen* of Morocco, may it be exalted, should be communicated through him, without any other intermediary, and nothing will be published unless that which is authorized through the said correspondent. Anything published in another paper will not be taken into consideration as true. Therefore, the paper and its correspondent will be appointed without restriction.

As to your praising of those three papers, this is known to Our Lord the Sultan, the Victorious by God, and it is sufficient honour for them to be under the rule and commands of His Majesty the exalted King Edward VII. May his reign endure. And may you be looked upon with consideration and honour and covered with glory and greatness, and finally this is the Chereefian command, may God prosper it, in the 11th day of Ramadan, the great of the year 1326.

Signed   Abdallah El Fasi (Vizier for Foreign Affairs)
May God be kind to him

The Director of the three London papers, may his happiness last.

APPENDIX IV

Comments on *Son Excellence*
by Members of the Old Régime

Babin writes that at the time of the death of Madani's and T'hami's mother, Lalla Zora, they were so poor that they could not afford the ritual cotton *suair*, and had to bury her dressed in wool, in her *haik*.

COMMENT: *Completely false. They were well off, even rich, in the time of the Sultan Moulay Hassan. Lalla Zora's husband, Mohammed El Tibibt, was* Caid. *She was decently buried in the normal way at Telouet. Moreover the Sultan Moulay Hassan had been received by El Tibibt at Telouet, and had left laden with the customary gifts – slaves, mules, dates, saffron, henna and silver.*

On the same page Babin recounts a conversation in derogation of the Glaoui, between himself and an authentic *Chereef* (descendant of the Prophet) who was Babin's servant.

COMMENT: *At that time* Chereefs *were very deeply respected, and it seems hardly probable that a* Chereef *would have been working for a Christian* (nasrani).

Babin suggests that at the death of Moulay Youssef in 1927 T'hami was engaged in some deep and treacherous intrigue. Babin says that he left hurriedly for Fez, and that the French had to give orders to the police at Ben Guerir to stop him and persuade him to return to his palace. He suggests that T'hami was trying to seize the throne.

COMMENT: *The Crown Prince, Moulay Idriss, brother of the late King Mohammed V and uncle of the reigning King H.M. Hassan II, was resident in Marrakesh. He was joined by the dead Sultan Moulay Youssef's Vizier, a certain Ababou, so that he might be taken to Fez and enthroned as the new Sultan. This did not suit the French, who wanted to put Idriss's brother Mohammed on the throne, and Idriss and Ababou were therefore arrested by French police at Ben Guerir. The Glaoui was required by the French to accompany their authorities to Fez and put pressure on the* oulemas *(religious councils responsible for electing a new Sultan) to elect*

Mohammed as Sultan. Between them, the Glaoui and his confederate Abd El Hay Kittani, chief of the powerful religious body the Kittaniyine, were successful in this assignment; Mohammed was elected Sultan, and brought by the Glaoui and the French authorities to Rabat. The Glaoui was thus responsible for the election of the Sultan who was to become his deadliest enemy, and whom, in the penultimate stages of the great drama, he succeeded in deposing in 1953. The idea that the Glaoui considered or was considered for the throne is a complete myth.

Babin writes that the fortunes of the Glaoua brothers dated from the usurpation of the throne by Moulay Hafid in 1908 from the only true and rightful Sultan Abd El Aziz.

COMMENT: *Abd El Aziz had showed himself incompetent. After the death of Bou Ahmed under whose thumb Aziz had been, Aziz embarked upon his frivolities, and Madani El Glaoui supported Moulay Hafid with men and with arms.*

Babin suggests that when Moulay Hafid dismissed T'hami from his post of Pasha of Marrakesh he did so because 'although he had never been known to be squeamish' he could no longer tolerate T'hami's infamies.

COMMENT: *Hafid dismissed Madani from his post of Grand Vizier and T'hami from his post as Pasha of Marrakesh because he was afraid of the ever-increasing power of the two brothers. Their conduct in office would have mattered nothing to Hafid one way or another. It has always been the same in Morocco – if a man or a family became too powerful it was only prudent to destitute them while there was still time.*

On the same page Babin writes that at that time T'hami had no house in Marrakesh and was compelled to rent, 'or more probably requisition', the palace of Abd El Aziz's former Grand Vizier and Minister of War, Hadj Mehdi El Menhebbi.

COMMENT: *The Glaoui was married to one of El Menhebbi's daughters. Menhebbi was living in Tangier, and put his Marrakesh palace at the Glaoui's disposal. Menhebbi's daughter (who was the Glaoui's only literate wife other than Chems, whom he married later) lived at this palace until the construction of her new one at Bab Doukkala (one of Marrakesh's principal gates). When El Menhebbi died, his heirs sold his own palace to the Glaoui. This is the kind of statement by Monsieur Babin that makes his book puerile, and it was beneath the dignity of the Glaoui to answer each of his insults categorically.*

Babin writes that while still a very young man he married for her money the elderly widow of an exceedingly rich merchant, Si Boubker Ben Bachir

Ghandjaoui, and appointed himself guardian of her children. He goes on to suggest that this marriage was never consummated, and that in fact she was merely imprisoned for fifteen years.

COMMENT: *Pure nonsense. She was far from old, and had small children at the time of Ghandjaoui's death. Another of his wives was T'hami's niece, daughter of Madani, and at Ghandjaoui's death they both came to T'hami's household. Here again Monsieur Babin simply ignores the customs of the country.*

Babin writes of the Glaoui's magnificent library, filled with rare editions evidently purloined from the Sultan's palace, since they carry the Sultan's stamp, and deplores such a library in the hands of an illiterate.

COMMENT: *Many books in the Glaoui's library had been the property of the Sultans, and were bought from those Sultans' heirs. Others who bought in the same way, and thus built up fine libraries, were Abd El Hay Kittani (who also did steal some), the Grand Vizier El Mokri, and Moulay Kebir Benzidane. For the rest, the Glaoui was not what we would call illiterate in Morocco. Certainly he wrote with a cut reed pen, and certainly his handwriting was coarse, but his signature, on the other hand, was exceedingly fine. His function in life was after all hardly that of a calligrapher or a scribe.*

'In order rightly to assess the Pasha of Marrakesh it is enough to look at his entourage – that "bad lot riddled with debts and crimes". Byaz, Salah, Morsi, Berrimoj: all of them greedy, slavish climbers, and complacent to the vilest whims.'

COMMENTS: *In the interests of historical accuracy we list below his 'cronies' at that time.*
  1. *His secretary and future* cadi *(religious judge)* Chereef Si Mohammed Ben Rhamoun, *who was his regular partner at the Spanish card game 'Los Tres'.*
  2. *His* khalifa *and half-brother Si Ahmed Zemmouri, who had been First Secretary to the Sultan Moulay Hafid. [Half brother would appear to be a slip for nephew.]*
  3. *Si Hadj Madani Kebbaj, a sugar merchant, still alive in 1964, aged eighty-eight.*
  4. *His barber, Si Mohammed Binbin. This man was a great talker, a great wit, and a great flatterer. He was also an expert on leg massage – a therapy widely practised in Morocco before retiring, to calm the nerves and assist the circulation.*
  5. *Hadj Bachir Chraibi, a dealer, who supplied textiles to the ladies of the harem.*
  6. *Moulay Abd El Malek El Amrani,* protégé obligé *of the Glaoui; also a*

dealer in textiles, who was another of his regular card partners. El Amrani might be described as a sort of talking newspaper, being a great expert on current Moroccan affairs and those of the recent past.

7. Hadj Abd El Krim Tichour.

8. Amine El Oumana, chief provost of the corporation, an old man long in the service of the central government, who had seen five Sultans pass.

9. Hadj Idder, the black servitor who had brought food and messages to him and the French hostages at the time of the Pretender El Hiba's entry into Marrakesh. Hadj Idder, T'hami's Chamberlain and later his closest personal confidant, was the son of a captive slave of Madani's, who had not freed him.

These were his intimates, who were faithful to him until they died or until he died, but they were essentially a circle of friends rather than counsellors, and all political matters he kept rigidly as a question for himself and the French. To describe any of these men as Babin described his so-called entourage is nothing short of absurd.

Babin refers to the myth that the Glaoui bore a charmed life, and had no fear of death.

COMMENT: *In fact, he lived in perpetual fear of being poisoned. For this reason he almost invariably refused invitations to any meal, except when his host was a man in whom he had absolute confidence. He also frequently employed a taster.*

Babin dreams of an exposé by Dr Françoise Légey, 'doctor to the House of Glaoua', of atrocities more horrifying than the confessions of Gilles de Rais, which made the Bishop of Nantes cover the image of Christ with his cloak.

COMMENT: *Really, Babin goes beyond all limits here. Dr Yvonne Légey, who published a well-known book* The Folklore of Morocco, *was a qualified French woman doctor who worked at the dispensary of Dar Si Aissa, (between the Ksour and the Mouassines). Being a woman, she was naturally chosen according to Islamic custom to look after the womenfolk of both the principal Glaoui households, that of Hammou at Telouet, and that of T'hami at Marrakesh. She had at first an assistant, a young Algerian woman, who was later sent to Paris. Dr Légey was hardly the type of woman to work in silence for a modern Gilles de Rais.*

Babin recounts how at the great feast of Aid El Kebir, at which the tribal chiefs come to render homage to their Sultan, T'hami El Glaoui had shown himself so reluctant to prostrate himself before His Imperial Majesty that the Grand Master of Ceremonies, *Caid* El Mechouar, had seized the Glaoui by force and pressed his forehead into the dust.

COMMENT: *This is a real Babinism! Moroccan protocol is intricate and traditional, and demands that the* Caid *or tribal chief, preceded by the* Caid *of the Mechouar (which is the description of a functionary, not the name of a man) advances to make obeisance before the Sultan. The Sultan's Chamberlain places his hand upon the subject's neck as he prostrates himself, keeping it there throughout the whole ritual of pressing his forehead to the ground. This is a spectacular ritual, and could obviously be misinterpreted by an observer who was completely unfamiliar with it. Babin might be forgiven this (but how, if he claims such profound familiarity with Morocco?); he cannot, surely, be forgiven the paragraph of pure invention that follows his description: 'This made a fine scandal at the Palace, and shook the dazzling protocol instituted by Marshal Lyautey, who so loved playing at Kings. The Resident-General, summoned by telephone from Rabat by the Sultan, hastened to Meknès, the scene of the drama, and lectured his "dear son" using all his influence to smooth the incident over.' A great many of Babin's castles are founded upon sand in this way – he might get away with invention if passages like this did not make it so obvious that he must be inventing. In fact, the Sultan and the Glaoui were at this time mutually trustful and close friends, and the Glaoui was one of the very few Moroccans who could obtain audience with the Sultan at a moment's notice and without prior notification. In recognition of this close liaison, the Glaoui was not required, as were other Pashas and* Caids, *to throw back the hood of his bernous in ceremonial submission at State occasions. The Glaoui was, naturally, proud of these prerogatives that set him above the other rulers; but he himself was a man of protocol, and he never abused them, even when, years later, he declared war upon the Sultan. The observance of tradition lay in his very roots.*

Babin writes that the *Caid* Abd El Malek M'touggi used to boast of having enjoyed from T'hami as an adolescent 'the favours which, according to *The Symposium*, Socrates refused to accept from Alcibiades'.

COMMENT: *Homosexuality between man and boy was never considered in any way abnormal or shameful in Morocco until the infiltration of European opinion with the French. It is perhaps interesting to note that scientific opinion in the United States and in Europe is now endorsing the old Moroccan notion that bisexuality is the normal human condition. Harkas were continually on the move, and boys were easier to take into battle than women. All the harkas of the period, including those of the M'touggi, Glaoui and Goundafi, were accompanied by numerous boys for the satisfaction of sexual needs, and no shame attached to the practice on either side. A boy lover was called an* ail or, *in the possessive sense a* 'd'rri'. *The universal existence of 'Greek love' was commented upon either directly or obliquely by nearly every French writer on Morocco, so Gustave Babin cannot have been ignorant of the facts. Some writers treated of the subject at great length and in great detail, notably Christian Houel in* Le Maroc, *and Maurice Privat in* Vénus au Maroc; *and chroniclers like Dr Paul Chatinières in describing the travels of his medical mission mention that this aspect of life that would have been embarrassing in France seemed in no way offensive in Morocco. Prostitution naturally existed, but to nothing like the extent of its female counterpart in other countries. In short, sexual relationships with boys were considered a normal and harmless convenience, and in making his 'allegation' M. Babin is removing the Glaoui from a Moroccan culture to one of puritan northern Europe – a clumsy mistake that recurs often throughout his whole book.*

Babin mentions a detail that, he says, makes everyone shudder who hears of it – that the Glaoui has a private cemetery – that of Sid El Sadafi. 'If one were to stamp on the ground of it,' says the Marrakshi with a shiver, 'it would spout fresh blood.'

COMMENT: *The inhabitants of the quarters of Tizzogarine, Halfaoui, Sidi Abd El Aziz and Bab Doukkala all had the right to free burial in the cemetery of Sid El Sadafi, which is a little more than a hectare in area. The cemetery was never other than* habous *(religious property). Sometimes when a cemetery is full, the older remains are removed elsewhere, or sometimes it is rented out for other purposes, as in the case of Sid El Sadafi, on whose ground there is now a garage, a charcoal depot, and a firewood depot. The shrine itself is roofless and neglected; the cult of saints or* marabouts *is frowned upon by the religious leaders, and plays little part now in the burial of the dead, which is not in any case attended by the Christian taboos. This was in no sense the Glaoui's private cemetery.*

Babin recounts an anecdote of how the Glaoui, receiving ill-prepared coffee on two successive days, wrote a note to the woman responsible, swearing never again to drink coffee that she had made.

COMMENT: *The Glaoui never had a single woman in his household – slave, concubine or daughter – who was literate, with the exceptions of his wife who was the daughter of Mehdi El Menhebbi, whom he divorced in 1943, and his Turkish wife Chems. There would therefore have been little point in writing a note to any of them.*

On the same page Babin describes how one of the Glaoui's servitors had killed a child, and came before the Glaoui for his offence. In answer to the punishment imposed upon him, he exclaimed, 'But I have often killed on your orders!' His punishment was severe, his eventual fate unrecorded.

COMMENT: *Certainly he was beaten and imprisoned – but no one in the whole world could have spoken like that to T'hami El Glaoui, least of all one of his own men. The Glaoui never pardoned, never forgave.*

Babin comments upon the Glaoui's enormous territories acquired by dubious means, and the fortunes in stolen gold and in jewels.

COMMENT: *Even Moroccans, in fact, believed in the myth of the Glaoui's inexhaustible coffers. At his death it was confidently expected that he would leave anything between fifteen and twenty milliard francs, whereas his total possessions did not exceed two and a half milliards. But three Moroccan citizens – Sebti (of Fez), Bennani (of Casablanca), and Benkirane, died worth more than the Glaoui. He spent gigantic sums in maintaining his prestige with foreign visitors, more especially the French and the Middle Eastern potentates. He was heavily in debt to France, largely because of the huge sums he spent in entertaining her higher officials. In this, as in everything else he did until 1955, the French encouraged and supported him. At his nomination as Pasha of Marrakesh he drew six thousand reals from the French (1 real = 5 old French francs); this loan increased and increased until it was finally twenty thousand reals over and above an entertainment allowance of ten thousand reals per month. Examples of current prices at that time are: one kilo of meat, one-twentieth of a real (0·25 old francs); one small house, one or two reals (5 or 10 old francs); an elegant outfit of clothes, one or two reals (5 or 10 old francs). It may be interesting to compare the Glaoui's spending with that of the late Sultan H.M. Mohammed V, who was on the throne at the time. His father, the Sultan Moulay Youssef, received on his succession to the throne ten thousand reals (50,000 francs). Mohammed V at his accession, apart from his inheritance, received an annual allowance of twenty thousand reals (100,000 francs) which was later increased to fifty thousand reals (250,000 francs). In addition he received by custom hediya, presents in cash and in kind from every town and district of his kingdom on the feast days of Aid El Kebir, Aid El Mouloud, and Aid Sghir. Pashas and Caids and khalifas of the Sultan, such as Hafid the Scurvy before he deposed his brother Moulay Abd El Aziz, were wont to divert the hediya to their own profit when opportunity offered. His Majesty Mohammed V put an end to the custom of hediya when he returned from exile in 1955, but, despite this, at his death in 1960 he left a gigantic fortune, made up almost entirely of hediya. Later, T'hami El Glaoui had serious disagreements with more than one French authority on the question of hediya, and on each occasion this dispute was with the French military commander of the Ouazarzat region. Briefly, Pasha T'hami El Glaoui insisted on two hediya, one for the Sultan and one for himself. This was after the death of Hammou, and he had stepped into Hammou's shoes as commander of all the South, by appointing his elder son Brahim Caid of all the regions that had been controlled by Hammou. He was merely following the custom instituted by Hammou, and to which Hammou owed much of his vast fortune. Colonel Doguant, Ouazarzat command, intervened, saying that the tribes were being destituted by the necessity to pay twice. The French civil authorities upheld him, but took no positive action, and the matter was shelved until 1949, when Colonel Ribaud, commanding the same area, took a firmer stand. The hediya in question was that of the Sektana tribes, and consisted of silver, carpets, almonds, butter, honey, dates and other valuables from the region of Taliouine. The French then proposed to the Glaoui that the Sultan's hediya should be shared between the Sultan and himself. But the Glaoui was as firm as Colonel Ribaud, and with better result. He said to the French delegation, 'Am I responsible for administering the tribes or are you? It has got to be one or the other. You are now on your way to see a French army officer who does not know the character, mentality or customs of the tribal peoples. The Residency-General knows enough to listen to me rather than to him.' The net result of this encounter was the recall of Colonel Ribaud, and the substitution of another who made no trouble and fell in with all the Pasha's ideas.*

Babin's fiercest attack of all lies in the allegation that the Glaoui lived upon the immoral earnings of not one but several thousand women. The red light quarter of Marrakesh was among the largest of any town in the world.

COMMENT : *Before answering this allegation in detail we should again explain that European and Moroccan attitudes differed widely in all matters pertaining to sex, and perhaps most of all as regards the two questions of homosexuality and prostitution. To be a prostitute was in no way a dishonourable profession or one to be ashamed of. As in other aspects of life, it was simply the will of Allah. The same Doctor Yvonne Légey, of whom we have spoken, has written accurately about this. The visit of a prostitute to a newly-married girl was a happy omen, because the prostitute carried on her forehead the magic sign which created love and desire in men. Sexual pleasure is one of the great gifts of Allah and is to be enjoyed as such. For this reason any well-to-do father would present his son with a girl slave at his first sign of puberty. In Fez this present was customarily made on the boy's thirteenth birthday. For this reason, also, a man on entering a prostitute's room would say 'Dief Allah' – 'I am the guest of God', and for this reason also many prostitutes (though not all, as Doctor Légey implies) had tattooed upon the* mons veneris *the* chahada *or profession of Islamic faith, 'La illa Lah Mohammed rassoul Allah' – 'There is no God but Allah, and Mohammed is his Prophet.' (In all Islam the sexual parts are depilated by religious custom.) Having made it clear that prostitution was a respected, even envied profession, I should go on to say that it owed its sudden, (and I admit spectacular) growth in Marrakesh entirely to the influence of the French Protectorate. Though all trades, without exception, were taxed, tax on prostitution had always and in every town been an important source of revenue; and it had been customary for a Sultan to pay his troops entirely from this tax; in this way, as some wit remarked, the soldiers had their fun and got their money back. In the early years of the French occupation the tax would have amounted for each* prostitute to about five francs a day and one cone of sugar per week, the sugar being sold to merchants so that the whole tax was readily available in cash. Even in the early days of the French penetration General d'Amade's army numbered some thirteen thousand men, and to meet their needs he established carefully surveyed brothels both for officers and for other ranks. These brothels were forbidden to Moroccans, and the number of prostitutes therefore increased sharply. Later these military brothels were taxed by the Caids or Pashas who ruled under the French, so that as a source of municipal revenue the trade became even more profitable than before. The precise history of the red light quarter of Marrakesh is as follows. In the early days of the Protectorate, the French authorities requisitioned a number of houses in the quarter called Arset Moussah, as brothels to serve solely the needs of French

Berber woman of the South

and Algerian soldiers stationed in Marrakesh, and units of the French Foreign Legion. These houses formed a closed quarter. As the number of French personnel, both military and civil, increased in number, so did the number of brothels. When units of Moroccan soldiery were recruited under the French, still further brothels were opened for them exclusively. It is difficult to recall the exact number of prostitutes in Marrakesh at the date at which Babin wrote, but they certainly numbered thousands. Later, two other great brothel quarters were opened on European initiative – the Arset El Ghezail and the Arset El Houta. These were not at first closed quarters, but little by little the regular inhabitants drifted away from them, so that they became given up entirely to prostitution, and also became closed quarters. It is true that this could not easily have been done against the Pasha's wishes, but he had no reason to refuse, and gave such assistance as was required. There was a plan for still further extension. A European company was formed; seventy million francs were required to launch this project, by which a new red light quarter would house still another six thousand prostitutes in the garden of Quechchich, near the gate called Bab El Khemis, where the Medina railway station was eventually built. The French Residency-General gave its written approval for the scheme, but the full sum was never raised, and the Resident-General had to ask the French Parliament for a loan of fifty million francs to reimburse El Glaoui for the money he had personally advanced. This was a business investment like any other; El Glaoui had also invested large sums in French industry in Morocco, and in mining projects in particular. In addition to the red light quarters mentioned above, there was a very large brothel composed entirely of European women. This brothel was involved in the Marseilles white slave traffic trial, in which El Glaoui was accused but exonerated. The defence employed the most famous of French counsels, Maîtres Floriot, Issors and Jean-Charles Legrand. The white brothel remained open until 1949; the rest were not closed until after the Sultan Mohammed V returned from exile in 1955, when the number of registered prostitutes in Marrakesh numbered, according to the khalifa, twenty-seven thousand, but others who had access to the facts put the figure at a maximum of sixteen thousand.

The Documents in Reply

On the subject of Babin's book, T'hami El Glaoui addressed himself both to the Sultan and to the Resident-General. Prefacing these letters by the text of his various citations, he assembled the whole under the title '*Son Excellence* – Some documents in reply to an infamous campaign'. I translate these in full as the first letter to the Sultan is of considerable interest in the light of subsequent events, and the lengthy epistle to the French Resident-General gives T'hami's version of his adult career.

The Glaoui as Lyautey and France saw him.

Text of citations obtained by the Pasha El Hadj T'hami El Glaoui. General Order No. 34, dated 16.12.1916.

El Hadj T'hami, Pasha of Marrakesh, commanding the *harka* sent against the Sektana of the South, by the vigour and energy of his action, assured the rapid submission of this tribe. Thereafter, working in liaison with the Pasha Haida ou Mouis, at the end of a fierce struggle lasting forty-eight hours, he forced the valley of the Oued Aghen, and took the reputedly impregnable fortresses of Ahelaghem. His courage, his bravery in battle, inspired the troops under his command; while at the same time by his political wisdom he pacified the region and the dissidence of El Hiba in the unconquered areas of the south-east and the centre. CROIX DE GUERRE AVEC PALME.

General Order No. 50, dated 18.6.1917.

El Hadj T'hami Ben Mohammed Mezouari El Glaoui, Pasha of Marrakesh, at the battle of Tizi on 11 April, went to the help of allied contingents beset by an enemy outnumbering them. Charging at the head of his cavalry with standards flying, he turned the tables by a brilliant counter-attack. On 17 April at Oued Tiguinit, in hand-to-hand combat and sabre charge, he displayed the most admirable bravery, killing several of the enemy with his own hand; and, though his own troops were inferior in number to those of the enemy, he finally repulsed them, taking both rifles and horses. During all that day he fought in the front rank, showing himself superior even to his reputation as a warrior and warlord. CROIX DE GUERRE AVEC PALME.

Text accompanying promotion to Grand Officier de la Légion d'Honneur dated 13.12.1920.

A great Moroccan leader, administrator and warrior, who for many years has not ceased to give proof of his constant loyalty to France during her days of trial as well as those of her glory. At the head of ten thousand men whom he had recruited, he came, by means of a brilliant diversion, to the aid of French troops in their action against the rebel *harkas* of the Chereef of the Sahara.

MÉRITE MILITAIRE CHEREEFIEN AVEC CITATION À L'ORDRE DE L'ARMÉE AVEC PALME dated 13.12.1920.

In July 1920, being placed in command of a *harka* in the Todgha region, he showed himself once again to be both a warrior and organizer of the highest order. In the battles of 31 July and 1 August at Timatraouine, he inflicted the bloodiest of defeats upon the troops of Ba Ali dispersing them and putting them to flight, adding by the skill of his dispositions yet another page of glory to his great deeds.

GRAND CROIX DE LA LÉGION D'HONNEUR MÉDAILLE MILITAIRE dated 24.10.1925.

El Hadj T'hami Ben Mohammed Mezouari El Glaoui, Pasha of Mar-rakesh, of the highest titles; magnificent warrior who since 1912 at the head of his *harkas* has put at the services of France his remarkable qualities of leadership. Of great courage and incomparable organizing ability, he has commanded the admiration of all. Once again he has brought us the most active and efficacious help in the task of pacifying the South.

To His Imperial Majesty the Sultan (may His power endure).

Sire, Very respectfully and humbly I lay before Your Majesty's feet my complaint on the subject of the humiliation and the damage done to my honour, of which the law is the safeguard. I must do this more especially because I am a slave in the service of our Master, and religiously scrupulous to approach Your Chereefian Majesty in sincerity and loyalty, attributes inherited from my ancestors, of whom since the reign of the great Sultan Moulay Ismael there is no memory of any of them breaking their loyal obedience in a way that might have dismissed them from the consideration of your holy and sacred ancestors.

The descendants of Mezouar (Glaoua) have never ceased, generation after generation, up to the time of this your blessed reign, to be docile auxiliaries of the Imperial authority, happy indeed to have for their lot the goodwill of the Alaouite dynasty and their administrative and military chiefs. This is attested by the historical records, and by the terms of decrees issued by the Alaouites, which are as decorations shining upon our breasts.

This unbreakable pact I have observed until the day when the splendid flag of the glorious government of the French Protectorate appeared in your fortunate Empire; I then from reasons of gratitude and loyalty remained heart and soul a firm and loyal commander at the service of Your Majesty and of the French cause, and to answer to Your Highness and to confirm his opinion in the attitude of the descendants of Mezouar towards the representatives of the glorious French Government.

In return I have reaped the satisfaction of Your Majesty, who has deigned to reward my perfect services in the profoundly sincere submission of His officer by conferring upon him all the Alaouite Orders. The chiefs of the Protectorate have in their turn honoured me with numerous and high French decorations.

I have continued to act to the very best of my ability; my merit lies in the nobleness of my mission, which has built up for me and my family a high citadel of glory, which the tests of time can only make more powerful and more solid.

Despite that, some newspapers such as *Paris Tribune* and others have lined themselves against me, attacking my honour with the clearly expressed intention of harming me in violation of the laws of human dignity – a thing that no human being endowed with self-respect can put up with.

The most astonishing thing, Sire, is that the writers in these journals are unknown to me, and do not know me personally; clearly, therefore, I have given them no reason to act in this way.

Thus Gustave Babin, who had committed the crime of attacking my honour, had been handed over at my request to the French tribunals and had been obliged to offer me his apologies, has reopened the offensive, and not content with writing for the newspapers, has written a book full of insults and base calumnies against me, of such a nature as to revolt anyone who hears them. These attacks have touched my honour and that of all my family, which until the present time has been preserved free from stain by the historic annals of the Alaouite dynasty and the regard of the French Government.

Sire (may God assist you), the action of newspapers like these, growing without encountering either contradiction or repression, could attack even the very highest personality, seeing that your commanders are the very corner-stones of your Empire.

May I add very respectfully that I should be very interested to know how Gustave Babin managed to print these slanders, and how he managed to ensure their dissemination throughout the land without any prohibition against either the work or its dissemination, seeing that at the Residency-General there is a controlling body for the censorship of literature introduced into Morocco.

I have already taken the necessary steps to demand justice from the French tribunals, whose impartiality is well known, and I have drawn up a complaint to the Residency-General, which Your Majesty may deign to find attached hereto, and which I beg them to have the goodness to send on to its proper destination by means of Your Government, so that it may receive the consideration it demands as a complaint emanating from a high member of the Government.

I salute most profoundly Your Majesty raised up by God.

Signed   El Hadj T'hami El Glaoui, Pasha of Marrakesh.

To the Ambassador the Resident-General of France in Morocco.

I have the honour to address you in your capacity of representative of the great protecting nation, in order to apprise you of the measures that I felt obliged to take in approaching His Majesty the Sultan, as well as the steps I have taken to safeguard my moral interests that have been outrageously called into question by certain unscrupulous persons.

A depraved publicist, Gustave Babin, of doubtful morality and habits, had settled in Morocco before 1927. To begin with he attached himself to a French group which, finding his attitude intolerable, abandoned him.

Brought to Marrakesh by a certain Abd El Hakim, a businessman and shady agitator long ago expelled from Morocco, he solicited and obtained from me a certain assistance. He then opened an extremely violent campaign against me in a newspaper that he started himself – *L'Ère Français*.

I was openly accused of murder, theft and falsehood. After several months of this my patience was exhausted, and I had recourse to the law courts at Casablanca. Immediately, Gustave Babin sent some of his friends to me to ask my pardon, and to the same end he caused the authorities to intervene.

The matter came before the court on 23 December 1927; Gustave Babin made public apologies, saying that he had been mistaken, that he had attacked me erroneously, and that he deeply regretted having done so. Faced with such cowardice, I gave instructions to my lawyer to act in a manner appropriate to Gustave Babin's public declaration, and I decided not to proceed further or to concern myself with such a man. Discredited in Morocco, Babin returned to France, and for some time I heard no more of him.

To the absolute astonishment of my friends, Babin published in 1932 a foul book entitled *Son Excellence*. The whole book is devoted to myself, though in passing Babin throws out assessments of both French and Moroccan personalities, which are more than derogatory.

This book, burning with hatred, contains nothing but lies. Babin coolly takes up again the theme of his articles in *L'Ère Français* and I am again represented as a murderer, a thief and a crook.

My disgust was so profound that I refused to recognize the existence of such a book or to take any interest in it whatsoever.

All French personalities in touch with Morocco, and all the notables of our own country, received a free prospectus. Babin, vexed by the negligible sales of his book and the hopelessness of his case, managed to interest a bi-monthly Paris periodical in his shameful campaign. This journal repeats Babin's accusations, and it is without doubt inspired by him. Following the same procedure, the issues are sent to French personalities interested in Morocco as well as to Moroccan notables.

Faced with the persistence of such a course of action I have decided not to be silent any longer. Having, under the control of France and with the full confidence of my Sovereign, the responsibility for governing important territories, I do not wish to take the direct action I had decided upon for the vindication of my honour without putting myself under the protection of His Majesty the Sultan and under the aegis of the great country of which you are the authorized representative. It was in this spirit that I obtained audience with the Sultan, which he very graciously accorded me, and in the course of which I explained to him the improper attacks to which I have been subject. It is also in that spirit that I address this letter to you.

In my ignorance of French law, I thought that the government of the Protectorate could take measures to ensure that these attacks directed against me by dishonourable persons be halted and punished. My hands being tied by the obligations of my responsibilities, I believed, and I still believe, that I have the right to efficacious protection.

I have had the great joy to receive from France the unequallable rank of Grand Cross of the Legion of Honour; and I have recently received, with undying pride, the Médaille Militaire, as a commanding officer in war. My sovereign has had the goodness to bestow upon me the highest order (Grand Cordon) of Ouissam, and that of a *Mérite Militaire Chereefien*. Having merited the highest decorations that can be awarded, both French and Moroccan, I thought myself sheltered from the kind of base intrigue with which I am surrounded. Nevertheless the force and persistence of these calumnies are such that I find myself today, on the advice of illustrious friends, under the necessity to come to my own aid by proclaiming before the tribunals of my Second Country both the villainy of its enemies and the inanity of their accusations.

I must also – a thing that is painful to me – recall the facts that have made me worthy of the Sultan's affection and the favour of the government of the Protectorate.

I have not hesitated to place myself wholly at the service of France and to show my devotion to her since her entry into Morocco. Well before the French occupation, under the Sultan Moulay Abd El Aziz, a certain Frenchman, the Marquis de Seconzac, was captured while on a perilous and courageous voyage of exploration of the South. The Quai d'Orsay made representations to the Sultan Moulay Abd El Aziz, who ordered the liberation of the prisoner, but he had been taken far from the South, and appeared lost for ever. With my brother Si Madani I discovered the whereabouts of de Seconzac and took him from his kidnappers and he was able to return safe and sound to France.

After the debarkation of French troops at Casablanca, and despite the fact that Marrakesh was far from the base of military operations, I was moved by profound personal feelings, and I entered into liaison with the Generals Monnier and d'Amade. My brother left for Fez with the Sultan Moulay Hafid, while I remained as my Sovereign's deputy at Marrakesh. I then took serious steps, with the object of helping and serving France. I used all my influence to prepare the attitude of the people, and when General d'Amade had reached Oum R'bia and arranged on the banks of that great Moroccan river, before the Protectorate, fêtes that symbolized the empire of France, it was I who sent as emissaries, to show my deference and love towards your great country, chiefs who might otherwise have been enemies and did thus become allies.

Time passes. We are now in 1912. Victorious troops of the Pretender El Hiba have installed their master in Marrakesh. The whole of the Sous has submitted to his rule; only our family, and to be more precise my brother Si Madani and myself, refuse to submit. Momentarily relieved of my functions as Pasha of Marrakesh, as a result of discord between my brother Si

Madani and the Sultan Moulay Hafid, the uprising of El Hiba is greatly facilitated by the intermediate Pasha of Marrakesh, Driss Mennou, a German agent associating with mining prospectors of that nation. At the risk of our lives, and despite the general hostility, our house remained independent under a guard of our soldiers, mountain men from our home, and in it we sheltered the Frenchmen Verlet-Hanus, the Consul Maigret, the police officer, and the Consul's interpreter.

Some weeks pass; in spite of everything the refugees are safe under our roof, until on the eve of the decisive battle which Mangin was to join, we are attacked in our own house by an enemy a hundred times our number, and the French refugees fall into the hands of El Hiba.

At that moment I impose as a condition that in the Imperial Palace occupied by El Hiba the prisoners should live with me and under my protection. Not one of them was mistreated, and I remained at their side until the end, El Hiba knowing full well the unfortunate consequences to himself which would have followed any act of violence towards myself.

General Mangin approaches. El Hiba goes forth to meet him with numerous troops, soldiers from the southern deserts and people of the Sous, trained by the Pretender under the command of a *cadi* Hida Ould Mouiss.

El Hiba is defeated on the Rehamna plains. General Mangin pursues him, and enters Marrakesh on 7 September 1912.

Alone, I and my tribespeople had remained stubbornly against the usurper.

Against the ascendancy of that man of the desert, and despite all his power, I continued to give aid to your troops.

The *harkas* of El Hiba and of Ould Mouiss were both beaten and put to flight, passing through Marrakesh in the direction of Taroudant.

I managed to take prisoner Ould Mouiss, El Hiba's principal lieutenant.

Of that ruthless enemy of France I made a precious ally, and at the same time I handed over to General Mangin the Frenchmen who had been sheltered at my house. I sent Ould Mouiss before the victorious commander, who granted him pardon.

Marshal Lyautey (then General) following the events with his genius and his gift of divination, understood at once that I was absolutely loyal to him and was only waiting to carry out for the great good of my country and of my master the Sultan his orders on the part of the French programme which concerned the territories adjoining my command.

El Hiba entrenched himself at Taroudant, where he prepared new armies and fresh onslaughts on the North. It was necessary to reduce him before his defeat became forgotten in the Sous, where he still reigned.

That mission was entrusted to me.

I took with me Ould Mouiss. The Marshal gave us two cannons and a French instructor to teach our men how to handle them.

These events are not long ago – they are still in everyone's memory. I may, however, be permitted to recall that it was I who, with the help of Ould Mouiss, surrounded by people of the Sous and the troops raised from my own command, attacked El Hiba alone and succeeded in dislodging him from Taroudant. On 22 May 1913 I had the honour to hoist above the *kasbah* of the town the Chereefian colours and the French flag at the same time.

I left Ould Mouiss at Taroudant, and on my return to Marrakesh I was proclaimed, with the assent of General Mangin, Pasha of that city.

To deny that page of Moroccan history one would have to be a veritable Babin.

Soldiers from the Sous and mountain men from my home fell in mass during the attack. All my brother Madani's resources, all my personal goods – everything was sacrificed to bring this campaign to a successful conclusion.

All this I did with joy, because I had once and for all sworn loyalty and devotion to your country.

Order comes to the South.

My help is devoted to your officers, and the archives of the offices of general information will show that in all the region and in all the territories I helped – without sparing my goods or counting my time – the protecting power which was faced with a task rendered even more difficult by the last convulsions of trouble evoked by El Hiba and the anarchy he had left behind him.

1914. The war breaks out. General Lamothe, commanding the region, brings together all the chiefs of the South, my brother El Madani and myself at their head. On the orders of General Lyautey, the General informs us that war has been declared. France, he tells us, has need of her troops. What will you do if we withdraw our soldiers? What will you do if the fortunes of war go against us?

All the chiefs gathered about Si Madani hesitated.

El Madani spoke for them, and as the eldest of our family declared the loyalty of all, saying that in the future his lot and that of his people was bound to that of France. He gave the most formal assurances possible. The French soldiers could go; we were the guarantors of order, and we assumed full responsibility for it.

These were no vain words. Despite German intrigues, despite the insurrection of Ma El Ainine, there were no incidents either at Marrakesh or at

Taroudant. France could continue her work of civilization in safety. More – the Marshal, to whom nothing was impossible, wished to continue the pacification and throw El Hiba and Ma El Ainine into the desert.

General Lamothe, accompanied by Si El Madani and his partisans, occupied Azilal after a successful campaign in April–May 1916. But it was necessary to go further.

Ould Mouiss is sent to Ait Bou Amrane, to engage El Hiba, who threatened to re-occupy Taroudant. The *harkas* of Ould Mouiss, supported by French artillery, encounter an outnumbering enemy. Ould Mouiss is killed, his *harkas* defeated, and his artillery captured.

General Lamothe forms a column. This time he chooses me to command the auxiliary troops. Battle is joined at Oujine, and lasts for an entire day. Nearly two hundred of my men die. I had two horses killed under me. The victory is ours. The General takes Ait Bou Amrane, and retakes the artillery of Ould Mouiss's *harka*. General Gouraud, replacing Marshal Lyautey, who has been named Minister of War, sends his official felicitations.

German intrigue increases more and more. Azilal becomes their objective. The enemy is better prepared, and more ruthless. General Lamothe forms the second Azilal column. My brother Si Madani accompanies him with a very strong contingent of Glaoua. A decisive battle takes place at Bou Yahia. We are victorious, but our losses are enormous. The Glaoua are decimated. The eldest son [*sic*] of Si Madani, his favourite, a warrior of remarkable spirit and a young man possessing very great beauty, is fatally wounded. His father was to die himself, inconsolable, a few days after his return to Marrakesh.

From December 1918 until March 1919, and from January until December 1920 two columns were formed under the command of General Lamothe. I was at the head of the auxiliary troops. These were the difficult and important operations which ended in the submission of tribes reputedly unconquerable.

From August until October 1922 I accompany General Dougan, who is operating in the territory of the Ait M'hamet tribe. I form a *harka*, and under the direction of the General we achieve the objectives laid down by the French plan.

From 1925 military posts are established in the territories dependent upon my own command, in the regions towards the south of the Atlas, where troops had not yet been installed. To aid in the establishment of these posts, I gave every facility in my power. This period of organization in a very difficult country lasted some years.

November 1931. New operations with their point of departure as Todgha.

November 1932. The campaign of the Ktaoua-Mohammed, and the occupation of Nekob-Tazzarine-Taghbalt. General Catroux commanded and directed the action. The French troops were supported by my irregulars, who gave them efficacious help. At Djebel Baddou and in the Ait Atta, the men of my tribe died in mass, but their loyalty to France never wavered for a moment.

Like my soldiers, and with them as far as the military side is concerned, but alone in political action from 1907 until this day, I have given myself wholly and entirely to France, whom I have served without ever breaking my sworn word.

'Blue men' from the South

Lost men like Babin and his acolytes attacked my actions and discussed them. For a long time I thought that their machinations of hatred and blackmail deserved nothing more than contempt. Today my friends no longer accept this silence. Therefore I have taken action. His Majesty the Sultan has given me his approval.

In your capacity of chief of the Protectorate and representative of France I ask more than this of you. France has heaped me with honours. The highest marks of distinction have been accorded to me. Before, that is to say, the ignominy of the lies so odiously gathered together by this vile detractor. Against these I solicit your moral guarantee.

It would not be admissible to blame a man publicly, in the heart of a country submitted to the Protectorate of France, for even one of the infamies he alleges against me, without the public authorities having their say. It may be useful to state that the facts impudently proclaimed by these dastardly blackmailers are appalling slanders, and if that were not so the French Government would never have tolerated them.

It is to this end that I have laid the matter before the tribunal, acting as a simple private citizen, but at the same time asking you to examine, from the point of view of the Protectorate, what are the best measures to take.

I beg you to accept, Your Excellency, Ambassador and Resident-General of France in Morocco, the assurance of my sincere allegiance and respectful loyalty.

Signed   Si El Hadj T'hami El Mezouari El Glaoui, Pasha of Marrakesh.

Select Bibliography

ANON. *Civilisation – Berbère ou barbare?* Privately printed, 1927.
ANON. *Quelle histoire.* Privately printed, 1935.
AYACHE, ALBERT. *Le Maroc.* Éditions Sociales, 1956.
BABIN, GUSTAVE. *'Son Excellence'.* Ficker, 1932.
BARRAT, ROBERT. *Justice pour le Maroc.* Éditions du Seuil, 1953.
BECHIR, MOSTAFA. *Hello Babitt! Voici le Maroc.* Cairo, 1954.
BENNOUNA, MAHDI. *Our Morocco.* Privately printed, 1951.
BENSUSNAN and FORREST. *Morocco.* Black, 1904.
BERQUE, JACQUES. *Structures Sociales du Haut-Atlas.* Presses Universitaires de France, 1955.
BLUNT, WILFRID. *Black Sunrise.* Methuen, 1951.
CATROUX, GENERAL. *Lyautey le Marocain.* Hachette, 1952.
CHATINIÈRES, DR PAUL. *Dans les Grands Atlas Marocains.* Plon, 1919.
DE CAMPREDON, DR. *Lyautey, Juin, Guillaume.* Durassie, 1955.
DEVERDUN, GASTON. *Marrakech.* Éditions Techniques Nord-Africaines, 1959.
EISENHOWER, D. *Crusade in Europe.* Heinemann, 1948.
EULOGE, RENÉ. *Cimes et Hautes Vallées du Grand Atlas.* Éditions de la Tighermt, Marrakech, n.d.
—. *Les derniers fils de l'ombre.* Éditions de la Tighermt, Marrakech, 1952.
FAJANS, ROMAN. *Alerte en Afrique du Nord.* Peyronnet, 1953.
FRENCH FOREIGN MINISTRY. *Documents Diplomatiques Français.* Various dates.
GABRIELLI, FRANCESCO. *Il risorgimento arabo.* Einaudi, 1958.
GODARD, LÉON. *Description et Histoire du Maroc.* Tanera, 1860.
GOUVION, M. and E. *Kitab Aâyane al-Marhrib 'l-Akça.* Geuthner, 1939.
GRANDVAL, GILBERT. *Ma Mission au Maroc.* Plon, 1956.
GROVE, LADY. *Seventy-one days' Camping in Morocco.* Longmans, Green & Co., 1902.
HARRIS, LAWRENCE. *With Mulai Hafid at Fez.* Smith, Elder, 1909.
HARRIS, WALTER B. *Morocco that was.* Blackwood, 1921.
—. *Tafilet.* Blackwood, 1895.
HOPKINS, H. *The White House Papers of Harry Hopkins.* Eyre & Spottiswoode, 1949.

JANON, RENÉ. *Sultans, Glaouis and Co.* Dominique, 1953.

JUIN, MARÉCHAL. *Le Maghreb en Feu.* Plon, 1957.

JULIEN, CH.-ANDRÉ. *Histoire de l'Afrique du Nord.* Payot, 1956.

JUSTINARD, COL. *Le Caid Goundafi.* Ed. Atlantides, 1951.

KAMMERER, A. *Du débarquement africain au mentre de Darlan.* Flammarion, 1945.

LACOUTURE, J. and S. *Le Maroc à l'épreuve.* Ed. du Seuil, 1958.

LANDAU, ROM. *Moroccan Drama.* Robert Hale, 1956.

—. *The Beauty of Morocco.* Evans, 1951.

LAOUST, E. *Mots et Choses Berbères.* Challamel, 1920.

LÉGEY, DOCTORESSE. *Essai de Folklore Marocain.* Geuthner, 1926.

LE GLAY, MAURICE. *La mort du Rogui.* Berger-Levrault, 1926.

LEPP, IGNACE. *Midi Sonne au Maroc.* Aubier, 1954.

MARTINIÈRE, HENRI DE LA. *Souvenirs du Maroc.* Plon, 1919.

MASPERO, FRANÇOIS. *Industrialisation au Maghreb.* Einaudi, 1963.

MASSIGNON, LOUIS. *Annuaire du Monde Musulman.* Presses Universitaires de France, 1955.

MEAKIN, BUDGETT. *The Land of the Moors.* Sonnenschein, 1901.

MINISTRY OF INFORMATION, RABAT. *Le Maroc à l'heure de l'Indépendance.* 1957.

MONTAGNE, ROBERT. *Les Berbères et le Makhzen dans le Sud du Maroc.* Felix Alcan, 1930.

—. *Révolution au Maroc.* France Empire, 1953.

—. *Villages et Kasbas Berbères.* Felix Alcan, 1930.

MOORE, FREDERICK. *The Passing of Morocco.* Smith, Elder, 1908.

M'TOUGGUI, LHAOUSSINE. *Vue générale de l'histoire Berbère.* Privately printed, n.d.

PAUL-MARGUERITTE, LUCIE. *Chants Berbères.* Berger-Levrault, 1935.

PÉRIGNY, CTE MAURICE DE. *Au Maroc.* Roger, 1918.

PIQUET, VICTOR. *Le Peuple Marocain.* Larose, 1925.

PRIVAT, MAURICE. *Vénus au Maroc.* Documents Secrets, 1921.

RESIDENCY-GENERAL OF MOROCCO. *Dix Ans de Protectorat.* Rabat, 1922.

ROBERT, JACQUES. *La Monarchie Marocaine.* Librairie Générale de droit et de jurisprudence, Pichon & Durand-Auziaz, 1962.

ROHLFS, GERHARD. *Adventures in Morocco.* Sampson Low, 1874.

TAILLARD, F. *Le Nationalisme Marocain.* Plon, 1947.

TERRASSE, HENRI. *Histoire du Maroc.* Atlantides, 1951.

THARAUD, J. and J. *Marrakech.* Plon, 1920; reprinted 1959.

—. *Rabat.* Plon, n.d.

THE MILITARY ATTACHÉ. *Journal of our Mission to Fez.* Harrison, 1909.

VARIOUS AUTHORS IN *Hesperis – Archives Berbères de l'Institut des Hautes-Études Marocaines.* Larosse, various dates.

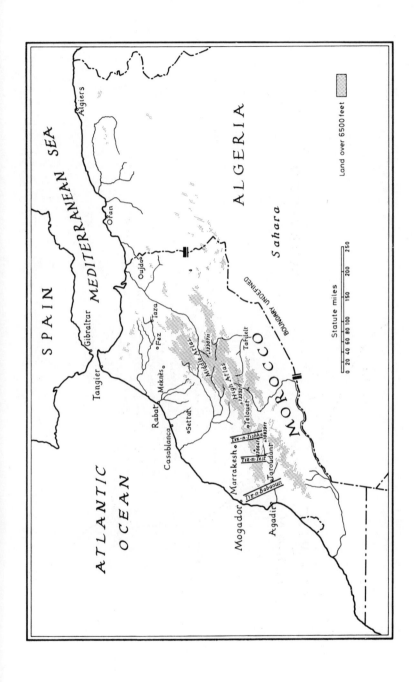

SPAIN

MEDITERRANEAN SEA

ATLANTIC
OCEAN

Algiers

Oran

Gibraltar

Tangier

Oujda

Taza

Fez

Rabat

Meknès

Casablanca

Settat

Marrakesh

Tiz-n-Tishka

Tiz-n-Test

Mogador

Telouet

Taroudant

Tiz-n-Babaoun

Agadir

Tafielt

Middle Atlas

High Atlas

MOROCCO

ALGERIA

Sahara

BOUNDARY UNDEFINED

Land over 6500 feet

Statute miles
0 20 40 60 80 100   150   200   250

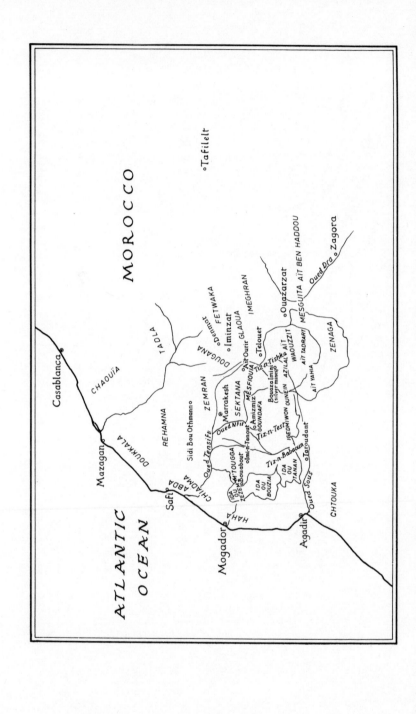

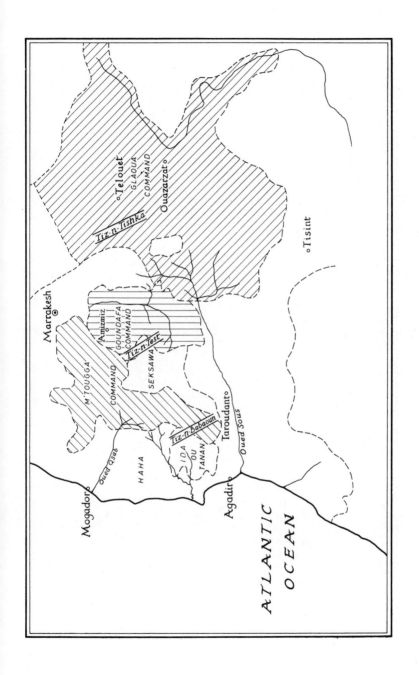

ATLANTIC
OCEAN

Mogador○

Marrakesh◎

○Teluet
GLAOUA
COMMAND
Ouazarzat○

Tiz-n-Tishka

Amizmiz○
GOUNDAFA
COMMAND
Tiz-n-Test

M'TOUGGA
COMMAND

SEKSAWA

Oued Qsab

HAHA

IDA
OU
TANAN

Tiz-n-Babaoun

Taroudant○

Oued Sous

Agadir○

○Tisint

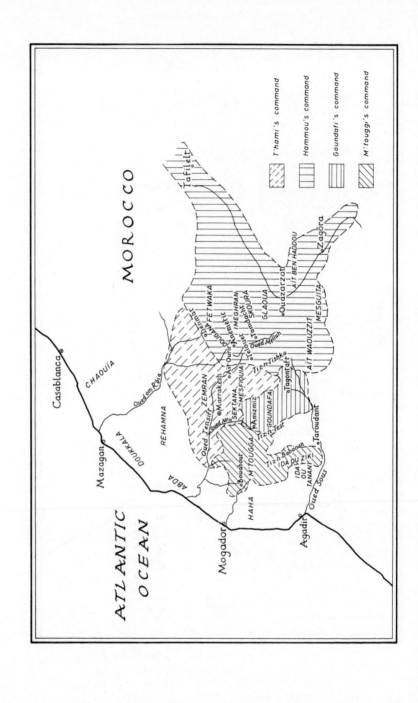

ATLANTIC OCEAN

MOROCCO

Casablanca

CHAOUÏA

Oued om Rbia

Mazagan

DOUKKALA

ABDA

REHAMNA

ZEMRAN

Oued Tensift

Marrakesh

Oued N'fis

SEKTANA

MESFIOUA

Amizmiz

GOUNDAFA

Tiz-n-Test

Tiz-n-Tishka

Tagontaft

AÏT WAOUZZIT

MESGUITA

Zagora

AÏT BEN HADDOU

Ouarzazat

GLAOUA

Tamdacht

Oued Mellah

Telouet

IMEGHRAN

Anemem

Ait Ourir

DOUANY-FET'WAKA

Tafieltt

HAHA

Mogador

M'TOUGGA

Bouabout

IDA OU ZIK

IDA OU TANANY

Tiz-n-Bahaoun

Taroudant

Agadir

Oued Sous

T'hami's command

Hammou's command

Goundafi's command

M'touggi's command

Index